WITHDRAWN

Chen Yun's
Strategy
for China's
Development

THE
CHINA
BOOK
PROJECT   Translation and Commentary

A wide-ranging series of carefully prepared translations of books published in China since 1949, each with an extended introduction by a Western scholar.

The People of Taihang: An Anthology of Family Histories
Edited with an introduction by Sidney L. Greenblatt

Fundamentals of the Chinese Communist Party
Edited with an introduction by Pierre M. Perrolle

Shang Yang's Reforms and State Control in China
Edited with an introduction by Li Yu-ning

Li Jui
The Early Revolutionary Activities of Comrade Mao Tse-tung
Edited by James C. Hsiung. Introduction by Stuart R. Schram

The Rustication of Urban Youth in China: A Social Experiment
Edited by Peter J. Seybolt. Introduction by Thomas P. Bernstein

Workers and Workplaces in Revolutionary China
Edited with an introduction by Stephen Andors

Fundamentals of Political Economy
Edited with an introduction by George C. Wang

Chinese Approaches to Family Planning
Edited with an introduction by Leo A. Orleans

Water Management Organization in the People's Republic of China
Edited with an introduction by James E. Nickum

Xu Liangying and Fan Dianian
Science and Socialist Construction in China
Edited with an introduction by Pierre M. Perrolle

Chen Yun's Strategy for China's Development: A Non-Maoist Alternative
Edited with an introduction by Nicholas R. Lardy and Kenneth Lieberthal

Edited with an
Introduction by
Nicholas R. Lardy and
Kenneth Lieberthal

Chen Yun's Strategy for China's Development

A NON-MAOIST ALTERNATIVE

Translated by
Mao Tong
and
Du Anxia

M. E. SHARPE, INC., ARMONK, NEW YORK
LONDON

830149

Copyright © 1983 by M. E. Sharpe, Inc.
80 Business Park Drive, Armonk, New York 10504

Library of Congress Cataloging in Publication Data

Ch'en, Yün, 1905-
    Ch'en Yün's Strategy for China's development.

    "Published simultaneously as vol. XV, no. 3-4 of Chinese economic
studies"—Copr. p.
    Includes bibliographical references.
    1. China—Economic policy—1949-1976—Addresses, essays, lectures.
I. Lardy, Nicholas R. II. Lieberthal, Kenneth. III. Title. IV. Title:
Strategy for China's development.
HC427.9.C52174 1982   338.951   82-16776
ISBN 0-87332-225-8

Printed in the United States of America

CONTENTS

INTRODUCTION   Nicholas R. Lardy and
                   Kenneth Lieberthal   xi

EDITOR'S NOTE   3

PREFACE   4

1. NEW ISSUES SINCE THE BASIC COMPLETION
   OF THE SOCIALIST TRANSFORMATION
   (September 1956)   7

2. METHODS OF SOLVING THE TENSIONS IN
   SUPPLIES OF PORK AND VEGETABLES
   (September 1956)   23

3. SPEECH AT THE ENLARGED
   MINISTERIAL AFFAIRS CONFERENCE
   (November 1956)   30

4. MANAGE COMMERCIAL WORK WELL
   (November 1956)   39

5. THE SCALE OF CONSTRUCTION SHOULD BE
   COMPATIBLE WITH NATIONAL STRENGTH
   (January 1957)   47

6. RESPONSES TO A XINHUA CORRESPONDENT'S
   QUESTIONS ON PROBLEMS OF
   MARKET PRICES OF COMMODITIES
   (April 1957)   58

  7. WE MUST SOLVE THE VEGETABLE
     SUPPLY PROBLEM WELL
     (July 1957)   63

  8. PAY ATTENTION TO GRAIN WORK
     (September 1957)   67

  9. PROBLEMS WE MUST PAY ATTENTION TO
     AFTER THE REFORM OF THE SYSTEM
     (September 1957)   73

 10. REGULATION ON THE IMPROVEMENT OF
     THE INDUSTRIAL MANAGEMENT SYSTEM
     (November 1957)   76

 11. REGULATION ON THE IMPROVEMENT OF
     THE COMMERCIAL MANAGEMENT SYSTEM
     (November 1957)   84

 12. SEVERAL MAJOR ISSUES IN CURRENT
     CAPITAL CONSTRUCTION WORK
     (March 1959)   88

 13. A LETTER TO COMRADES IN THE CENTRAL
     FINANCE AND ECONOMICS SMALL GROUP
     (April 1959)   112

 14. THE PROBLEM OF MAKING PRACTICABLE
     THE STEEL TARGET
     (May 1959)   117

 15. A LETTER TO COMRADE MAO ZEDONG
     CONCERNING PROBLEMS IN THE STEEL TARGET
     (May 1959)   127

 16. SPEED UP DEVELOPMENT OF THE
     NITROGENOUS CHEMICAL FERTILIZER INDUSTRY
     (May 1961)   129

 17. MANAGE FOREIGN TRADE WORK WELL
     (May 1961)   139

18. AN IMPORTANT WORK THAT RELATES
    TO THE OVERALL SITUATION
    (May 1961)   144

19. AN INVESTIGATION OF
    RURAL QINGPU [COUNTY]
    (August 1961)   155

20. TALK AT THE FORUM ON COAL WORK
    (October 1961)   174

21. HOW WE CAN ACHIEVE A SOMEWHAT MORE
    COMPREHENSIVE UNDERSTANDING
    (February 1962)   181

22. THE CURRENT FINANCIAL AND ECONOMIC
    SITUATION AND SOME METHODS
    FOR OVERCOMING DIFFICULTIES
    (February 1962)   185

23. TALK AT A MEETING OF THE CENTRAL
    FINANCE AND ECONOMICS SMALL GROUP
    (March 1962)   202

ABOUT THE EDITORS   212

ACKNOWLEDGMENTS

We want to thank Mao Tong and Du Anxia for their excellent translation work. Mao Tong did the basic translations of documents number 3-6, 8-9, 13-18, and 20-23, and Du Anxia did the same for documents number 2, 7, 12, and 19. (Document number 1 is the official translation provided by Foreign Languages Press, and documents number 10-11 are based on translations originally done by the Union Research Service in Hong Kong.) Anthony Marr, Curator of the East Asian Collection of Sterling Memorial Library at Yale University, acquired the volume which is translated here. We are also indebted to David Bachman, Nina Halperin, Roderick MacFarquhar, Lyman Miller, Michel Oksenberg, and Roger Thompson for comments and assistance at various stages of this project. For the mistakes that remain, we have no one to blame but each other.

N.R.L. and K.L.
September 1982

WEIGHTS AND MEASURES

1 <u>jin</u> = 0.5 kilogram
1 <u>mu</u> = 0.0667 hectare
1 <u>dan</u> = 50 kilograms (or 100 <u>jin</u>)
1 <u>li</u> = 0.666 square meters
1 <u>liang</u> = 50 grams (or 0.1 <u>jin</u>)
1 <u>zhang</u> = 3 meters (approximately)

Nicholas R. Lardy
and
Kenneth Lieberthal

INTRODUCTION

"Had Chairman Mao died in 1956, there would have been no doubt
that he was a great leader of the Chinese people, a respected,
loved and outstanding great man in the proletarian revolutionary
movement of the world. Had he died in 1966, his meritorious
achievements would have been somewhat tarnished but still very
good. Since he actually died in 1976, there is nothing we can do
about it."

> Chen Yun at the Central Party Work
> Conference, November-December
> 1978, cited in Ming-pao (Hong Kong)
> January 15, 1979, p. 1.

Since Mao Zedong's death the Chinese have been debating the future character of the country's political and economic system.
While discussions of this type have occurred periodically since
1949, this latest round has been remarkably unconstrained. Fundamental premises are not being spared searching reexamination,
and approaches that once lay beyond the range of articulated choices
surface regularly in the media. Indeed, Red Flag and People's
Daily no longer monopolize the public dissemination of alternative
possibilities, as they did during the 1960s and 1970s. Dozens of
new journals, many associated with China's major universities and
research institutes, have joined the fray. No longer, also, do suggestions for reform come only from an annointed few at the Center;
a broader circle is now actively involved.

The present collection of Chen Yun's writings must be read
against the backdrop of this ongoing policy discussion. Chen has
been, and remains, an advocate of economic policies that are central to this debate, and since 1978 many of his views have become
state policy. In this context, the publication in China of this volume of

xi

Chen's writings and speeches from 1956 to 1962 undoubtedly is designed in part to bolster Chen's point of view in current policy discussions. For again and again the implicit message of this volume,[1]
translated here in full, is that had Chen's views been heeded earlier,
China would have developed rapidly and successfully. Indeed, Deng
Liqun, vice-president of the Academy of Social Sciences, staff member
of the Central Committee Secretariat (who in 1982 was promoted to
head the Propaganda Department), and compiler of both the Chen
volume and a companion text,[2] has made this argument explicit.

> Thirty-one years of practice have proved that Comrade Chen Yun's opinions
> are in conformity with China's national conditions. If we act according to his
> opinions, we can do our economic work well. In the past we sometimes put his
> opinions aside and even acted contrary to them and suffered a great deal.
> Therefore, if we want to do our economic work well, we should from now on
> follow the principles and proposals put forth by Comrade Chen Yun.[3]

The collection Deng compiled makes a major addition to our
knowledge of Chen's thinking and activities during three critical
periods — the decentralization debate of 1956-57; the Great Leap
Forward of the late 1950s; and the post-Leap economic recovery.
In 1956-57 Chen's writings and speeches primarily reflect his role
as Minister of Commerce (a post he officially assumed in the late
fall of 1956), although he simultaneously served on the State Planning Commission and was the most senior Party leader primarily
involved in economic work. While Chen nominally remained as
vice-chairman of the Central Committee of the Party during the
Great Leap, his influence in economic affairs diminished until the
spring of 1959, when for a few months he again became a key de-
cision-maker. Finally, during 1961-62 Chen played a key role in
the Central Finance and Economics Small Group, headed by Li
Fuchun, which helped to shape the recovery from the Great Leap
and was a brain trust for Deng Xiaoping and Liu Shaoqi.[4]
Much of Chen's writing goes beyond economic issues, narrowly
defined. Indeed, his rich and varied background qualifies him to
speak with authority on a range of questions. Chen is one of the
few truly proletarian leaders of the Chinese Communist Party,
having been a communist labor union organizer while he worked for
the Commercial Press in Shanghai in the 1920s. He left the Long
March to spend the mid-1930s in Moscow, and soon after his return headed the Party Organization Department. In this position,
he authored one of the key texts on Party organization and rectifica-

tion used in the famous rectification campaign of 1942-1944 in
Yanan.[5] In the early 1940s Chen increasingly turned his attention
to economic work, and after the communist victory in 1949 he became virtually the economic czar of New China. From 1949 to
1954 the new government had a committee in charge of both financial and economic work, and Chen headed this powerful body. Following the purge of Gao Gang in 1954, Chen was identified as the
fifth-ranking leader of the Chinese Communist Party (behind Mao
Zedong, Zhou Enlai, Liu Shaoqi, and Zhu De).[6]

Thus, by the mid-1950s Chen Yun had garnered vast experience
in Party organization and rectification and in various aspects of
financial and economic work. He had an intimate knowledge of the
Soviet Union, although ironically his recommendations for China
flew in the face of key tenets of Soviet orthodoxy. In sum, Chen's
views as expressed in these documents of the 1956-62 period reflect greater insight into both the Chinese and Soviet systems than
one might normally expect from an official concerned primarily
with economic affairs.

The Chen Yun Collection

The present collection contains twenty-three of Chen's speeches,
articles, reports, and letters from September 1956 through March
1962, only a few of which were previously available.[7] There remain major chronological lacunae, with no pieces from December
1957 through February 1959 or from June 1959 through April 1961.
Perhaps significantly, also, the essays included in this volume have
been edited for publication. It is impossible to determine how radical the surgery performed on some of the original texts has been.

There are basically two types of articles in this collection: those
that discuss the overall situation, and those that focus on particular
issues. Seven of the pieces belong in the former category: "New
Issues Since the Basic Completion of the Socialist Transformation"
(September 1956); "The Scale of Construction Should Be Compatible
With National Strength" (January 1957); "Several Major Issues in
Current Capital Construction Work" (March 1959); "An Important Work
That Relates to the Overall Situation" (May 1961); "How We Can Achieve
a Somewhat More Comprehensive Understanding" (February 1962);
"The Current Financial and Economic Situation and Some Methods for
Overcoming Difficulties" (February 1962); and "Talk at a Meeting of the
Central Finance and Economics Small Group" (March 1962).[8] While
these seven are in general the most interesting pieces for under-

standing Chen's overall analysis, the other essays also add a great
deal to our knowledge of both the political agenda and policy process
during 1956-1962.

These documents thus enrich our understanding of Chen's basic
economic principles and of the evolution of the debate over economic policy from before the Great Leap to mid-1962. Section I below
explains three of the most central elements in Chen's economic
thought — markets and prices, balanced growth, and types of centralization — while the following section places these and related
ideas into the concrete political context in which they were debated.

I. CHEN'S ECONOMIC STRATEGY

Markets and Prices

Chen has consistently supported the use of market forces in
agriculture, commerce, and parts of light industry. In his well-
known speech to the Eighth Party Congress in the fall of 1956, he
muted his praise of the so-called socialist transformation of private
industry and commerce (that had been accelerated by Mao Zedong)
because state control had produced a host of new problems. A
state monopoly on purchases of many agricultural products had de-
pressed prices and output. For industrial products, inefficient state
wholesaling companies had reduced market competition and effectively curtailed the range of goods available. The solution for industrial products, Chen argued, was to make manufacturers do their
own marketing, either directly or through agents working on commission. Chen also opposed the amalgamation of small firms and
handicraftsmen into large cooperatives that either stopped producing their original products or produced less efficiently. Agricultural collectivization, Chen felt, had undermined household manufacturing and marketing of subsidiary agricultural products, thus
affecting peasant income. "The state of affairs where everything is
indiscriminately managed by the cooperative," he argued, "must be
altered." Fei Xiaotong had arrived at a similar conclusion based
on his investigation of Gaixiangong Village in Jiangsu after collectivization.[9]

Chen's analysis led to policy positions. First, he supported
rural free markets for agricultural products and opposed the
state monopoly on the rural distribution of manufactured consumer goods. During the "high tide" of collectivization in the

winter of 1955-56, many peasant markets had closed. Cnen very
likely called for reopening these markets, a policy adopted in the
summer of 1956. He also, as indicated above, advocated multiple
channels for distribution of consumer goods in the countryside to
compete with state-owned commerce and thereby increase the
volume and range of consumer goods available in the countryside.

Second, Chen supported the use of agricultural prices not only
for accounting but also as a tool to influence the allocation of resources. Chen was bold and direct in his advocacy of this highly
controversial use of "active" prices, arguing that "we must frame
our price policy so as to facilitate production." Tnus, prices should
be adjusted to provide incentives to produce the output mix favored
by the central authorities. Quality differentials should also be enlarged. Perhaps most daring, given the sensitivity of the issue,
Chen even opposed the fetish of price stability, particularly for
subsidiary agricultural products. If prices went up when constraints
on marketing were released, he argued, state intervention was still
not warranted. The higher prices would induce increased output,
which in turn would bring prices down. This concept is still not
widely accepted within the Chinese leadership.

Finally, Chen's belief in market incentives made him argue per-
sistently for the retention or expansion of rural private plots. He
raised this issue explicitly in his two speeches to the Eighth Party
Congress, reiterated it in the midst of the Leap in 1959 when private plots were under attack, and returned to it in his investigation
report on Qingpu Village in 1961. One interesting dimension of his
concern with private plots was his linkage of private plots with the
production of fodder for private household production of pigs. In
turn, private production of animals was, he felt, vastly superior
to collective production.

Balanced Growth

These documents highlight Chen's consistent opposition to
very high rates of investment as counterproductive. High targets
for new construction, he argued, inevitably led state organs to recruit new labor into urban construction and manufacturing enterprises. These workers received relatively high pay and benefits.
But to feed them China's agriculture had to grow at a fast pace —
rapid enough that the state in an average year would not have to
draw down its grain reserves to meet the demand for food by
the nonagricultural population. But agriculture did not grow at

sufficient speed in most years because the peasants had inadequate incentives to produce more. The resulting food shortfalls created strong inflationary pressures in the system that could get out of hand without the firm application of corrective measures. Chen was willing to tolerate short-term inflation as part of price adjustment in rural markets but blanched at a structural inflation growing out of overly high rates of state investment.

Thus, Chen has been a persistent advocate of balanced growth, what the Chinese refer to as "comprehensive balance." He was a critic of the high investment rates that prevailed in 1956, 1958-59 and, at least in retrospect, evisaged for the ten-year plan that was unveiled at the Fifth National People's Congress in January-February 1978. And his views on rates of state investment were linked with his position on market incentives in China's countryside.

Chen's analysis of China's peasants allowed little room for increasing production on the basis of political exhortation or of coercion for, unlike Mao, he felt that neither of these could produce the results desired. Peasants responded to material rewards based on their individual effort. Therefore, Chen advocated lower levels of collective ownership in the rural areas during the early 1960s (larger collective units of ownership and distribution led to poorer performance of the peasants). As discussed above, he also wanted fewer constraints on private plots and private marketing of both agricultural commodities and manufactured consumer goods. Finally, Chen in general supported higher state prices for the procurement of agricultural products. To work, however, these policies required that the urban economy produce enough consumer goods to entice the peasants to give up their output to the cities. Neither raising the level of requisition sales to the state nor allowing private markets without sufficient consumer goods could make the peasants increase their efforts. Allowing peasants to sell their output directly on private urban markets would stimulate production and marketing in the short run. But this would also shift buying power to rural areas. If the supply of consumer goods in rural markets subsequently was not increased, the incentives for increased production and marketing would be undermined. Thus, only sufficient consumer goods could induce peasants to part year after year with a growing share of their products.

Chen's vision of balanced growth therefore had specific implications for the rate and composition of investment. He actively opposed the periodic surges in investment rates that occurred during

the First Five-Year Plan. For example, he argued in January 1957[10]
that investment would have to be curtailed to eliminate the 1956
state budgetary deficit and to reduce the growth of the wage bill.
Moreover, Chen's balanced growth policies required restructuring
investment to provide a greater supply of manufactured consumer goods. These were essential to increasing the output and
marketing of agricultural products.

Important theoretical writings by a group of economists associated
in the 1950s with the Economic Research Institute of the Academy of
Sciences accompanied the development of Chen's policy position. Indeed, the mid-1950s appears to mark the beginning of a symbiotic relationship between Chen and these economists, one that would reemerge
in a much stronger form in 1962-63 and again in the late 1970s, when
well-known economists such as Dong Fureng and He Jianzhang wrote
major articles supporting Chen's policy and celebrating the compilation of the Chen Yun collection.[11] These writings, first published in
1956 about the time that the Second Five-Year Plan was being formulated, sought to repudiate the cardinal principle of socialist development that had been adopted from the Soviet Union — the priority
growth of the producer goods sector. The first such article, by
Deng Xiaogui, appeared in August 1956 in the journal of the Institute
and sought to trace out the implications of the principle in mathe-
matical terms. More rapid producer goods growth could be sustained either by investing an ever larger percentage of gross national
product or by increasing the capital/output ratio continuously.[12] The
first alternative was not feasible in the long run, while the second
was undesirable for a capital-short developing country.

Chen's advocacy of balanced growth as expressed in his views on
the appropriate rate and composition of investment alone differen-
tiated him from most other Politburo members. But his perspective
also differed from that of his colleagues in more profound ways.
First, Chen realized that economic growth was stimulated by interactions among and between various sectors of the economy — agriculture, industry, and services, as well as state, collective, and
private. His Politburo colleagues tended instead to believe that
growth in one sector could be achieved only at the expense of the
remaining sectors. This latter perspective, derived from Marx
and widely held within the Soviet leadership at least since the time
of Stalin, has been called the "predatory" view of economic growth.[13]
Chen's advocacy of agricultural and private sector development
(private plots, flourishing handicrafts, higher price levels for farm

products sold to the state), in short, did not mean that he opposed the heavy industrial sector. Quite the opposite. Chen agreed that heavy industrial growth formed the core of China's development program. He did not believe, however, that ignoring the rest of the economy was the most effective way to achieve this growth.

Relatedly, Chen believed planning must be based on a careful consideration of the interrelationships among economic sectors and among particular branches of the economy. He thus tended to articulate, in ways many others could not, the interindustry relations of the whole system. Was the Ministry of Metallurgy's proposed 1959 steel target of 16 million metric tons feasible? To Chen the methodology for addressing this question was obvious. What was the quantity of iron required for smelting to produce the steel sought while not neglecting inventory demands? In turn, how much iron ore and coke would be needed to produce the iron? Could existing mines and processing equipment meet the demand? How much washed coal would be required to produce the coke? How much coking coal would have to be mined? What quantity of refractory material would need to be mined? What additional mining equipment (for both coal and refractory material), washing equipment, and ore benefication equipment, would each of these imply? What additional transport capacity, including trucks, locomotives, and railroad cars, would have to be available to move all the necessary materials?[14] In short, Chen would trace out the quantities of all the necessary raw materials and intermediate goods required to meet a single final output target, in this case steel products.

By contrast, because of his faith in political mobilization as a means of increasing production in the late 1950s, Mao Zedong embraced economic planning techniques that encouraged initiative, flexibility, and storming. Mao thus believed, for example, in a "dynamic balance" in planning, essentially basing the "plan" on optimistic projections of future output in the country's priority sectors with other related sectors expected to go all out in order to catch up and permit the economy to surge ahead.[15]

Centralization

Chen's concern for balance made him a strong advocate of centralized planning. That position might seem somewhat anomolous given his preference, discussed above, for the use of markets and prices to allocate resources. But on closer examination this seeming contradiction largely dissolves. Chen saw the market solely as a supplement to centralized planning. Markets were necessary because the state could not efficiently direct all resource and commodity allocation. Markets also provided greater incentives for production in handicrafts and agriculture. But Chen never advocated consumers' sovereignty whereby market demand determined the allocation of investment resources and thus the pattern of production. These were decisions that in Chen's view properly rested largely in the hands of the state. Similarly Chen preferred to rely on bureaucratic allocation of skilled labor and bureaucratic control of the size of the entire nonagricultural labor force. The latter was critical in that it determined the overall wage bill and therefore the urban demand for consumer goods, especially food.

Chen's views on the proper distribution of decision-making authority among various levels of government administration emerge at several points in his selected works and the companion volume of Deng Liqun. For example, at a 1953 Finance and Economics Work Conference that was considering interprovincial flows of grain, a deadlock emerged over whether the quantity of exports from surplus provinces should be subject to annual adjustment by the Center or set at a fixed amount over a period of several years. The issue was referred to Zhou Enlai, who discussed the issue with Chen. Chen came down strongly on the side of central authority. Recognizing that any system that fixed set amounts for several years would give high performance provinces increased control over their additional output, Chen argued that the proposed fixing of the flows was inconsistent with the complexity of the agrarian situation. He noted that surplus provinces could become deficit provinces in years of localized bad weather and normally deficit provinces might be able to export in some years. He thus preferred that the Center retain the ability to reallocate the grain of provinces with surplus production in any given year. Zhou concurred with Chen's opinion and reserved to the Center the prerogative of adjusting interprovincial flows of grain on an annual basis.[16]

Chen's writings provide additional information on his views on this issue. Chen made a major report at the Third Plenum of the Eighth Central Committee, a meeting that made important decisions on the reform of China's economic system. But for some reason Chen's speech was not published at the time, and even the current collection contains only a fragment of this speech. This fragment makes clear he favored imposing severe constraints on the pro-

posed devolution of resource allocation authority to provincial and
local governments, fearing that excessive devolution could unleash
major centrifugal forces. The appropriate policy, Chen argued, was
for the Center simultaneously to strengthen overall balance work as
it devolved limited authority to local governments. In practice,
Chen's cautionary approach was embedded in the decentralization
decisions approved by the Plenum, two of which Chen drafted and
are included in this collection. [17]

Chen came back to this issue in his March 1959 article on investment, which reflected the expansion of Chen's area of direct bureaucratic responsibilities that had occurred in November 1958
when he was appointed director of the newly established State Capital Construction Commission. In this article Chen sought to lay
out explicitly the rationale for integrated investment planning. He
opposed the incipient attempt to establish, during the early phases
of the Leap, what were known as complete industrial systems
(wanzheng di gongye tixi) in each large region [18] and province.
Rather, initially China should seek to establish such a system nationally based on specialization in production and building on the
strengths of the few regions with strong industrial bases. Contradictions between national and regional interests should be resolved
on the basis of the part yielding to the whole. Chen thus stressed
the theme that "the whole country is like a chessboard," which was
first popularized in December 1958.

In sum, for Chen, centralized planning was advantageous because
it allowed the state to direct the intersectoral and interregional
flows of producer goods and agricultural products, especially cereals. It also permitted the state more control of the size of the
modern sector work force and the allocation of employees, particularly skilled workers. Finally, centralized planning of investment
and finance enabled the Center to limit the unified state budget — a
policy on which Chen had relied heavily in 1950-51 when, as head
of the Government Administrative Council's Finance and Economics
Commission, he led the effort to bring the budget deficit fueled
hyperinflation inherited from the Nationalist government under control. Chen's sensitivity to budgetary deficits as a source of inflationary pressure was to reemerge forcefully, both in 1961-62 and
again in 1978-1981, two important periods when the government
budget was unbalanced.

Chen preferred not merely concentrating authority of resource
allocation power at the Center but also vesting it primarily in the

hands of the State Planning and State Economic Commissions, if necessary at the expense of the ministries. In 1962, for example, when Chen sought to restructure the composition of investment to support agricultural development (including industries that produced modern inputs for agriculture), he urged that the commissions be made responsible for carrying out the new investment priorities.[19] To achieve this goal, Chen advocated reducing the authority of the ministries to control the distribution of commodities they produced. He charged, for example, that the Ministry of Metallurgy could not be relied upon since it diverted its products to its own purposes, contrary to broad state interests.[20]

In sum, Chen had developed in the 1950s his own model for China's economic development. This strategy stressed heavy industry and central planning but also recognized the limits imposed on the country's capabilities by a weak agricultural sector and the state's inability to mobilize or coerce the peasants into higher production. Chen therefore advocated a strategy of adequate incentives for peasants, which required in turn more investment in consumer goods, utilization of private plots and free markets, and toleration of short-term inflation for market adjustment purposes. This strategy of necessity demanded lower overall investment in industry, but Chen recognized that over the long run it would produce the most rapid industrial growth. This strategy differed in both fundamental assumptions and practical recommendations from that being advocated at the time by Party Chairman Mao Zedong. We turn now to an analysis of what this collection of newly released documents reveals about the political debates over Chen's policies during the late 1950s and early 1960s.

II. CHEN AND MAO

According to Deng Liqun,[21] Mao's relations with Chen Yun remained excellent through the early years after 1949, and Mao relied heavily on Chen's judgment in finance and economic work. The close collaboration evidently lasted until the socialist transformation of industry and commerce in late 1955-early 1956, around which time the two men's views began to diverge. Chen became alarmed at the inflationary pressures generated by a concatenation of circumstances growing out of the socialist transformation, and thus he joined a rising chorus of voices arguing by June of 1956 against "rash advance."[22] Chen called for a slowdown

at a late June Politburo meeting that Mao did not attend, and an
editorial in People's Daily of June 20, 1956, supported Chen's
position.[23] Although Chen is known in general for maintaining good relations even with those with whom he disagrees, little information is
available on the actual personal interactions between Mao and Chen
from mid-1956 until early 1958. But, as the following discussion details, the substance of the two men's views clearly diverged with increasing sharpness as this period wore on.

During the last half of 1956, policy tended to move in the directions Chen advocated: toward consolidation of the cooperatives and
increased efficiency of the newly transformed industrial and commercial system. Mao evidently personally moved in this direction
also. With the failure of the Hundred Flowers Campaign in June
1957, however, Mao put his full weight behind a radicalization of
politics and the search for a development strategy that could be
carried through even without the cooperation of the specialists
against whom he had just turned.

In the summer and fall of 1957, Mao thus moved back toward a
policy of rash advance,[24] which directed China's strategy away
from the balanced, controlled development that Chen had advocated.
In his September 1957 piece printed below, Chen focuses attention
on the inequalities that decentralization will inevitably produce,
perhaps as an argument against the direction in which Mao was
moving policy. But to no avail. As the Great Leap Forward strategy took shape and gathered steam, Chen Yun's influence diminished.

At the January 1958 Nanning Conference, Mao Zedong attacked
experts in the state apparatus who constantly raised technical issues that had gotten in the way of the thinking of the "proletarian"
Politburo. He lashed out at the conservatives who during 1956-57
had opposed bold advance, and he said that in the future what was
needed was bold advance while correcting errors. Chen Yun was
not the only target of these remarks — indeed, Zhou Enlai quite
clearly also came under the gun — but the entire thrust of the
Nanning Meeting and its aftermath ran directly counter to Chen's
prescriptions over the previous two years.[25] Thus, the sharp decline
in public appearances and documents by Chen Yun from November
1957 through February 1959 almost certainly reflects the fact that
he was pushed off center stage by the exuberant Party Chairman
in the latter's quest for a way to circumvent the constraints to
which Chen always pointed as he argued for a balanced and steady
strategy of economic development.

By the late fall of 1958, though, the Great Leap began to run into trouble, and Mao called for restraint and consolidation lest the movement produce a disaster. The initial indication of this shift came at the First Zhengzhou Meeting in early November[26] and was reinforced in a succession of meetings during the following months (at Wuchang in late November-December, the Second Zhengzhou Meeting in February-March 1959, and a Shanghai conference followed by the Seventh Plenum of the Eighth Central Committee in March-April). Considerable evidence indicates that Mao led the effort to stress central planning (to regard the whole country like "a single chessboard"), to lower targets for steel production, and to constrain the cavalier approach by the new people's communes toward the rights and property of the peasants.[27]

Mao met resistance to his demand that targets be lowered and the Great Leap Forward be brought under control.[28] Confronting this opposition, Mao evidently welcomed Chen Yun's support to move China's economic planning and policies back into directions that Chen thought were reasonable. Indeed, the evidence presented in Chen's articles provides graphic confirmation of the fact that management of the economy had fallen into disarray since the fall of 1957.

Planning of steel production for 1959 illustrates well the degree to which economic decisions of the Great Leap Forward had been made arbitrarily — at least until Mao asked Chen Yun and the Central Finance and Economics Small Group to focus on the issue in the spring of 1959. The Sixth Plenum at Wuchang in November-December expressed the original 1959 target as a range of 20-30 million tons.[29] By the Shanghai Conference in April 1959, pressure from Mao had reduced the target to 16.5 million tons, and it fell further to 15 million tons shortly thereafter. To judge from Chen's report to the Politburo,[30] even this revised target had not been based on careful calculations. Indeed, the evidence suggests that three separate agencies continued to work at cross purposes on the steel target well into the first quarter of 1959. The Ministry of Metallurgy advanced the highest targets. It wanted steel output of from 13 to 15 million tons (although a 16 million ton variant also was mentioned). The State Economic Commission's Metallurgy Bureau also plumped for a 13-15 million ton target. Finally, a slightly more conservative proposed target, 12.5 to 14 million tons, came from the State Planning Commission's Heavy Industry Bureau.

Thus, well into the second quarter of 1959 no target had been determined, as three separate agencies and ministries promoted

their own, apparently independent, plans. The State Planning Commission, which should have focused on long-term planning, took an
active part in the design of the annual plan. And the Ministry of
Metallurgy, headed by Wang Heshou, although nominally subordinate
to the State Council commissions, pursued the politically risky
strategy of presenting its own apparently self-serving targets directly to the Finance and Economics Small Group and protesting
the Group's endorsement of a lower target.

Under Chen's leadership the Small Group recommended to the
Politburo a compromise target of 13 million metric tons of steel
(9 million tons of steel products) but deleted any mention of a "higher target to strive for." The Politburo, and subsequently Mao, approved this recommendation.[31]

Steel [Steel Product] Targets
millions of metric tons

Meeting/Agency	Reliable target	Target to strive for
Sixth Plenum (Wuchang, November-December 1958)	20	30
Shanghai Conference (April 1959)	16.5	
Proposals to Finance and Economics Small Group (May 1959)		
A. Ministry of Metallurgy	13 [9]	15-16
B. State Economic Commission, Metallurgy Bureau	13	15
C. State Planning Commission, Heavy Industry Planning Bureau	12.5-13 [8.5-9]	14 [9.5]
Chen Yun proposal	13 [9]	

Statistics were equally chaotic in agriculture. Chen's writings
make it clear that planning for 1959, which included a significant
reduction in grain sown area and a substantial increase in investment and in urban employment, was based on the internal acceptance of the 1958 output figures of 375 million metric tons of grain
and 3.5 million metric tons of cotton which were announced in the
communique of the Sixth Plenum of the Eighth Central Committee.

But Peng Dehuai has revealed how these figures were reached, as follows:

At the time of the Wuchang meeting [November 1958], I participated in the Northwest small group. When the small group discussed announcing the 1958 figures for grain and cotton, some comrades said that there were more than one trillion jin [500 million metric tons]; some comrades said more than 900 billion jin [450 million metric tons], with cotton amounting to 60 to 70 million dan [3–3.5 million metric tons]; and some other comrades said that regardless of how much grain and cotton there is, industry is now vastly behind agriculture. I [Peng Dehuai] said that there is not so much grain and cotton. At that time, some comrades gave me some polite criticism, saying, "Old Marshall! You doubt this and doubt that; what should we do?" I said, "If we announce figures that are a bit low, then later when we find out the figures things will be relatively active; if we announce figures that are high, the future will be passive." Afterwards, the Chairman said to announce 750 billion jin [375 million metric tons], and at that time I agreed, but in my heart I still had doubts about this figure.[32]

Significantly, government procurement of cereal crops was also based largely on inflated local reporting of crop output. Chen Yun carried out his own investigations of the actual situation in the countryside in the spring of 1959, and produced a scathing indictment of the inaccurate reporting by local officials that had been accepted by the upper levels. Chen pointedly focused his investigations — and his ire — on the work of Henan's Wu Zhipu, the provincial Party secretary on whom Mao had relied in 1958 in developing China's commune program.[33]

Despite Chen's accusations against Mao's Henan model, Deng Liqun argues that as late as the eve of the Lushan Conference Mao highly praised Chen Yun as a person who all along had been right in arguing for the need first to arrange the market and then to arrange capital construction.[34] Deng thus implies that as long as Mao saw himself as trying to rein in a campaign gone wild he called on Chen Yun's support. The situation, however, was very likely more complex and subtle than this. Mao in the spring of 1959 saw that the entire concept of the Great Leap Forward was being put in jeopardy by the overzealousness of local-level cadres and hotheaded provincial leaders. He thus turned to Chen Yun as part of his effort to bring the situation back under control and save his enormous gamble from disaster. But while Mao wanted to control the Great Leap, Chen evidently sought to prove that the entire idea had been fallacious in its fundamentals. Thus, the partnership between the two had im-

plicit limits — ones that would become crucial if Mao again
turned to attack the critics of the campaign he was trying to
salvage.

This subtle dynamic may explain a curious dimension of the letter
to Mao in the following collection that comes directly after Chen's
report to the Politburo on the steel target. The report itself pulled
no punches in its analysis of the problems or prescription for
changes. At the same time, though, Mao did not attend the
May Politburo meeting at which this report was presented, even
though it concerned a matter of great importance to him. Unfortunately, it is not possible with the information currently available to
determine whether Chen's letter to Mao reporting the results of the
Politburo meeting was in fact a cover letter to accompany the complete text of his remarks to the meeting. If it was not — that is, if
Chen's letter is all that Mao saw from this meeting — the omissions
and phrasing in the letter are fascinating. For while the letter suggests the lower steel target, it leaves out the complex rationale
Chen used to justify this, a rationale that includes all the differences between Mao and Chen on issues of planning the economy.
Chen also hedges his recommendation for the new steel target more
in the letter than he seemed to in his report to the Politburo.[35]

Whatever the nuances of the relationship between Mao and Chen
in the spring of 1959, Chen had dropped out of the political scene
by the time of the Lushan Conference. Deng Liqun notes simply
that Chen "took a rest" until 1961.[36] Since Deng later uses the
same phrase to indicate that Chen was ill, the implication is that
Chen's health deteriorated to the point where he could no longer
shoulder the burdens of office. At the same time, Chen's pur-
ported illness set in at an auspicious time, since the dynamics
of the Lushan Conference resulted in Mao's initiating an anti-
rightist campaign that produced a new upsurge in the Great
Leap Forward. Chen also fully recovered from his "illness"
at a politically appropriate moment — during the increasingly fran-
tic deliberations in the spring of 1961 over how to extricate the
country from the economic disaster that the policies since 1958 had
produced. It is possible, therefore, that Chen Yun's indisposition
as of the summer of 1959 was political as well as physiological in
origin.

Aftermath of the Great Leap

The Great Leap entered a new upsurge after the 1959 Lushan

Plenum, and Chen's influence evidently remained minimal until 1961, when Zhou Enlai apparently personally asked him to resume a major role in policymaking. According to Deng Liqun, Zhou had drafted the "Urgent Directive on Rural Work" known as the "Twelve Articles" that officially was approved in November 1960.[37] The negative assessment contained in the directive on China's rural situation was reflected in an important editorial in People's Daily in late November.[38] The editorial endorsed a shift in the basic unit within the three-level rural structure (commune-brigade-team) from the commune to the brigade level and even sought, in several ways, to enhance the power of the teams vis-à-vis the brigades. Mao personally felt that the agricultural situation was not as critical as the directive implied. It was at this point that Chen began to play a more active role in policy formulation. Indeed, the most revealing documents in the Chen collection deal with the period 1961-62.

As of May 1961, Chen weighed in with recommendations in areas ranging from fertilizer production, to xiaxiang of workers, to foreign trade. He then investigated rural areas near the Yangtse and wrote an extensive set of reports that called for reintroduction and enlargement of private plots, among other measures.[39] In this period, Chen seems to have been acting on Mao's general injunction made at the Guangzhou Conference in March 1961 to carry out more investigation work in order to learn appropriate lessons from the Great Leap Forward experience.[40] The Red Guards subsequently charged that Deng Xiaoping and Peng Zhen took advantage of this injunction to carry out investigations with the specific object of demonstrating the disastrous consequences of the Great Leap Forward and their causes,[41] and they may well have been right. Chen Yun during this period reported his own field investigations directly to Deng Xiaoping,[42] and Chen's writing during 1961 certainly paints a very grim picture of the Chinese economy.

These documents reveal that Mao's skepticism on the extent and depth of China's agricultural crisis was shared widely. They also reveal Chen's belief that the rural situation was more desperate than appreciated and that recovery would take longer than expected.

Chen's first piece from this period concerns the development of the chemical fertilizer industry. While the report concerned technical issues, its recommendations amounted to a clear repudiation of Mao. First, the report was premised on the notion that agricultural growth should be achieved through increased supplies of mod-

ern industrial inputs — not through labor mobilization schemes such
as the Leap Forward. The entire First Five-Year Plan had included funds for the construction of only two new nitrogenous and two
new phosphate fertilizer plants.[43] Among heavy industrial investments in this First Plan, less than three percent were allocated for
fertilizers, pesticides, and farm machinery.[44] In 1961 Chen recommended that the Central Committee authorize construction of
fourteen additional plants, four to be initiated in 1962, followed by
five each in 1963 and 1964. Each plant would have an annual capacity of 50,000 tons of synthetic ammonia and would take a year to complete. Thus, total capacity under the plan would rise 200,000 to 250,000
tons per year in 1963, 1964, and 1965, compared with incremental addi-
tions of less than 50,000 tons in 1950-1960.

Second, the report repudiates the Maoist concept of "walking on
two legs" in which small-scale plants with less advanced technology
were developed simultaneously with modern facilities. Chen's report contains a scathing indictment of the small-scale plants that
could produce 800 or 2,000 tons of synthetic ammonia annually that had
been built since 1958. Only a fourth of the 800-ton plants operated normally. Even these had unstable production, high levels of consumption of raw materials and electric power, and low quality output.
The 2,000-ton plants were also repudiated by the report.

Finally, the report rejected the Maoist concept of self-reliance.
The new large-scale plants recommended by Chen each required
about 10,000 different types of metal products, many of which were
not produced in sufficient quantities or could not be produced at all
in China. Chen recommended allocating a total of 45 million (U.S.)
dollars of foreign exchange to import these materials.

Chen's other major recommendation on foreign trade also reflected his assessment of the dire state of affairs in the countryside. While after several years increased use of chemical fertilizers and other inputs would raise agricultural production, in the
short run Chen argued that China had to import significant quantities of grain. Chen had previously been intimately involved in the
procurement system and the supply of cereals and other staple
commodities to the urban population. His recommendation for imports reflected his assessment that urban food needs could not be
met from domestic procurement and that stocks had already been
drawn down to a dangerously low level. Procurement in the recent
past had been excessive. In Chen's words, "Because we procured
too much and left too little to the peasants ... [in the final analysis]

the peasants did not like to work and...we did not collect anything."

In the 1950s China had been a net exporter of cereal products. The recommendation that China import grain must have
dealt a devastating blow to Mao's prestige. While the immen-
sity of the agricultural disaster induced by the Leap, including
the deaths of many millions of peasants, would be concealed
from the world for two decades,[45] China's import of cereals
for the first time since 1949 signalled to all that the Leap had
failed. The cereal import program troubled Mao, and throughout the early to mid-1960s he actively opposed it.[46] When Mao
fully regained his influence after 1965, he quickly and strongly
advocated local self-sufficiency as a mechanism for reducing
China's dependence on imported cereals.[47]

Even after the leadership had accepted cereal imports and an expanded chemical fertilizer program based on imported components,
debate continued over the severity of the rural crisis. Throughout
1961 and 1962, Chen conceded that agricultural production was improving but argued that the crisis remained far from over. He
pointed in particular to three factors.

First, the urban population had grown explosively during the
Great Leap. At year-end 1957 the state provided grain through the
rationing system for 99 million urban residents. By Chen's May
1961 report to the Central Party Work Meeting that number had
grown by a third to 130 million. Second, grain production in 1960
had fallen in aggregate terms to 143.5 million metric tons, 52 million less than in 1957. Although production began to recover in
1961, the aggregate level of output (147.5 million tons) was still
below that of any year in the First Plan (1953-57).[48]

Third, and equally critical from Chen's point of view, urban China
largely had been insulated from the agrarian crisis in 1960 and the
first half of 1961 by drawing down state controlled stockpiles. By
the spring of 1961 the cupboard was bare. Data on state stockpiles
of grain are among the most closely guarded of all secrets in China,
and the Chen Yun collection provides some of these data for the
first time. Stocks at the end of June 1956 (the end of the grain
year) were 21.35 million tons. Because of the surge in investment
and urban employment in 1956 they had declined to 18.2 million
tons by the end of June 1957.[49] In the subsequent four years, reserves almost had been exhausted. Chen estimated the July 1,
1961, level would be only 7.4 million tons, of which 5.05 million
tons represented carryover of old grain while 2.35 million tons was

an estimate of the over-wintering wheat crop that would be harvested and procured in the late spring and early summer of
1961 and in state stocks by the end of June. The carryover of 5.05 million tons represents less than 40 kilograms per urban resident —
slightly more than a month's average ration. It is unlikely that the
distribution system could operate effectively with inventories representing not much more than a month's outgo. In short, stockpiles
had been drawn down by almost 11 million tons, partially cushioning
the urban population from the effects of sharply declining output.
By mid-1961 this cushion was exhausted and stocks were at a dangerously low level.[50]

   Thus, Chen in 1961 held the view that agricultural recovery would
take several more years, but it is clear from his speeches that
there remained widespread resistance to this position. The skepticism apparently was so pervasive that Deng Xiaoping directed
several high-ranking Party members to investigate rural conditions. Chen headed a group that went to Qingpu County, his native
place in Jiangsu Province not far from Shanghai, and his investigation apparently confirmed his worst fears. Even in a relatively
prosperous Yangtse Valley commune Chen found that "there is not
enough grain to eat" and that mismanagement by Party cadres undermined production incentives. He also noted that exaggerated
production claims were still being reported by cadres anxious to
conceal the magnitude of the debacle in the countryside.[51]

   Chen's views of the agricultural catastrophe led to strong
policy prescriptions. He declared that the state must resettle back
to the countryside as many as possible of the 30 million peasants
who had moved to the cities since 1957 to reduce the burden on
state grain supplies. Many objected on the ground that these resettled urban residents would not add appreciably to grain output,
at least in the first year, and that since agricultural production
was recovering rapidly they soon could be provided for by the
state. Indeed, only a week later Liu Shaoqi suggested at the same
conference that only 10 million of these people need be sent down.[52]

   Chen rejected the arguments against sending people down,
pointing out that many of those resettled would become the responsibility of their families and that, in any case, they would, along
with other peasants, share in the output of collective production and be
assigned private plots. These, in Chen's view, would provide 225 kilograms of unprocessed grain per capita by the second year, an amount
sufficient for their own consumption. Even in the first year Chen

proposed that state support for resettled urbanites be limited to an
average of 75 kilograms. Thus there were both immediate and
longer term savings from the point of view of demand for state
grain.[53]

Chen's resettlement recommendation implicitly endorsed a range
of related — and controversial — urban and rural policies. These
included: closing thousands of enterprises that had sprung up during
the Great Leap Forward but had proved to be inefficient; expanding
private plots and providing other incentives in the countryside; reopening private rural markets; and fixing output quotas based on
individual households (part of the "three freedoms and one contract
system").

During the first half of 1962, Chen became closely identified with
Liu Shaoqi's assessment that it would take a long time to rectify the
damage done by the Great Leap Forward. Indeed, shortly after the
Seven Thousand Cadre Meeting in January-February 1962 (which had
adopted a somehwat more optimistic appraisal) Chen learned from the
Ministry of Finance that the government faced a potential 1962 budget
deficit of 2 to 3 billion yuan, and he felt that this new danger required a reassessment of the entire prospect for recovery. Mao
was in Wuhan at the time. Liu Shaoqi convened a meeting called
the Xilou Conference where Chen presented his analysis. They in
turn decided to convene a meeting of top Party people in the State
Council to consider Chen's analysis. Chen's report to that meeting
is translated below.[54]

The State Council meeting enthusiastically accepted Chen's report and referred it to the Secretariat. Under Liu Shaoqi's urging,
the Secretariat circulated Chen's report as a Central Committee
document, with a comment by the Standing Committee of the Politburo appended. When the issue was raised as to whether Chen's
portrayal of the difficulties stemming from the Great Leap Forward
should be toned down somewhat in the version of the document to be
circulated, Liu insisted that the stark facts be presented. Once the
Secretariat had adopted a resolution to circulate this report and an
accompanying comment, Zhou Enlai, Liu Shaoqi, and Deng Xiaoping
traveled to Wuhan to report the entire sequence of events and decisions to Mao to obtain his approval. Mao assented to the circulation of the document. After Chen's speech was circulated as a
Central Committee document, the newly reconstituted Central Finance and Economics Small Group met to discuss it.[55] His report
to this meeting is the final document translated below. A separate

major document on commercial work was also drafted that reflected Chen's opinions. But then Chen faded from active political involvement, again purportedly for reasons of health. Remarks in the Deng Liqun volume imply that he remained too "ill" to take part in national political affairs (with the possible exception of an appearance at the August-September 1962 Beidaihe Meeting) again at least until 1965.[56]

Substantively, Chen's assessment of China's rural situation and the looming financial deficit led him in 1962 to dissent strongly from the proposed Third Five-Year Plan that was being formulated at that time. The origins of this clash are evident in Chen's February 1962 speech to the State Council. Chen charged that most of the central ministers in charge of various branches of industry, transportation, finance, etc., were insufficiently familiar with the magnitude of the agrarian problem and, more importantly, with what it portended for the speed of recovery of industrial production.

In Chen's view, expressed in February 1962, the Ten Year Plan then being discussed internally should be divided into a recovery and a development phase. The recovery phase would require five years (1960-65), during which agricultural output would recover and (more importantly from the point of view of the audience) industrial growth would remain very slow. Thus, the plan would have to give priority to agricultural recovery, and the State Planning and State Economic Commissions had to begin the process of planning with agriculture in mind rather than to consider it as an afterthought. Steel and coal production were fine if they contributed to agricultural recovery. Otherwise, "it will be fine not to produce so much." Chen invoked Mao's slogan of "taking agriculture as the foundation" to justify his approach.

Chen and his allies were fighting an uphill battle. A month after this speech, at a meeting of the Finance and Economics Small Group, he made his most pessimistic assessment of agriculture — even within five years (presumably meaning by 1965) the previous peak level of grain output would not be achieved. He tried to defer a scheduled July meeting at which the Third Five-Year Plan was to be approved, apparently because he felt the target for steel production was too high. Now he argued the ultimate pace of agricultural recovery would not be clear for another year or two. He appealed to the experience in formulating the First Plan, pointing out that it was not put forward to the Party Congress until the spring of 1955, almost two and a half years after its scheduled beginning.

The situation was now more complex, Chen argued, and the Five Year Plan should not be fixed prematurely. The scheduled July meeting should consider only an outline of the 1963 annual plan and defer decisions on the Third Five-Year Plan that was then scheduled for 1963-67.

Chen suggested that the meeting adjust the 1962 plan in order to meet what he described as a deteriorating food situation. The construction of fishing boats should be stepped up so that urban supply of fish could increase by a kilogram a year, which in turn would improve protein supplies significantly. This proposal, as well as his earlier suggestion that soybean supplies of 50 grams daily (i.e., a kilogram every three weeks) be assured, was endorsed on the spot by Zhou Enlai. Chen also suggested steps to raise urban meat consumption by one quarter of a kilogram per month by the end of 1963.

"Chen's" economists, including some associated with the Economic Research Institute, Wu Shuqing, Shih Xue, Sung Zexing, and particularly Liu Guoguang and Dong Fureng, again supported his policy position with theoretical writings.[57] These authors from 1961 through 1963 sought to show that the traditional Marxian preoccupation with the constraint of the producers goods sector on economic growth was incomplete and that the growth of the consumer goods sector posed a constraint on the growth of producer goods. Thus a minimum investment required for consumer goods imposes an upper limit to investment in heavy industry.

In the midst of the agrarian crisis in which millions were starving to death, Chen and a few supporters were focusing their energies on how to raise per capita fish consumption by a mere kilogram per year. But the Ministry of Metallurgy was undaunted. They proposed that China's planning take an inflated steel target — now placed at 25 to 30 million tons by 1970 — as its central goal. Chen reiterated his plea for balanced growth to deflect this proposal. Planning must proceed on the basis of constraints. In this case Chen pointed out that China could not produce or afford to import the estimated 50,000 tons of nonferrous metals such as copper, aluminum, lead, and zinc that were required to produce each million tons of steel.

In the late spring of 1962 Zhou Enlai took charge of the Finance and Economics Small Group from Chen and elaborated on Chen's ideas in a major speech. Zhou convened a meeting early that summer that brought together the secretaries of the six regional Party committees, along with members of the Politburo to determine whether to circulate his speech nationally. During the subsequent discussion, Ke Qingshi, the most pro-Mao participant, objected to Zhou's characterization of the situation in far bleaker terms than the assessment of the Seven Thousand Cadre Conference in January. Liu Shaoqi responded that the budget deficit had become known only after that conference and that the reassessment was, therefore, necessary and correct.[58]

In the end, Chen appears to have gained a partial victory on the Third Five-Year Plan. He and his allies successfully extended the period of readjustment until 1965, thus postponing the beginning of the Third Plan to 1966. They also succeeded in talking down the initially proposed target of 25 to 30 million tons of steel by 1970. The final choice came down to two plan variants: A target of 20 million tons requiring a 30 percent rate of investment or an 18 million ton target, reportedly favored by Chen, that could be achieved with a 25 percent investment rate. The higher target won. Thus, after the conclusion of readjustment in 1965, not only the proportion but even the absolute magnitude of agricultural investment declined compared to 1963-65. The share of heavy industrial investment allocated to farm machinery and chemical fertilizers in the Third Plan also fell compared to 1963-65.[59]

How did Mao feel about these events? The little evidence available indicates that Mao believed his interests were being poorly served by the assessment that painted a very bleak picture. Thus, for example, when Liu Shaoqi in the early summer of 1962 ordered the compilation of a volume of Chen Yun's writings that ran to more than 40,000 characters and sent a copy to Mao, the Chairman simply left the copy on his desk for months — through the Beidaihe Conference of August-September 1962 — without commenting on it. But at this summer conference Mao launched a stinging attack against commercial policy and against the finance and economic organs, accusing the latter of not consulting with him and of always forcing him to sign things. Mao also used this conference to demand that class struggle be put high on the agenda and that continuing retreat from collective forms of organization in agriculture be brought to a halt.[60] Mao clearly based his assessment on a far more optimistic view of the state of China's economy than that found in Chen's writings during early 1962.

Thus, Chen Yun's evaluation of China's situation as of the spring

of 1962 differed significantly from Mao's, and Liu Shaoqi, Zhou
Enlai, and Deng Xiaoping used Chen's analysis as a key component
of their own critiques of the Great Leap Forward. Indeed, the
writings in this volume make more certain than previously the degree
to which Mao and his top colleagues disagreed over basic issues during
this critical period. The solution adopted by the Tenth Plenum in September 1962[61] incorporated some elements of both analyses, calling
for technical transformation and other pragmatic measures in industry
and agriculture at the same time that it sparked major political campaigns to rectify the Party apparatus. But even on substantive economic issues, as indicated above, many of Mao's views prevailed for
the Chairman had important allies in heavy industry. Indeed, in terms
of priority to heavy industry over other sectors, Mao was more Stalin-
ist than is ordinarily appreciated.

In sum, the present collection permits a more textured understanding
of the relationship between Mao Zedong and Chen Yun during 1956-
1962. This relationship worked when Mao sought to bring the Great
Leap Forward under control and deteriorated when the Chairman tried
to use political campaigns and high investment targets to increase production. At its core, though, the rocky relationship between Mao and
Chen centered on their fundamentally different approaches to developing China's economy. Mao totally dominated the Chinese political stage
during 1966-1976, and he left an exhausted country in his wake. Chen
Yun did not suffer as badly as did many of his colleagues during the Cultural Revolution, but returned fully to power only in 1978, two years
after Mao's demise. What has been Chen's impact on China since then?

Chen Yun Since 1978

Although Chen Yun appeared regularly in public identified as a "Party
and State leader" starting in the early 1970s, little is known of his specific activities until 1978, when apparently at the request of Deng Xiaoping he began again to play a conspicuous role in policy formulation.
According to Deng Liqun, Chen sharply criticized China's new Ten Year
Plan. This plan, announced in early 1978 at the first session of the
Fifth National People's Congress by Party Chairman Hua Guofeng,
had proposed an extraordinarily ambitious heavy industrial investment program and a goal of 60 million tons of steel production by
1985, more than double the 23.7 million tons produced in 1977.
Chen's critique (delivered at a November-December 1978 Central
Party Work Conference) followed the familiar refrain that the plan
must give first priority to agricultural production and allow for
balanced growth. Hu Qiaomu, recently appointed president of the

newly created Chinese Academy of Social Sciences, had laid the
groundwork for Chen's analysis. In a July 1978 speech that was
finally published only on October 6 in People's Daily, Hu pointed out
that average per capita grain production in 1977 was actually no
greater than in 1955.[62] Materials presented at the Third Plenum
that December revealed that not only was per capita production unchanged, but food distribution also remained heavily skewed, with
up to 200 million peasants living in a state of "semi-starvation"
(i.e., consuming less than 150 kilograms of cereals annually).[63]
Prior to this plenum Chen had recommended increasing cereal imports, then running at about 10 million tons per year, to 20 million tons.

The December 1978 Third Plenum effectively undermined the entire rationale of the Ten Year Plan announced only eleven months
previously. The Plenum simultaneously formally rehabilitated Chen
and signalled his prominence through both the offices it gave him
and the policies it adopted. Chen became a member of the Politburo
and its Standing Committee, a vice-chairman of the Party, and head
of the newly created Discipline Inspection Commission. He thus effectively fully regained the positions he had held from the mid-1940s
until he had been officially dropped from the Politburo in 1969.
The Plenum also approved a major price increase for agricultural products purchased by the state and paved the way for
the reemergence of increased specialization in cropping patterns
based on regional comparative advantage, the reopening of rural
private markets, and the legitimation of the so-called "responsibility system" in agriculture that devolved production responsibilities from the team to smaller subgroupings or even households.
All of these were policies Chen had advocated in the 1950s or in the
first half of the 1960s.

While the plenum gutted the old Ten Year Plan, it failed to produce a new one. As discussion of a new plan resumed in the State
Council in early 1979, the problems appeared to multiply. Deng
Xiaoping, supported by Li Xiannian, recommended the establishment of a Finance and Economics Commission to be headed by
Chen Yun. The Central Committee quickly endorsed this suggestion. In March of 1979, shortly after the new commission was
established, Chen resurrected still more elements of his former
strategy. He recommended to a Central Committee Meeting that
the 60 million ton steel target adopted only the year before be
lowered to 45 million tons and that China enter a three-year period
of "readjustment." The Ministry of Metallurgy, Chen said, should
devote its energies to improving the quality of its products, not to

an unlimited expansion of output. Indeed, Chen argued that even
as late as the year 2000 China need produce only 80 million tons of
steel. Deng Xiaoping reportedly endorsed Chen's recommendation
without reservation.

The ascendency of Chen's views and the reemergence of a symbiotic relationship between Chen and the Institute of Economic Research (formerly with the Academy of Sciences and now shifted to
the Academy of Social Sciences) was apparent in People's Daily as
early as December 1978. An article by Tian Jinghai and Liang Wensen, both associated with the Institute, opened the debate by attacking the view that plans should contain gaps (quekou), i.c., that targets for key products should be set at unrealistically high levels
in order to stimulate output. Without attacking the steel target explicitly, they called for proportionate development.[64] By February
1979 a People's Daily editorial advanced the same view more explicitly. Plan figures, the editorial charged, "have not been set
forth after investigation, study, and calculation but are decided upon
impetuously," a view that was identical to Chen's criticism of the
setting of the steel output target in 1959. For the benefit of readers
too obtuse to read between the lines, later the editorial specifically
attacked the use of the Great Leap slogan "take steel as the key
link" to justify setting the target for steel production "arbitrarily,
irrespective of reality."[65] In April Chen's supporters in the Academy, including Liu Guoguang, wrote another set of articles in People's Daily explaining and advocating the concept of balanced
growth.[66]

In June 1979 the Second Session of the Fifth National People's
Congress adopted "readjustment" as official policy, although
speeches made by Hua Guofeng and Yu Qiuli (head of the State Planning Commission) at the congress suggest that they still held views
substantially at variance with those of Chen.[67] Chen continued to
press his case for readjustment, most notably in a major speech
in September 1979 at a meeting of the Finance and Economics Commission.[68] The debate apparently was not yet over, but had merely
entered a new round. By November 1979 an authoritative People's
Daily "commentator" article spoke of the readjustment process as
being a "hard battle." "Everyone agrees with the new policy in
principle. However, differences still exist as to how it should be
implemented."[69] By late 1979 and early 1980, as the size of the
(unanticipated) 1979 budgetary deficit must have become widely
known, Chen's argument for the need to curtail capital investment

expenditures apparently seemed more persuasive. As late as June
1979, Zhang Jingfu, the Minister of Finance, reported to the Second
Session of the Fifth National People's Congress that revenues and
expenditures in the 1979 budget were balanced.[70] But Zhang's pro-
jection was wide of the mark. The deficit was reported by the new
Minister of Finance Wang Bingqian to have been 17 billion yuan,
mostly because expenditures were in excess of the budgeted
amounts.[71] By the spring of 1980, Yu Qiuli, whose State Planning
Commission long had been dominated by the Ministry of Metallurgy
and other advocates of growth centered on heavy industry, was
shifted to the newly created State Energy Commission. His replace-
ment, officially announced in September of 1980, was Yao Yilin, a
long time protégé of Chen Yun who had succeeded Chen as Minister
of Commerce in the late 1950s. At the same September meeting of
the National People's Congress, Zhao Ziyang, a Deng protégé, replaced Hua Guofeng as premier, and the Ministry of Metallurgy was
criticized severely for its promotion of the Baoshan steel plant in
Shanghai.

A year later, by the time the Fourth Session of the Fifth National
People's Congress convened in December 1981, Chen's views had
gained wider acceptance among the leadership. The session officially extended the original "three years of readjustment" through
at least 1985. Premier Zhao Ziyang announced ten important principles, generally incorporating Chen's balanced growth philosophy,
to govern economic construction. Conspiciously, however, the National People's Congress was unable to ratify the annual plan or
budget for 1982 or discuss the long-awaited draft five-year plan for
1980-85. While all agreed on the principle of "readjustment,"
evidently debate on the actual allocation of resources remained
tense.

With Chen's advanced age and the uncertainties of succession,
it is not possible to anticipate the impact his views will have on
China's development strategy in the future. But Mao's mobilization
approach largely has been discredited, and the strategy revealed
in the documents of the Chen collection is the most complete
set of alternative principles by a ranking Chinese leader. China
is changing. Chen's suggestions of the 1950s and 1960s will not
be applied in a rigid way now. But Chen's strategy has about
it the aura of having provided a potentially viable alternative
to what are now seen to have been two decades of partially
destructive and costly efforts. The fundamentals of Chen's ap-

proach will continue to be debated in the coming years as the Chinese grope for an effective formula for modernization. The documents in this volume should enable observers of the Chinese scene to better appreciate the richness and texture of this debate.

NOTES

1. Chen Yun tongzhi wengao xuanbian, 1956-1962 (Selected Manuscripts of Comrade Chen Yun, 1956-1962), Renmin chubanshe, March 1981, 180 pp. Hereafter abbreviated as: Chen Yun Collection. This volume was put together by the Research Office of the Secretariat of the Central Committee (Zhonggong zhongyang shujichu yanjiushi). After this introduction was already in page proofs we obtained a copy of a second volume, Chen Yun wengao xuanbian, 1949-1956 (Selected Manuscripts of Chen Yun, 1949-1956), Renmin chubanshe, June 1982, 328 pp. This volume contains 49 essays and speeches by Chen from August 1949 through July 1956 and a nineteen-page postscript providing historical background on the issues discussed by Chen. About three-fourths of the selections have not been available previously.

2. Deng Liqun, the head of Research Office of the Secretariat of the Central Committee, wrote this companion volume of study notes to provide background for the pieces and to explain their contemporary significance. The study notes consist of four lengthy lectures Deng gave at the Central Party School during November-December 1980, totaling 120 pages of Chinese text: Deng Liqun, Xiang Chen Yun tongzhi xuexi zuo jingji gongzuo (Study How to Do Economic Work from Comrade Chen Yun), Zhonggong zhongyang dangxiao chubanshe, March 1981. Hereafter abbreviated: Deng Liqun.

3. Deng Liqun, "Seriously Study Chen Yun's Economic Theories," Shijie jingji daobao (World Economic Bulletin), June 15, 1981, pp. 4-5. Translated in Foreign Broadcast Information Service (FBIS), July 27, 1981, pp. K15-K21.

4. Deng Liqun, p. 6. Chen was asked to head this group but demurred on grounds of ill health.

5. The text of Chen's "How to Be a Communist Party Member," written in 1939, is available in Boyd Compton, Mao's China: Party Reform Documents, 1942-44 (Seattle: University of Washington Press, 1966), p. 88-107.

6. Donald Klein and Anne B. Clark, Biographical Dictionary of Chinese Communism, 1921-1965 (Cambridge: Harvard University Press, 1971), pp. 149-152. A full biography of Chen Yun unfortunately remains to be written. The present volume is not so ambitious. The most comprehensive study of Chen's life currently available is William E. Belk, "Chen Yun: A Preliminary Study of Moderate Chinese Communist Political-Economic Policies," MA Thesis for Interdisciplinary Studies Program in Asian Studies, University of Oregon, 1982.

7. David Bachman of Stanford University has traced carefully the previous availability of these materials in whole or in selected excerpts in his "Chen Yun and the Chinese Political System, 1956-1982," May 1982, unpublished manuscript.

8. Deng Liqun, p. 17. These are selections nos. 1, 5, 12, 18, 21, 22, 23 in this volume.

9. Fei Xiaotong, "A Revisit to Gaixiangong," Xin Guancha (New View)

1957, No. 11 and No. 12. In Fei Hsiao-t'ung: The Dilemma of a Chinese Intellectual, translated and edited by James P. McGough (Armonk, N.Y.: M. E.
Sharpe, 1979), pp. 39-74.

10. See document 5 in this volume.

11. Dong Fureng, "Develop a Socialist Economy That Is Beneficial to the
People — Rereading Comrade Chen Yun's Speech at the Eighth Chinese Communist Party National Congress," Renmin ribao (People's Daily), January
29, 1981, translated in FBIS, February 24, 1981, pp. L6-L10. He Jianzhang,
"The Basic Guideline of Socialist Construction Should Be to Work for the
Welfare of the People — An Appreciation Based on Studying Comrade Chen
Yun's Works on Economic Theory," Jingji yanjiu (Economic Research),
1981, No. 11, pp. 23-27. Dong is the Deputy Director of the Institute. He Jian-
chang was a member of the Institute as early as the 1950s but more recently has
become a member of the Institute of Economic Research subordinate to the State
Planning Commission.

12. Deng Xiaogui, "Using Marx's Expanded Reproduction Formula to Study
the Principle of the Priority of Producer Goods," Jingji yanjiu, August 1956,
pp. 23-40, cited in Cyril Chihren Lin, "The Reinstatement of Economics in
China Today," The China Quarterly, No. 85 (March 1981), p. 27. Lin's article
is the most illuminating account of these developments available.

13. James Millar, "A Reformulation of A. V. Chayanov's Theory of Peasant Economy," Economic Development and Cultural Change, Vol. 18, No. 2.

14. See document 14 below.

15. Deng Liqun, pp. 83-85. See also, Stuart Schram, "Mao Tse-tung and the
Theory of Permanent Revolution," The China Quarterly, No. 46 (April/June
1971), pp. 221-244.

16. Deng Liqun, pp. 3-4.

17. Documents 10 and 11. Chen supervised the drafting of these documents.

18. Chen's phrase "large region" (daqu) referred to the seven economic cooperative areas (da jingji xiezuo qu), the antecedents of which were the six
"large administrative regions" (da xingzheng qu) that were abolished in June
1954. The decentralization decrees of 1957, however, made no mention of
these economic cooperative areas, and it is not clear what decision-making
power they possessed. Liu Zaixing, "Problems Concerning the Establishment
of Complete Industrial Systems in Cooperative Regions," Xin jianshe (New
Construction), 1958, No. 10, pp. 45-51, 57, sets out the geographical bound-
aries of the seven regions.

19. See document 22 below.

20. See document 23 below.

21. Deng Liqun, p. 11.

22. See documents 4 and 5 below.

23. Deng Liqun, pp. 11-12, indicates that Liu Shaoqi approved this editorial
and sent a copy to Mao, presumably before its publication. At the Nanning
Meeting in January 1958, Mao railed against this editorial, arguing among
other things that it twisted his meaning in a quotation from him that it employed. This editorial appeared during the middle of the Third Session of the
First National People's Congress (NPC).

24. The turning point seems to have come at the July 1957 Qingdao Conference, when Mao reversed the judgment given in the September 1956 First Ses-

sion of the Eighth Party Congress that class struggle had ceased to be a major contradiction in China. At Qingdao, Mao argued that class struggle remained a primary issue in both urban and rural policy and demanded that a political situation conducive to rapid economic growth be created. Mao Zedong, "The Situation in the Summer of 1957," in Selected Works of Mao Tse-tung, Vol. V (Peking: Foreign Languages Press, 1977), pp. 473-482.

25. Mao's January 11 and 12, 1958 speeches to the Nanning Meeting are available in Mao Zedong sixiang wan sui! (Long Live Mao Zedong Thought!) (1969), pp. 145-154. See also Deng Liqun, pp. 12-13. Deng also notes that throughout 1958 Chen Yun continued to oppose the high steel targets that were adopted that year: Ibid.

26. For documentation on Mao's speeches to this meeting, see Mao Zedong sixiang wan sui! (1967), pp. 116-120, and Mao Zedong sixiang wan sui! (1969), pp. 247-251.

27. Details on these and related meetings, with supporting documentation, are provided in: Kenneth Lieberthal, A Research Guide to Central Party and Government Meetings in China, 1949-1975 (White Plains, N.Y.: International Arts and Sciences Press, 1976), pp. 123-138.

28. See, e.g., Mao's speeches at the Second Zhengzhou Meeting, Mao Zedong sixiang wan sui! (1967), pp. 8-49.

29. 1957 output was 3.5 million tons. In 1958 output was 11.08 million tons including the steel, mostly of low quality, produced by so-called indigenous methods.

30. See document 14 below.

31. See Deng Liqun, pp. 13-14, 116. Deng comments here that Chen's investigation of steel production capabilities took three months.

32. Peng Dehuai zi shu (Peng Dehuai's Account) (Beijing: Renmin chubanshe, 1981), p. 265. Chen Yun uses 350 million metric tons as the figure arrived at by the Sixth Plenum. He is mistaken, as is indicated both by Peng's account and by the plenum's communique: Renmin shouce (People's Handbook), 1959, pp. 37-38.

33. Deng Liqun, pp. 54-55. Peng Dehuai also criticized the validity of these figures. After the Wuchang Conference in December 1958, Peng visited his hometown in Hunan and found that "the masses were in danger of starving." Peng immediately sent a telegram to the Central Committee warning that the 1958 production figures were overstated. Li Rui, "Reading Peng Dehuai's 'Account,'" Dushu (Reading), 1982, No. 4, translated in FBIS, April 16, 1982, pp. K5-K6. The Communique of the Eighth Plenum of the Eighth Central Committee, at which Peng officially was charged with heading an anti-Party rightist clique, revised downward the 1958 output figures to 250 and 2.1 million metric tons for grain and cotton respectively. More recently the figures were disclosed to have been 200 and 1.708 million metric tons: Chinese Agricultural Yearbook Compilation Commission, Zhongguo nongye nianjian 1980 (Chinese Agricultural Yearbook 1980) (Beijing: Agricultural Publishing House, 1981), pp. 34, 36.

34. Deng Liqun, pp. 13-14, 16.

35. See below, documents 14 and 15.

36. Deng Liqun, p. 14. Chen did not attend the Lushan Conference.

37. Deng Liqun, p. 8.

38. "Summarize the Experience of the Communes and Strengthen Commune Construction," Renmin ribao, November 20, 1960.

39. Three of these ten reports are printed below as document 19.

40. Gongzuo tongxun (Bulletin of Activities), April 5, 1961. Translated in: J. Chester Cheng (ed.), The Politics of the Chinese Red Army (Stanford: Hoover Institution, 1965), p. 405; and JPRS, No. 41202: May 29, 1967, p. 121.

41. Dongfang hong (East Is Red), April 20, 1967. Translated in SCMP-S, No. 187: June 15, 1967, pp. 23-36.

42. See document 19 below.

43. First Five Year Plan for Development of the National Economy of the People's Republic of China in 1953-1957. (Beijing: Foreign Languages Press) 1956, p. 82.

44. Yang Jianbai and Li Xuezeng, "The Relations Between Agriculture, Light Industry and Heavy Industry in China," Social Sciences in China, 1980, No. 2, pp. 181-212.

45. Sun Yefang, "Strengthen Statistical Work, Reform the Statistical System," Jingji guanli (Economic Management), 1981, No. 2, pp. 3-5, reports (page 3) that the death rate more than doubled from 10.8 per thousand in 1957 to 25.4 per thousand in 1960, implying increased mortality in 1960 alone of over 9.5 million. Estimates by Ansley Coale and John Aird place the number of excess deaths (i.e., over and above those that would be expected under normal conditions) for 1958-1962 at about 16 million. John Aird, "Reconstruction of an Official Data Model of the Population of China," unpublished manuscript, 1980. Ansley Coale, "Population Trends, Population Policy and Population Studies in China," Population and Development Review: Vol. 7, No. 1, March 1981, pp. 85-97.

46. See, for example, Mao's writings of 1960-61 in A Critique of Soviet Economics, translated by Moss Roberts (New York: Monthly Review Press, 1977), pp. 102-103, and his statements at a Work Conference of the Chinese Communist Party Central Committee in June 1964, cited in Lieberthal, Research Guide, p. 211.

47. For an analysis of this policy see Nicholas R. Lardy, Agriculture in Chinese Economic Development (Cambridge University Press, forthcoming).

48. Zhongguo nongye nianjian 1980, p. 34. It is possible that the figures that formed the basis for Chen's analysis in early 1962 were higher than the data cited in more recent reports. Chen in February 1962 thought 1961 output was about forty million tons less than 1957. The figures in the Yearbook show a difference of 47.5 million tons.

49. This number differs from an estimate of 20.84 in Kang Chao, Agricultural Production in Communist China 1949-1965 (Madison, Wisconsin: University of Wisconsin Press, 1970), p. 247. Chao's estimate was based on information originally contained in Tongji gongzuo (Statistical Work), 1957, No. 17. Reprinted in Xin Hua banyue kan (New China Semimonthly), 1957, No. 22, pp. 171-172.

50. This had been reported in the fall of 1961 by Viscount Montgomery, who quoted Mao as having said that reserves were virtually exhausted by mid-1961. Times (London), October 15, 1961, cited by Chao, op. cit., p. 248.

51. See document 19 below.

52. Liu's recommendation to this Central Work Conference at Huairentang

in Beijing's Zhongnanhai was made in a speech on June 6, 1961. The text of the first part of this speech was on display in the spring of 1981 in the Liu Shaoqi memorial exhibition at the Museum of the History of the Revolution in Beijing.

53. See document 18 below.

54. See document 22 below.

55. Deng Liqun, p. 6.

56. This history is related in Deng Liqun, pp. 6-7, 45. Deng also notes that Chen Yun enjoyed Deng Xiaoping's strong support during this period.

57. Cyril Lin, op. cit. Names are rendered according to Lin's romanization.

58. This history is related in Deng Liqun, pp. 6-7, 45.

59. Yang and Li, op. cit., pp. 191, 200.

60. See Mao Zedong sixiang wan sui! (1969), pp. 423-429.

61. Peking Review, October 5, 1962, pp. 1-5.

62. Hu Qiaomu, "Act in Accordance with Economic Laws, Step Up the Four Modernizations," Renmin ribao, October 6, 1978.

63. Lin Shen, "The Inside Information on China's Economic Readjustment," Zhengming (Contention), May 1979, pp. 9-13.

64. Tian Jianghai and Liang Wensen, "It Is Not Permissible to Leave Any Gap in Drawing Up Economic Plans," Renmin ribao, December 31, 1978, translated in FBIS, January 8, 1979, pp. E17-E19.

65. Editorial, "Emancipate the Mind for Overall Balance in Economic Development," Renmin ribao, February 24, 1979. Translated in FBIS, February 26, 1979, pp. E12-E16.

66. Liu Xianzhao and Huang Zhenqu, "Practice Comprehensive Balancing in Light of Actual Conditions," Renmin ribao, April 6, 1979. Translated in FBIS, April 19, 1979, pp. L6-L8. Liu Guoguang, "Several Questions Regarding Comprehensive Balancing," Renmin ribao, April 13, 1979. Translated in FBIS, April 30, 1979, pp. L4-L8. See also Liu's longer analysis co-authored with Wang Xiangming, "A Study of the Speed and Balance of China's Economic Development," Social Sciences in China, Vol. 1, No. 4 (December 1980), pp. 15-43.

67. Dorothy J. Solinger, "The Fifth National People's Congress and the Process of Policymaking: Reform Versus Readjustment," unpublished paper, 1982.

68. Deng Liqun, pp. 10-11.

69. Commentator, "Make Concerted Efforts in Fighting Well the Hard Battle of Readjustment," Renmin ribao, November 23, 1979. Translated in FBIS, November 28, 1979, pp. L8-L14.

70. Zang Jingfu, "Report on the Final State Accounts for 1978 and the Draft State Budget for 1979," Beijing Review, No. 29, July 20, 1979, pp. 17-24.

71. Beijing Review, No. 39, September 29, 1980, pp. 11-23.

*Chen Yun's
Strategy
for China's
Development*

EDITOR'S NOTE

This selection includes a portion of the important manuscripts by Comrade Chen Yun on socialist construction from September 1956 to 1962. Among these manuscripts, some are speech transcripts which have never been sorted out, and we have polished them stylistically. We have abridged, supplemented, and revised very few transcripts. The selected manuscripts are arranged chronologically.

There might be important omissions in the manuscripts selected in this book, and inappropriate editing may have occurred at certain points as well. Please make suggestions in order to facilitate future corrections.

The Research Office of
the Central Committee of
the Communist Party of China

PREFACE

For twenty-eight years from starting to carry out the First-Five Year Plan in 1953 up until now, our Party has been leading the Chinese people in socialist construction. This has been a more complex struggle than any of our past revolutionary battles. Just as in our revolutionary battles, we have won great victories and also suffered serious reverses during this great struggle. We went forward on a tortuous road, and we paid a high price. Looking for the reason, except for the special conditions during the ten years of the Great Cultural Revolution, the basic point is whether we have followed or violated the basic Marxist principle of seeking truth from facts that Comrade Mao Zedong advocated repeatedly. The practice of twenty-eight years really gives such a proof: the constructive course is developed quickly when we firmly adopt the style of seeking truth from facts; otherwise, it suffers damage or even stagnates and falls back. To carry out socialist construction in a large country, which was originally quite poor and backward, is a specially complex and specially arduous course. Besides other factors, whether it develops quickly or slowly, goes forward or backward, or succeeds or fails is mainly subject to whether or not the guiding ideology of the party in power is correct. Doubtlessly, it is very significant to the construction of modernization in the next twenty years to profoundly understand this point, then carefully handle affairs; to strive not to make this or that kind of mistake in each work item, and therefore strive not to make mistakes on the major issues.

A very important stage of socialist construction occurred in our country, from the basic fulfillment of socialist transformation of individual farming, handicraft industry, and capitalist industry and commerce in the autumn of 1956, to the implementation of the Eight-Character Policy of readjustment, consolidation, filling out

and raising standards in 1962.[a] A notable characteristic of that
stage was the movement from success to failure and then from
failure to success again. Our work of socialist transformation had
a problem — the rashness of the steps and the roughness of the
work — but generally speaking, it was successful. In 1958, the
movements of the Great Leap Forward and the formation of the
People's Communes caused our constructive course to suffer a
serious reverse, and in 1959 and 1960 our economy faced difficulties that it never had before experienced. Nevertheless, advancing
the Eight-Character Policy and its unanimous and firm execution
from the top to lower levels again opened up a road of victory for
us. The economy basically recovered by 1962, and by 1965 a picture of national economic prosperity had emerged.

This volume of selections contains the main articles by Comrade
Chen Yun from this period. They total twenty-three. We can learn
many things from these articles, yet what is most necessary for
us to learn is the scientific attitude and dialectic method of seeking
truth from facts. In Comrade Chen Yun's words, all leaders should
give orders "not according to higher authorities, not according to
books, but according to facts." Methodologically, they should know
and analyze the factual conditions comprehensively, make comparisons of different kinds of opinions, suggestions and plans in
many aspects, and must consider them repeatedly before making
the final decision. In short, this is the six-character phrase "comprehensive, comparative, and repeated." During the period when
Comrade Chen Yun was in charge of financial and economic work,
he always insisted and practically applied the principle of seeking
truth from facts, and he earnestly practiced what he advocated and
correctly conducted the socialist construction of our country.

Comrade Chen Yun advanced his views and opinions in regard to
all the important issues of socialist construction. Among all of
these views and opinions, some were then adopted and carried out,
but some were not adopted and were even misunderstood and criti-

---

a) The so-called eight-character policy, "tiaozheng, gonggu, chongshi, tigao,"
was officially endorsed by the Ninth Plenum of the Eighth Central Committee
in January 1961. The development policy approved at the Third Plenum of the
Eleventh Central Committee in December 1978, popularly known by the phrase
"readjustment," is summarized in a similar eight-character slogan, "tiaozheng,
gaige, chengdun, tigao" (readjustment, reform, consolidation, and raising standards). It differs primarily by the inclusion of reform as a specific policy objective. — Eds.

cized. History, however, has proved that his views and claims not only were correct and applicable at that time, but also that they are still correct and applicable. For example, the view that we should allow a certain amount of individual management in addition to industry, agriculture, and commerce run by the state and collectives; the view that we should allow a certain freedom to enterprises under the direction of the national plan; the view that we should develop each undertaking, especially capital construction, according to our capability; the view that we should pay attention to comprehensive balance and leave some leeway when the plan targets are set, in order to achieve proportionate development; the view that in planning work at all times and places we should pay attention to and organize the three balances of materials, finance, and credit; the view that in the arrangement of goods and materials we should arrange production prior to capital construction; the view that in the arrangements for production and livelihood we should give first priority to the peasants who make up 80 percent of our population; the view that finance and trade should serve socialist production, the livelihood of the masses, the political power of the people; the view that it is much more difficult to correct deviation of rash advance than conservative deviation in economic construction; and so on. All of these still have practical significance today. Certainly, as conditions change, we must adopt new directions, specific policies, and measures in economic construction, but these basic views of Comrade Chen Yun should be respected continuously. From a Marxist perspective, any view or claim that is raised strictly according to the principle of seeking truth from facts holds great and enduring vitality because it conforms to the demands of objective laws.

We ask our readers to kindly give opinions if there is anything improper or omitted in the editing of this book.

Editor
September 25, 1980

1

NEW ISSUES SINCE THE BASIC COMPLETION
OF THE SOCIALIST TRANSFORMATION
(September 1956)*

Comrades:

I am in full agreement with Comrade Mao Zedong's opening
speech, and also with the reports made by Comrades Liu Shaoqi,
Zhou Enlai, and Deng Xiaoping. I agree to the revised Party Con-
stitution and the proposals for the Second Five-Year Plan.

Socialist transformation in our country has achieved a great and
decisive victory. Whether in the field of industry or handicrafts,
agriculture or commerce, the socialist sector is now the only important form of our economy. But both the scope and tempo of this
movement in which the nonsocialist sector was changed and merged
into the socialist sector made it inevitable that we should be faced
with new problems and tasks. I should like to give my views on
some problems which have arisen in the wake of the socialist
transformation of the nonsocialist sector, primarily capitalist industry and commerce, including some problems which the movement has brought to state-owned enterprises.

For seven years our Party and the government have been carrying out the socialist transformation of capitalist industry and commerce. It will take us several more years to bring this work to
completion, as much still remains to be done. Following the
change-over of capitalist industry and commerce to joint state-
private management by whole trades, we have had to consider our
practical work from the following three main aspects: (1) in regard
to the capitalists; (2) in regard to the workers and employees; and
(3) in regard to the conversion of capitalist industry and commerce
into socialist industry and commerce.

Much has been done already in regard to the capitalists. For ex-

---

*This is a speech made by Comrade Chen Yun at the Eighth National Congress
of the Communist Party of China. [Translation from Eighth National Congress
of the Communist Party of China, Volume II: Speeches (Peking: Foreign Languages Press, 1956), pp. 157-176.]

ample, we have fixed the rate of interest on their investments; in-
ventoried their stock and capital; made arrangements regarding
their work and livelihood and that of their associates; gradually
improved their working relations with the state representatives
in enterprises, and so on and so forth.

As to the workers and employees, we have promoted a number
of the more outstanding ones to the position of representatives acting for the state in joint state-private enterprises. Meanwhile a
new wage scale is being worked out. Under the new scale there
will be a gradual increase in wages for those workers and employees in joint state-private enterprises who are getting lower pay
than those working in similar state-owned enterprises in the same
locality, but there will be no reduction where the wages are higher
than those paid in state enterprises. It should be stated that far
from enough has been done for the workers and employees in
joint state-private enterprises in the last six months, and this is
gross negligence on our part. These workers and employees have
given warm support to the change-over to state-private management, and everywhere they have organized socialist emulation
drives. But because we have not done enough work for them, some
of them are asking: "How is it that we have even fewer rights and
functions than before the change-over?" "Why are the former
capitalists still in positions of authority?" The fact that workers
and employees entertain such doubts reveals the unsatisfactory
state of our work and our shortcomings.

The change-over of capitalist industry and commerce into joint
state-private enterprises is a fundamental change of ownership, a
change which consists in the transformation, in the main, of capitalist ownership into socialist ownership. This transformation has
resulted in the change of all kinds of relations in joint state-private
enterprises. Following the struggle waged in 1952 in all private
enterprises against bribery, tax evasion, theft of state property,
cheating on government contracts, and stealing of economic information from government sources, it became the rule in every
capitalist enterprise for the workers to supervise production and
for the trade union to enjoy wide powers over the management of
the enterprise. Prior to the recent change-over of private enterprises, it was absolutely necessary to have such supervision of
production by the workers. It had a good effect on production in
capitalist enterprises and on the process of their transformation.
But now that these enterprises have been converted into joint state-

private enterprises, the working class should take a further step forward and, instead of merely supervising production, should put into effect direct management by the state, which is led by the working class. Needless to say, in managing these enterprises, the state must rely on the workers and employees, promote the more experienced and outstanding ones from among them to positions of leadership and other administrative jobs, improve and vigorously enforce the various systems of democratic control in the enterprises. The change in the role played by the workers from supervision over to management of production, together with the state-share representatives appointed by government organs is no deterioration, but a further rise in the powers of the working class in the joint state-private enterprises. It is not a setback, but a step forward. As to the capitalists and their associates, whatever position or authority they may still retain in the joint state-private enterprises differs fundamentally from what it was prior to the change-over. The position and authority which they had in the enterprises prior to the change-over consisted in their right to the ownership of the property, and their rights to manage the enterprise and its personnel. After the change-over, insofar as their right to property ownership has not been entirely abolished, the capitalists can still for a certain period of time draw a fixed interest on their investments. Apart from this, the rights to manage the enterprise and its personnel now no longer belong to the capitalists, but to the state's "special companies for whole trades." The position and authority which the capitalists and their associates still have in joint state-private enterprises has nothing in common with the three rights they enjoyed prior to the change-over. The position and authority given them by the state is no more and no less than what is given to ordinary technical personnel or managerial staff. It is given to the capitalists not as such, but as public servants of the state.

Do industrial and commercial capitalists in our country possess a knowledge of the techniques of production and management? We should say that, unlike the landlords and bureaucrat-capitalists, the overwhelming majority of the national capitalists do in fact possess, in varying degrees, a knowledge of modern techniques of production and management. We need such useful knowledge as they possess. In the future there will certainly be a growing number of engineers, technicians and administrative personnel coming from the ranks of the working class itself; in fact, they have already begun to appear. But under existing circumstances in our country, the national bourgeoisie with its intellectuals has, as a class, a relatively high level of cultural attainment. We should make it clear to all workers and employees that it will not be to the advantage of the cause of the working class if they fail to enlist into its service those national capitalists who are willing to do their bit to build China into a prosperous and powerful socialist country. It does conform to the interests of the working class if these people are allowed to take part in production and management in socialist enterprises, and accorded the same political rights as the rest of the people of the country. We should explain these things on a wide scale among workers and employees, so that they may understand the changes which take place in the capitalist enterprises; and we should continue to promote a number of those workers and employees who have the proper qualifications of leading positions in enterprises. Leading personnel in enterprises should see to it that the management of their units is democratic, and that, wherever necessary and possible, the working conditions and livelihood of the workers and employees are improved. If these tasks are well carried out, then the misgivings which some workers and employees entertain will naturally disappear.

Such are our tasks with regard to the capitalists and to the workers and employees. Now I wish to deal with some new questions of principle relating to industrial and business management which have cropped up in the transformation of capitalist industry and commerce.

First, as a result of the decisive successes we have achieved in the socialist transformation of capitalist industry and commerce, certain measures taken by state economic departments in the past few years, and particularly in the past two years, to restrict capitalist industry and commerce have now become unnecessary. These measures were indispensable and effective at the time. Now, however, they are quite unwarranted. Not only that, they were not without shortcomings at the time they were enforced. To continue them now would inevitably hamper the further development of the national economy.

The measures I refer to are the following: (1) It was necessary in the past for state commerce to give capitalist industrial enterprises orders for processing and manufacturing goods, and to purchase and market all their products. From now on, it will still be necessary for state commerce to purchase and market all the important products of light industry. But continued indiscriminate application of this method would tend to make certain factories pay less attention to the quality of their products than they used to do when they were marketing their own products, and, consequently, it would hinder the raising of the quality of some industrial goods.

(2) When orders are placed for processing and manufacturing goods and when the state purchases and markets all the products of industrial enterprises, the relations between the state wholesale companies of various levels become such that, in most cases, goods have to be allocated for sale by state wholesale companies at higher levels to those at lower levels. The result is that the work of placing orders with factories is handled only by a few wholesale companies, and shops at the primary level cannot buy directly from the factories in accordance with the needs of consumers. Consequently, the variety and specifications of goods ordered by commercial departments from the factories have become less. It is also unavoidable that the distribution of goods by state wholesale companies to the various localities has in some cases got out of step with local needs as regards both quantity and variety; this has resulted in cases of overstocking in some places while other places are short of supplies.

(3) The methods used for control of markets have put restrictions on private merchants in purchasing, transporting and marketing goods. These methods make the local supply and marketing cooperatives or state commercial enterprises virtually the sole purchasers of agricultural products and products of subsidiary occupations in the villages. There is no competition whatever, and when supply and marketing cooperatives and state commercial enterprises neglect to purchase certain agricultural products and products of subsidiary occupations or offer too low a price for them, the result is a drop in the output of these commodities.

Second, in the upsurge of socialist transformation of agriculture, handicrafts, and capitalist industry and commerce, it was not easy for us to give guidance to concrete organizational work so as to keep pace with a situation that was developing so rapidly. Mistakes of a temporary and local nature have occurred which we must now rectify as soon as possible. These mistakes are as follows:
(1) While cooperation was extending into the field of handicraft industry, too much emphasis was laid on amalgamation and unified management with profit and loss shared in common by all the different units drawn into a cooperative. This has not benefited the management of handicraft production. That is why some handicraft products have deteriorated in quality or become less varied

since the handicraftsmen ceased working on their own. Furthermore, both customers and handicraftsmen themselves have experienced many inconveniences since some handicraft service establishments were brought together and placed under unified management. (2) Cases in which amalgamations were blindly carried
through also occurred when the transformation of capitalist industry
and commerce was at its height, and this gave rise to the same
problems as ill-considered mergers of handicraft establishments.
(3) When bringing cooperation to agriculture, we did not pay sufficient attention to those subsidiary occupations which were only
suitable for cooperative members to run as household industries.
Coupled with negative influences from other directions, this has
caused a certain drop in the output of some agricultural subsidiary
occupations. All the above-mentioned mistakes are of a temporary
or local nature. Some of them have been put right while others
still remain to be corrected.

What measures should be adopted now to replace those taken in
the past to restrict capitalist industry and commerce, and also to
effectively rectify mistakes made through lack of experience in the
course of socialist transformation?

First, we should change the purchasing and marketing arrangements now established between industrial and commercial enterprises. The system of state commercial departments giving the
factories orders for processing and manufacturing goods should be
replaced by the system of the factories themselves purchasing raw
materials and marketing products. In purchasing industrial products, the commercial departments should adopt the following two
methods:

(1) The practice of exclusive purchasing and marketing should
be continued so far as this concerns products closely affecting the
national welfare and the people's livelihood and products whose
variety is limited, for example, cotton yarn, cotton piece-goods,
coal, table sugar, etc. This ensures a regular supply of these
commodities and a stable market.

(2) As for those consumer goods which exist in a wide variety,
the practice of exclusive purchasing and marketing should be
gradually discontinued, and replaced by a system of selective purchasing. That is to say, the practice which we followed prior to the
winter of 1953 should, in general, be restored on the new basis of
our socialist economy. The state commercial departments will
have priority in buying commodities of this category. In case they

relinquish this priority, or if certain quantities are left over after they have done their purchasing, the goods will be marketed either by the factories themselves or by the commercial departments acting as their commission agents. When contracting to supply factories with raw materials, state commercial departments should not fill the orders partly with materials of standard quality and partly with materials of poor quality. With the exception of the raw materials in short supply, which are distributed by the state alone, all other raw materials should be purchased by the factories on the free market. Wholesale companies at higher levels should not allocate commodities for sale to those under their control. Shops at lower levels may make such purchases as they think fit from any wholesale organization in the country; they may also make purchases directly from the factories. Such a system of selective purchasing to govern relations between industrial and commercial enterprises as well as between higher and lower commercial organizations is meant to make the factories pay close attention to market conditions and improve the quality of their products. The new arrangements are also designed to make the shops keener about the needs of customers, and prevent any reduction in the range of goods offered for sale. Such a system of selective purchasing is also applicable to many handicraft products.

Second, it is essential that a considerable proportion of industrial and handicraft establishments, agricultural subsidiary occupations and commercial enterprises should be separate units of production under separate management. The tendency to blindly amalgamate and unify managements which results from a one-sided view of things must be checked.

True, some joint state-private factories should be merged and put under unified management. But taking the country as a whole, most of them should continue to be operated separately, either exactly as before or with some necessary readjustments. The great majority of joint state-private factories are manufacturing consumer goods, and the people's needs for such goods are very varied and constantly changing. If a large number of small factories are merged into larger ones, producers will become less responsive to the changing conditions of the market. Take cotton prints for instance. A small machine-dyeing works may use a pattern for only 50-60 bolts of cloth. That is why it is able to suit the people's needs by constantly changing its patterns. But this is not the case with large machine-dyeing works where each pattern is used for

300-500 bolts at least, because any change in the pattern involves
a major change in the working process. If we were to merge all
our small factories into larger ones, we would never be able to
satisfy the people's diverse and ever-changing demands for consumer goods.

We should remember that, before the liberation, the patterns and
variety of consumer goods were no less than at present, and that
most of the factories producing such consumer goods were of
small size. Some comrades, thinking that production can be increased by merging small factories into larger ones, are bent on
amalgamation all the time. We must, of course, have a certain
number of large factories, because many of the most important industrial products have to be manufactured on a large scale. The
increase in production of many consumer goods achieved after a
merger of factories is, however, mainly due to a decrease in the
variety and specifications of commodities made and, hence, a
greater concentration of production effort. Such "rationalization"
cannot meet all the people's demands for consumer goods. That is
why we should not encourage ill-advised amalgamations.

Part of the handicraft trades engaged in manufacture can be appropriately amalgamated, but the great majority of the service
trades and many of the manufacturing trades should not be amalgamated. In order to put an end to the uniformity of products and
the drop in the quality of service resulting from blind amalgamation and blind implementation of the method of unified management
with profit and loss shared in common by the various units drawn
into a cooperative, many big cooperatives must be reorganized into
small ones, and the calculation of the overall profit and loss of
the whole cooperative society should be replced by another system,
that is, the different cooperative teams and individual households
should themselves shoulder responsibility for their own profit and
loss. Such a change will be suitable not only for the great majority
of service trades but for a number of manufacturing trades as well.
Handicrafts are generally of a scattered and local character; therefore, the primary-level cooperatives should, in the main, engage
in purchasing and marketing on their own. The central authorities
as well as the provincial and municipal leading organs of the handicraft industry and the combined cooperatives of most trades should
only give guidance in respect of principle and policy and not undertake purchasing and marketing operations themselves.

In the field of commerce, there should also be appropriate de-

centralization where too many organs have been amalgamated. The
method with which small traders and pedlars ply their separate
trades within a cooperative team should be preserved for a long
time to come. Certain state wholesale concerns, such as department stores and stationers, should try to get back those business
personnel of different trades and specializations who were formerly employed in the privately owned wholesale shops but have
now changed their trades. And wholesale shops of separate trades
should be set up within state wholesale trading companies, so that
the oversimplified division of labor and low level of professional
skill which at present characterize state wholesale concerns such
as department stores and stationers may be gradually rectified.
In order to meet the needs of factories, shops, cultural and educa-
tional departments and other organizations for the numerous kinds
of imported commodities, the Ministry of Foreign Trade should
organize those import companies which were formerly privately
operated but are now under joint state-private management into
import shops specializing in those commodities in which they used
to or can specialize. It should get part of the professional personnel who did various kinds of import work in concerns run by foreign
merchants in the past, to participate in the work of these import
shops. The few state import companies which monopolize the
whole import business at present and still have a low level of professional skill cannot meet the needs of society. We must put an
end to this state of affairs.

The production of grain and industrial crops and part of the
subsidiary occupations in the agricultural producers' cooperatives
should be collectively managed by the cooperatives. But many
subsidiary occupations should be separately managed by members.
The state of affairs where everything is indiscriminately managed
by the cooperative must be altered. Only by giving a free hand to
the members in their individual management of many subsidiary
occupations can the production of different sorts of subsidiary occupations be increased, the needs of the market be met and the
cooperative members' income raised. In places where cooperative
members, on the average, have more land, we should, if it does
not affect the yield of the staple farm products of the cooperative,
consider whether it is advisable to let the members have a bit
more land for their private use, so that they can plant crops for
fodder to raise pigs and increase the production of subsidiary
occupations.

The work of reorganizing former capitalist industrial and commercial enterprises is just beginning and we are arranging the collective and scattered management of industry, commerce and agriculture. We must correct our mistake of focusing attention on centralized production and management while neglecting scattered
production and management. Otherwise, the defects already seen
in production, in circulation and in service to consumers will get
worse.

Third, we must cross out from our regulations governing market
control all those provisions which were meant to restrict the speculative activities of capitalist industry and commerce. In order to
control grain, industrial crops and various other kinds of farm
produce and check the speculative activities of the capitalists, the
state, in the past, restricted the private merchants' purchases in
the rural markets. This was, of course, justified. In future, it is
still necessary for all grain, industrial crops and important products of peasant subsidiary occupations to be purchased by the state
or by the supply and marketing cooperatives as agents of the state;
but part of the products of peasant subsidiary occupations, for instance, minor local products, now purchased in a unified way by
local supply and marketing cooperatives, should be allowed to be
freely purchased, transported and marketed by state shops, cooperative shops, cooperative groups and supply and marketing cooperatives in different parts of the country. Mutual exclusiveness in
purchasing should be prohibited. By so doing we shall be able to
prevent the production of minor local products from being reduced
because of any negligence on the part of the supply and marketing
cooperatives or because of low prices. This will also help the
goods circulate more freely. If everybody wants to buy something
and a drain on supplies results, we should, with the leadership of
the local authorities or the Party, distribute the available supply
according to the degree of the urgency of the needs of various purchasing units. If supply exceeds demand for a period in a certain
range of goods and all purchasing agencies are on the point of reducing prices, the supply and marketing cooperatives should purchase the goods in question at ordinary prices so that the peasant
producers will not suffer a loss. Those provisions in the regulations for controlling industry and commerce which are out of keeping with the situation today should be revised in order to meet the
needs of free purchasing, marketing and transportation. In our
regulations governing payments of bank remittances we must alter

all those mechanical restrictions which lead to such absurdities as not permitting "money allocated to buy vinegar to be used to buy soya bean sauce," or which prevented money remitted to one place from being used in another. All those regulations drawn up by the departments in charge of tax-collecting or transport and the post offices which were meant to restrict speculative activities in their respective fields should be revised in the light of changed conditions to permit a free exchange of commodities.

Fourth, we must so frame our price policy as to facilitate production. Since March 1950, the government has slightly raised procurement prices for farm produce, and marketing prices for industrial and agricultural products have been generally stable. The price policy has been correct and has successfully stimulated the growth of our industrial and agricultural production. Our procurement prices for staple farm produce have been correct. But procurement prices for some farm produce were fixed somewhat too low, thus harming production. These should be readjusted. Since the practice of placing orders by the state with enterprises for processing and manufacturing goods was replaced by that of allowing factories to purchase their own raw materials and market their products, the unfair procurement prices fixed for some industrial products have been adjusted.

Our present price policy has an element which is unfavorable to production. That is, in marketing, we think of stabilizing prices simply as "unifying prices" or "freezing prices." As a result, differences in prices between goods of different quality are very small and high-quality goods are denied high prices. Such a price policy cannot encourage improvement in the quality of goods; it will only encourage the lowering of quality. In our market control, use of the method of fixing prices through consultation played its role for a time in stopping private merchants from raising prices. Before March 1950, the country had passed through twelve years of currency inflation and price fluctuations. It was quite understandable therefore that the people throughout the country should be afraid of price fluctuations and demanded stabilized prices. But we must note that a wrong price policy is bound to impair production. Therefore, we should not become worried if prices go up for a time within certain limits under one of the three conditions described below:

(1) Since we will fix prices according to the quality of goods, prices for high-quality products whose production costs are higher

will be duly raised. We should take note of the fact that deterioration in the quality of goods is the worst price jump. For instance, if an electric bulb, otherwise good for a whole year, can now only last three months because its quality has fallen off, this means that its price has actually gone up four times. As the quality of certain consumer goods is found to be falling off, we are actually reducing commodity prices if we arrange that high prices will be paid for high-quality goods.

(2) New varieties of consumer goods should be allowed to be sold at somewhat higher prices than ordinary during the period when they are being manufactured for the market for the first time, and as long as consumers are willing to pay such prices. This is necessary because when they are first made the cost of new varieties of goods is generally high. But once they are being produced in large quantities and consequently at lower costs, they may reduce their prices as far as conditions permit. The situation at present is that there are less varieties in certain consumer goods; and unless we adopt such a price policy, there will be no incentive to produce new varieties of consumer goods.

(3) With regard to certain minor local products, immediately after the loosening of market controls and the introduction of free purchasing, transporting and marketing, purchasing prices will be apt to go up, which in turn will cause a corresponding rise in marketing prices in the cities. It should be noted that if we fail to adopt the policy of free purchasing, transporting and marketing and, instead, allow the local supply and marketing cooperatives or the state trading companies to continue as sole purchasers of these minor local products, the production of many of these items will fall off. When the supply of these local products falls short of urban demand, with the government unable to do anything about it, then people needing such products will all help to boost their prices. The present steep rise in the prices of several kinds of medicinal herbs is a proof of this. On the other hand, when some of these local products are again brought into the market through free purchasing and free trading, rising prices will only be a temporary phenomenon. Moreover, the range of the price rise can still be kept under our control. The increased prices will give an impetus to the production of these commodities; and when a balance is reached between supply and demand, prices will come down to their normal level. In regard to these minor local products, we should adopt the policy of free purchasing and free trading without

getting alarmed at a certain temporary rise in prices that may
well be anticipated. What we must avoid is a steep rise in prices
due to a drop in production. It should be understood that marketing
prices are determined by purchasing prices and that price stability
comes only as a result of a considerable increase in production.

People may wonder if we can still keep prices stable after we
have adopted the above-mentioned price policy and put into effect
the system of selective purchasing of articles of daily use by the
state commercial departments. We believe we can. In the case
of such daily necessities as grain and cloth, we shall continue the
system of planned purchase and planned marketing by the state.
Now the annual value of output of minor local products which are
to be bought and sold on the open market is no more than 4,000
million yuan. The value of output of the articles of daily use falling within the scope of the selective purchasing scheme is also
approximately 4,000 million yuan. The handicraft products to be
purchased by the state on a selective basis, or directly marketed
by producers, come up to another 4,000 million yuan. All told, the
value of output of these commodities is 12,000 million yuan. This
will make up only a little more than one-fourth of the total turnover of this year's retail trade, which will be 46,000 million yuan,
while the important commodities which constitute three-fourths of
our domestic trade will still be bought and distributed by the state.
Besides, up to 1954, most of the 4,000 million yuan worth of the
annual output of minor local products and the 4,000 million yuan
worth of the annual output of daily necessities, which will be
brought under the selective purchasing scheme, used to be bought
and sold by private merchants. And the 4,000 million yuan worth
of the annual output of handicraft products had always been freely
sold by the handicraftsmen themselves before the cooperative
movement reached the handicraft industry in the spring of this
year. And as we succeeded in stabilizing prices in the years preceding 1954, why can't we do the same at a time when all capitalist
industry and commerce have come under joint state-private ownership, when the overwhelming majority of handicraftsmen and pedlars have been organized into cooperatives, and when the forces of
socialist economy have been greatly strengthened? There is absolutely no reason for us to doubt this. We shall certainly be able to
keep prices stable.

Fifth, suitable changes should be made in the state's planned
control over certain products. Our state plans, whether long-term

or annual, make provisions only for a few kinds of articles of daily
use, handicraft products and minor local products. Apart from
these, no detailed plan is made for particular commodities in these
categories. This arrangement is justified. On the other hand, the
state plan does specify the value of their annual output and, in the
case of departments manufacturing articles of daily use, targets
are set for reduction of costs, raising the level of productivity of
labor and the amount of profits to be handed over to the state treasury. Not all these targets are based on fully accurate data; most
of them are based only on estimates. Because these targets are
set in the state plan, which is handed down from one rung of the
administrative ladder to another, and because the marketing of the
products of a factory is done exclusively by the state commercial
departments, the factories manufacturing articles of daily use often
concentrate only on the fulfillment of targets relating to value of
production and profits, while giving insufficient attention to whether
their products meet the needs of consumers. Henceforth, these
targets in the state plan should be taken merely as figures for
reference. Factories manufacturing articles of daily use should be
allowed to make their own production plans in the light of market
conditions without being tied down to the reference figures in the
state plan. As for the profits to be handed over to the state treasury, the amount should be determined by the factories' actual receipts at the end of the year. Provided the enterprises concerned
strictly abide by the financial regulations of the state governing
their expenditure, the state will not suffer any loss if the profits
to be handed in to the national treasury are fixed according to
actual receipts at the end of the year.

Since there is no need for the state plan to set rigid targets for
many of the factories and commercial departments, we should not
waste more money and labor in collecting much statistical information that has turned out to be useless. Thus, the number of statisticians can be drastically reduced. At present, many statisticians
in commercial departments are working on figures that are not of
much use.

As we are engaged in converting capitalist industry and commerce into socialist enterprises, we might ask ourselves what
should be our principles in directing the production and management of such enterprises? Certainly we shall not allow consumer
goods to deteriorate in quality or decrease in variety; nor shall
there be any drop in the output of agricultural subsidiary occupa-

tions or deterioration in the work of the service trades. On the contrary, we must improve the quality of consumer goods, increase their variety, expand industrial and agricultural production and improve the work of the service trades. The five measures mentioned above are designed precisely to help the conversion of capitalist industry and commerce into socialist industry and commerce in the interests of the people.

To sum up: In regard to a part of our commodities, we should use either the method of selective purchasing by state commercial departments or allow the producers to market their own products. A large number of small factories should continue to operate independently, while many handicraft cooperatives should be split into smaller ones with the component teams or households managed separately. Members of agricultural cooperatives should be allowed to take up different kinds of subsidiary occupations on their own. Minor local products should be freed from market control. We need not fear that the prices of some commodities will rise for a short time within certain limits. The methods of planned management of some branches of the economy should be suitably modified.

Will all these measures combine to bring about the danger of reemergence of a capitalist free market in our country? No, that will never be the case. The adoption of the above-mentioned measures will never lead to reemergence of a capitalist market, but will further the growth of a socialist market adapted to our conditions and the needs of the people. The general state of our socialist economy will be as follows: In the production and management of industry and commerce, the mainstay will be either state or collective management, to be supplemented by a certain minor proportion of individual management. As regards planning, the bulk of the industrial and agricultural output of the country will be produced according to plan; but, at the same time, a certain amount of production will be carried on freely, with the changing conditions of the market as its guide and within the scope prescribed by the state plan. In industrial and agricultural production, planned production will be the mainstay, to be supplemented by free production carried on within the scope prescribed by the state plan and in accordance with market fluctuations. This kind of market under a socialist economy is in no way a capitalist free market, but a unified socialist market. In this unified socialist market, the state market is the mainstay, and attached to it is a free market of certain proportions under the guidance of the state. The free market

is under the guidance of the state and supplements the state market. Consequently, it is a component part of the unified socialist
market.

The adoption of the above-mentioned measures will help us solve
a number of problems now existing in our state market. At the
same time, however, it may bring forth new problems, the solution
of which will require further efforts. As we still lack the necessary experience in these matters, the measures I have just described must therefore be implemented with caution, that is, with
a view to steady advance and gradual extension on the basis of experience gained through trial.

2

METHODS OF SOLVING THE TENSIONS IN SUPPLIES OF PORK AND VEGETABLES
(September 1956)*

There are currently some problems in the supply of pork and vegetables, our two major nonstaple foods.

Since 1955, there has been no increase in the export of pork, the supply of pork in big and medium-sized cities has declined, and small cities and rural towns are often out of it. In a word, pork supply is tense in both cities and rural areas. I think that the problem of pork supply is no longer a simple and ordinary question of some goods being out of stock but a major problem affecting the relations between the Party and the people. The people have complaints against us in this respect. From a long-term point of view, as more and more people become employed, the purchasing power of the urban and rural inhabitants will increase and the demand for pork will increase, too. This contradiction will become sharper unless effective measures are adopted to resolve it.

The main reason for the short supply of pork is insufficient production. Production of pork since national liberation can be divided into two stages. In the period before 1954, national output of pork increased consistently and basically kept pace with the increasing purchasing power of urban and rural residents. Ever since 1955, output has declined while people's purchasing power has kept on increasing — hence the major problem of supply falling short of demand. The only way of resolving this contradiction is to try every means to boost production so that output can meet the increasing demand.

The first measure to increase pig-raising is to increase fodder, which can be done as follows: (1) restore the original system of grain-processing and stop the practice of extracting oil from rice

---

*This is a speech made by Comrade Chen Yun at the Eighth National Congress of the Communist Party of China.

bran; (2) appropriately disperse the industries for processing
grains, oil crops, and bean noodles as well as wine-making and
appropriately reestablish workshops in rural market towns for
processing grain, oil crops, wine, and bean noodles so as to increase the supply of fodder; (3) as of this autumn, set aside more
grain as feed during the period when the state purchases grains;
(4) make it an important task of the agricultural producers' cooperatives to organize the masses to collect a great amount of greenfeed. It could be expected that once the shortage of grain supply is
somewhat alleviated, more pigs can be raised if for one to two years
we adopt a policy of reducing the rate of increase in grain reserves.
Raising more pigs will increase the fertilizer which in turn will
help promote grain production.

The second measure to increase pig-raising is to raise the procurement price. Pig prices have been increased yearly since
liberation. When pigs were raised by individual peasants, labor
and some of the feed were excluded from costs and, with cheap
rice bran, peasants benefited from pig-raising. However, things
have changed with the state monopoly for purchase and marketing
of grain and with the cooperativization of agriculture. Nowadays,
rice bran is quite expensive to both cooperatives and peasants who
raise pigs so that feed has to be counted as cost. Moreover, cooperatives have to count labor in the cost of pig-raising. Therefore, the procurement price must be further raised. Production
has already been affected by our not deliberating on this question
in time and our making a decision late on it. It is estimated that
most areas can benefit from pig-raising if the procurement price
is raised by an average of 15 percent.[a] For areas where this still
would not cover the cost, a further increase could be effected. In
some other areas, the price should be increased by a smaller margin. The procurement price in areas near big and medium-sized
cities can be increased more so as to encourage more pig-raising
to meet the demand of the cities and to cut down long distance
transportation and reduce intermediate links. At the same time
that the procurement price is raised, taxes should be reduced and
commercial profits minimized in order basically to stabilize the
selling price.

---

a) The average state procurement price for pigs was raised 13.89 percent in
February 1957. State Council, "Directive Concerning the Readjustment of Pig
Procurement and Sale Prices," in Compendium of Laws and Regulations of the
People's Republic of China, vol. V, pp. 181-182. — Eds.

The third measure to increase pig-raising is to give priority to
pig-raising by individual cooperative members, help them overcome difficulties in feed procurement and allocation of time, and
set a proper price for manure so as to enable pig-raising to continue to be a major household sideline.

In addition, in areas where forced designated procurement [paigou]
is practiced, peasants should be fully consulted and forced designated
procurement quotas should be fixed according to needs and possibilities.[a] There should be no increase in purchase quotas even if
production has increased. Peasants should be permitted to keep
some of the pigs for their own, to butcher, to eat, to share with
others or to sell. When a pig is purchased, it should be ensured
that the peasant who has raised the pig is left with several jin of
pork and cooking oil. The purchasing organs should do both the
buying and the selling so as to meet the needs of the local people.
They should not simply buy pigs and ignore selling pork. Special
attention should be given to doing good supply work during holidays
and festivals. In grading and pricing, realistic and effective measures should be worked out according to traditional customs of the
area and after consulting with the peasants. What should be avoided
or corrected are downgrading and down-pricing or purchasing pigs
with full stomachs. All these are policy questions in procurement
work. In the past few years, some areas have gained pretty good
experience in this regard where there is no loss suffered by the
state while there is satisfaction on the part of the peasants. However, serious problems still exist in some areas. Commercial departments haven't done enough in summarizing and popularizing
these experiences. Henceforth, they should pay attention to this.

Now I would like to say a few words about the supply of vegetables. Vegetables are not like pork, which affects areas far and
wide. The question here is the supply of vegetables in big and
medium-sized cities as well as industrial and mining areas. Vegetables, usually not suitable for long-distance transportation and
wide-ranging allocation, are basically locally produced and locally
sold. In the last two years, thanks to the enlarged vegetable-growing areas in the suburbs of various cities, supply of vegetables has
greatly increased except in a few new industrial and mining areas.

---

a) Designated procurement, "paigou," is the system used by the state for the
procurement of category two agricultural products. — Eds.

Therefore, the present problem is mainly how to combine vegetable producing with its selling and to find proper ways of marketing.

In some big and medium-sized cities as well as industrial and mining areas, vegetables grown by the peasants are all purchased by the state-operated vegetable companies, and marketing is exclusively done by these companies. Trading markets of the peasants are banned and no direct transactions are allowed between producers and consumers. This is an erroneous policy with bad consequences in production and supply in the following respects: (1) Producers give first priority to quantity at the expense of quality. In order to obtain a bigger quantity and sell more for more money, they keep the fresh and young vegetables growing in the fields until they have overgrown. What's more, the mass harvesting and mass delivery as a result of mass sowing in large acreage lead to overfull markets in peak periods, which causes a huge amount of waste and tremendous losses. (2) Producers one-sidedly seek high yield. Acreage for many low-yield but high-quality vegetables has thus been reduced. The result is that there are less varieties in the markets, and all the markets have only common vegetables in large quantities. (3) The state-operated vegetable companies, in their effort to introduce a unified distribution of vegetables, have set up a huge management structure, which has increased the number of links and led to high expenditures and all kinds of formalities. This has caused a lot of inconvenience to the consumers and has deprived them of fresh vegetables. Such managerial methods do not conform to the objective commodity circulation laws for vegetables.

Vegetables are a seasonal commodity that rot easily. Great variety is needed and they must be fresh. The only vegetable that can be preserved for a longer period of time are Chinese cabbages, turnips and potatoes, some dry and pickled vegetables, as well as beans for bean sprouts, bean curd, and other bean products. No vegetables except these few can be preserved for long. Considering these characteristics, the following points must be dealt with in the production and supply of vegetables: First, leave some time between the sowing of the same and different vegetables so that there will always be a great variety of fresh vegetables in the market. Second, encourage people to consume more during peak periods and provide markets in the off seasons with Chinese cabbages, turnips, potatoes, and bean products. Third, stress direct transactions between producers and consumers, minimizing the intervening links.

In order to meet the above-stated requirements in vegetable management, the state monopoly policy for purchasing and selling should not be implemented. One cannot assume that vegetable prices must remain unchanged all year round. There must be a certain degree of price flexibility.

The following measures should be adopted in vegetable management to meet the demands of both producers and consumers. First, in accordance with the overall situation of the market, the commercial departments should put forward reference quotas for vegetable growing. With the approval of the Party and government organizations, these quotas will be presented to the agricultural producers' cooperatives in the suburbs for their reference, and the agricultural cooperatives can change these quotas whenever necessary in light of the market situation. Second, the cities and suburbs can set up a number of vegetable markets to let the agricultural cooperatives, cooperative members, and individual peasants sell fresh vegetables freely and at the same time allow all the urban vegetable shops, small retailers, government organizations, army units, schools, factories, and individual consumers to purchase freely and deal directly with the producers. State-operated vegetable companies can also manage a portion (of this business). Third, in light of the needs in the off seasons in particular areas, the state-operated companies can sign contracts with the agricultural producers' cooperatives, ordering procurement of a certain amount of preservable vegetables, such as Chinese cabbages, turnips, and potatoes. They can also store some beans in order to provide the market in off seasons. To facilitate transportation and storage, the vegetable companies should arrange for the catering offices of government organizations, army units, schools and factories as well as vegetable retail shops to go straight to the cooperatives for the vegetables and to store them separately. Fourth, producers and buyers can negotiate among themselves prices of the fresh vegetables in the market, and usually prices should not be stipulated by the state. To avoid excessive rises in vegetable prices, the state can impose price ceilings in accordance with different seasons and different varieties. A unified arrangement by vegetable companies is advisable when there is a shortage of supply. List prices should be stipulated for vegetables in large quantities sold in state-operated companies, such as Chinese cabbages, turnips, potatoes, and bean products. Though fluctuations of prices blindly following supply and demand of the market are not allowed,

there should be some seasonal and qualitative price differences.
Fifth, generally speaking, small vegetable retailers should not be
organized into cooperative shops which are engaged in joint purchase and joint selling and assume a joint responsibility for their
profits and losses. They should take cooperative teams as a main
form, each taking responsibility for its own profits and losses. By
doing so, the auxiliary laborers in families can be better used and
the existing defects in the cooperative shops, such as too many
links, high expenditures, low individual incomes, lack of enthusiasm, etc., can be eliminated.

Should the above-mentioned measures be adopted, the urban
vegetable market, instead of being a state market with state monopoly for purchase and marketing, will become a free market under
the leadership of the state. The state leadership is manifested
through providing production plans for reference to the cooperatives, selling large quantities of vegetables under the list price by
the state-operated companies in the off seasons, and imposing price
ceilings and making unified arrangements during periods of shortage. This market is also free to a certain extent because the producers can make and change their plans according to the demands
of the market, freely negotiate prices with consumers, and have
direct transactions within the range stipulated by the state. With
the adoption of these measures, on the one hand, the enthusiasm of
the agricultural cooperatives can be greatly boosted. They will
then study the changes in the demands of the urban population and
properly arrange the timing and variety of vegetable growing.
Thus, not only the demands of the consumers can be satisfied; the
income of the cooperative members will increase, too. On the
other hand, as long as the suburbs grow enough vegetables and the
state-operated companies have large amounts of vegetables and
beans at their disposal, supply in off seasons will be basically
guaranteed. What's more, there will only be seasonal fluctuations
of vegetable prices, and it is unlikely that prices will always go up
and never fall. As a result, the problems of combining vegetable
production with marketing and the problem of supply methods will
be properly tackled.

There is another question that needs an answer, i.e., will the income of vegetable growers be ensured after the adoption of these
measures? I think it can be ensured so long as the cooperatives
set aside the right amount of land for vegetable growing so that
they do not grow more than can be sold. Facts in the last few years

have proven that income from growing vegetables has greatly out-
stripped that from growing grain and cotton no matter whether or
not purchase and marketing are monopolized by the state. To further ensure the income of vegetable growers, various big and medium-sized cities can consult the cash value of a work point in
grain- or cotton-growing cooperatives and fix a minimum cash
value of a work point for the vegetable-growing cooperatives. If
this minimum is not reached in the year-end settlement of accounts,
agricultural taxes could be reduced or remitted or subsidies be
granted so as to ensure a reasonable income for the vegetable
growers.

3

SPEECH AT THE ENLARGED
MINISTERIAL AFFAIRS CONFERENCE
(November 1956)

During the several days of this meeting, comrades have raised
many questions. They can be summed up into three main areas.
One is that commercial work is poorly managed. People who want
things from you demand them, but things that should be given to
you do not arrive. Like wheat between grindstones, you are attacked from both sides. Another is that organizational work in
commerce is chaotic, and its relation with each field is not har-
monious enough. Third is the question of how to evaluate the work
of the past few years. With regard to these questions, I will now
give some opinions.

We will first talk about the problem of the shortage of commodity
supply.

The shortage of commodity supply did not fall from heaven, but
rather, it is a reflection of the situation of finance, trade, and economic construction in the whole nation. The shortage of commodities this year is greater than that of the past six years. Is it going
to be like this every year in the future? No, it cannot. If it were
like this every year, then the problem would expand. It would be
a problem not simply of commerce work or even of economic work
more generally but would repeatedly call into question the appropri-
ateness of our policy of construction. The condition of supply shortage
that appeared this year is due mainly to the shortcomings in our work.

It is not difficult to obtain a superficially balanced budget; it
would be "evened" if we put in less. For example, this year we
did not enter 2.5 billion yuan of agriculture loans in the budget because we plan to rely on reserve funds, so the budget seems to be
balanced. It was said in the past that there was no imbalance in
cash; if currency in circulation was excessive, we could collect it
back through selling things or through savings deposits. This year
we must rely on hidden commodity reserves to avoid imbalance.

This year the currency in circulation has increased by 1 billion yuan compared to the same time last year. If there is nothing to buy, it will become reserves in the hands of the people. Therefore, it will not work if we look for the cause of supply shortages simply in the field of commerce; we must look for the cause in the economic condition of the whole country, especially the financial situation. Only then can we explain the problem.

With regard to the economic condition this year, the Second Plenary Session of the Eighth Central Committee has given this estimation: production developed, employment increased, and people are happy This is the first. Second, construction investment is mostly appropriate; only a part is inappropriate or overspent. The total that is overspent is about 2 or 3 billion yuan, of which about 1.5 billion yuan was on capital construction, and also a little bit on education, culture, farming, forestry, and water conservancy. Agricultural credit is necessary but it has not been included in the budget; moreover some of it was excessive. Of 2.5 billion yuan in agriculture loans, about 1.5 billion yuan is necessary. In order to get 500 million peasants organized without chaos, it is worthwhile to extend some loans. But, agriculture loans should be listed in the budget because we have to cut down other expenses if the budget is unbalanced. The salary of workers has not been increased for three years, so it should be increased this year as well. Following this, the purchasing power increases, and commodities are in great demand. Not only this, construction materials are also in short supply. For example, as to iron and steel, there was still not enough even after the accumulation of four or five years was used up.

In economic construction, there was a little rashness in 1953, and there is a little rashness again this year. It is a little bit bigger than that in 1953, so the exposed problems are more obvious. As long as we take the lesson of this first half year and we are not rash any more in the future, commodities will not be in such short supply.

Comrades might say: Why is man so stupid? Actually it is hard to say. At the beginning of this year, it was said, first in the Ministry of Commerce, that there would be more coal and even more distribution. It is very difficult to work without making mistakes. People who worked for elimination of counterrevolutionaries and for land reform all understand this truth. It is easy to write the articles opposing left-leaning as well as right-leaning, but it is very difficult to do. This year, during the high tide of nationwide socialist transformation, it is hard to avoid a little bit of rashness in economic construction. It is hard to guarantee not making the same mistake in the future. Social economic life is complex and changeable, and it is not as simple as watching movies. We have gained rich experience from the rashness of the first half of the year, so it is also an advantage.

The economic construction and people's livelihood must both be considered and must be balanced. It seems, for quite a long period, that this kind of balance will be basically a comparatively tight balance. I think that it is rather difficult to have both ample economic construction and a comfortable life for the people. Our cultivated lands are limited, but the population is big. We all depend on these lands for food and clothing. If we do not promote construction, the unemployment and semi-employment will be the same, and since social purchasing power is very low, the supply of commodities would not be tense for a while. But it is out of the question not to promote construction. If we carry on construction, we will increase employment, a portion of the population of the countryside will move into cities, and people will eat more, wear more, and use more. Social purchasing power will increase, and commodity supply will be tight. But it must not be so tight that the balance is broken down; instead, it should be a tight balance. In the so-called tight balance, frequently some things are insufficient. Pork meat, for example, is often not enough. And cotton cloth would still be in short supply even if we increased cotton production by 1.5 million metric tons, because each person would have only a little more than 4 zhang. We should be mentally prepared for this condition. It is a temporary phenomenon that some commodities have increased. For example, it was said few years ago that there was more paper, but it was used up within a year. There is also a similar situation with respect to the five metals and electrical equipment. The commercial departments should not proceed on the basis of simply speeding up commodity turnover and turning more profits over to the state in order to find an easy way to say that there are more commodities. We cannot put undue emphasis on the speed of circulation, because we are not pedlars on the streets, or the Yong An Company,[a] and also, the situation is different from

---

a) A reference to the popular Wing An Department Store Company of prewar China. — Eds.

that in the early period of Liberation. Now we have the responsibility of regulating production and balancing demand and supply.
Therefore, we should consider both rapid turnover as well as necessary reserves of society.

It is very important to see clearly the cause of commodity shortages. In that way we will be unable to argue that the cause is simply within each department and does not lie in overall financial and
economic work. If we argue that it is only within each department,
the problem will not be solved even by a head-breaking fight.

Now I will talk about the issue of improving commercial work.

First, the whole organizational form and work method in the
commercial field in the past seven years was appropriate to the
condition of utilizing, limiting, and transforming private capitalism.
Now the three major transformations have won a decisive victory.
Circumstances have changed radically, so commercial work should
be changed accordingly as well.

Second, though the whole system of commercial work in the past
was advantageous to the struggle against private capitalism, there
were still many things disadvantageous to the people. Our state-
owned commerce is a business of "only this one," so there is
really a touch of monopoly. The secretary of the Shanxi Provincial
Party Committee recalled an old woman who wove a little bit of
cotton cloth and went to sell it in a country fair, but a cadre said
it was illegal. She was so scared she ran away without her cotton
cloth. Of course this was not an order of the minister or vice
minister of commerce, but we must consider that there are 2.5
million workers and staff in the commercial system. There are
many people who do not have the good art of policymaking and who
have complex class status. The leading organs should complete
tasks, as well as consider the interests of people. It is easy to
say, but not so easy to do. Especially in regard to purchasing
agricultural products, there are many problems in our work, and
peasants are filled with anger. We absorbed much from peasants.
For example, there is a lot of extra grain in warehouses. It should
have something to do with some of our grain purchasing units which
measured in with a big steelyard and measured out with a small
steelyard. The state-owned commerce is "both official and merchant"; thus it is hard for common people to deal with us. In general, there are many cases of work that is divorced from the
masses, and what is said in the newspapers is all true.

Third, too much centralized power and too little local power.

This is created by history. After Liberation, we needed centralization in order to recover quickly economically and to unify finance and economics. We also needed centralization to struggle
against private capitalism. However, the line of the commercial
system is just a line for making clothes, and it is not as strong as
a cement post. In the field of commercial work, the important affairs must be handled by the Party and government at each level.
I think that we will have "great order across the land" if a deputy
secretary of the county Party committee can be in charge of commercial work, and the county Party committee can often discuss
commercial work. There is an experimental center in Taigu
County, Shanxi Province. Four companies were put under county
administration, 40 percent of the profit was turned over to the
state, 50 percent belonged to local government, and 10 percent belonged to the enterprises. Thus, the county Party committee vigorously took charge of commercial work. Unsold commodities were
sold, and unpurchased things were purchased. In one year the
revenue of the whole county increased by 100,000 yuan, while there
were only 12,000 yuan of flexible funds a year before. Even if each
county has 100,000 yuan a year, 2,00 counties in the whole nation
will have only 200 million yuan; if each county has 50,000 yuan,
these will be only 100 million yuan for the whole nation. If the
county has power as well as an interest, the commercial problems
will be largely solved. Now the whole burden is put on our shoul-
ders. We cannot see the problems at the lower levels, and they
cannot be solved. What is good about this? Unifying financial and
economic work and carrying out planned economy both demand
centralization. However, the centralization cannot be overdone,
and we must consider the fact that our country has a large population and territory, and the circumstance of each place is different.
We often say that the policy should be specified according to local
practical circumstance. Who does this specification? It should be
mainly the county Party committee.

Fourth, adjust the relationship between leaders within the
commercial system and the masses. The minister, bureau of-
ficers, and managers can only take charge of important issues,
and specific execution still depends on 2.5 million workers and
staff. We can handle affairs well only by relying on them and
bringing their initiative into full play. We definitely cannot do
commercial work well if we think that they know nothing except
how to listen to orders, like abacus beads which only move after

being touched. A comrade at the meeting of the Party's Eighth
Plenary Session suggested that worker's representative assemblies
should be able to dismiss a factory director or manager. I think
this opinion makes sense. Although the supervising work is important, it doesn't work if we only rely on supervising work. We
must let the masses all speak out and all have initiative. To develop democracy, we can use workers' representative assemblies,
sales clerks' representative assemblies, and other forms. Many
big issues should be discussed by representative assemblies. They
can make suggestions to higher levels for the dismissal of factory
directors or managers. Our Party has been maintaining the mass
line. We should mobilize the masses and rely on the masses in
all types of work. After relations were cut off with the Soviet Union
in 1948, finding no way out, Yugoslavia let workers manage factories by themselves, and that had considerable utility. In the
early period of the War of Resistance, He Yingqin did not give us
money. Chairman Mao told us two things: one was disbandment,
the other was production. As a result, we found a way out. We
launched a big production movement, and we all ate well and had
clothes to wear. It is thus clear that there is always a way out by
relying on the masses. Under the condition of not giving up national plans and centralized unification, what is wrong with supporting workers' representative assemblies? As long as 2.5 million people in the commercial system get organized and everybody
has a sense of responsibility, we are not afraid of "great chaos
across the land." This is a major political issue. What is called
exclusive concern about economy means not relying on the masses
and the local Party committee. In the past, the mass work of the
commercial system was very poor. It is an important question to
strengthen ideological and political work, and it should be discussed
often at ministry affairs meetings.

I have explained above that commercial departments have a relationship with the masses and the local Party and government; there
also is a relationship between leaders within the system and the
masses. What is called policy is nothing more than handling each
of these relationships well. I think that if we improve our work
according to the methods mentioned above, we can say in principle
there is hope that commercial work will be done well.

Last, I will talk little bit about estimating achievements and
shortcomings.

I think that in seven years of commercial work there have been

achievements as well as mistakes, but there have been mainly
achievements. We have had achievements both in the field of promoting production and stabilizing markets and in the field of transforming private capitalism. As for shortcomings and mistakes,
some were created by objective causes. For example, in order to
carry on socialist transformation of private capitalism, we should
have had our present set of organizational institutions. Of course,
among them, some were created by the lack of subjective efforts.
The purchase of pigs, for example, both for local sale and export,
is divided into four grades. This gives purchasing personnel one
more chance to lower the grade and price. As to the shortcomings
in the transformation of private capitalism, some were caused by
work that was not done well. In estimating achievements and shortcomings, I think there should be several dividing lines. One, we
affirm that there have been mainly achievements. Two, among
shortcomings and mistakes, some were caused by objective factors, and some were caused by work that was not done well. Three,
the upper and lower levels are both responsible for shortcomings
and mistakes, but mainly, the Ministry of Commerce at the central
level should be held responsible. Many policies and methods were
decided by the upper level, so the leading organs should be held
responsible. Of course, I am also responsible. Now, it is understandable that comrades from lower levels are filled with anger
and they want to release a little bit here. We should make this
clear.

Also, I will mention a view on getting scolded. Somebody said
that in commercial work, you get scolded every day. I think that
there is a bad side as well as good side in regard to getting
scolded. It is easy to correct, if there is somebody scolding as
soon as there is a mistake. If people shout "long live" every day,
once you make a mistake it will be a big one. In commercial
work, there are many people who put on a rival show, but this
can promote our improvement. Failure is the mother of success. If there are mistakes and we correct them, we shall
progress continuously. If there were nobody mentioning mistakes in five years, and we had been climbing up, we would
fall from the fifth floor in the sixth year. That would be ter-
rible. For example, during the construction of the Yangtse
River Bridge at Wuhan, if the problems had not been pointed
out and we had been just shouting "long live," it would have been
disastrous once there was a sudden collapse. The Baocheng

Railroad has been built,[a] it now caves in all the time just because we shouted "long live."

We should not mention it all the time if we have achievements. It is enough to mention it several times a year. Having achievements is a very obvious thing; it does not need to be mentioned every day. However, we should pay attention to shortcomings and mistakes continuously. Commercial work is being watched by 600 million people every day. They criticize and expose the problems in our work. What is bad about this? We are not capitalists; we are not bureaucrats; we are people who make revolution. In the past, we promoted commerce to overthrow reactionaries, to obtain revolutionary victories, and to establish a people's regime. Now it is for stabilizing the people's economic life, and to benefit socialist construction. We are merchants; however, we are not ordinary merchants but revolutionaries who engage in commercial work. We should stand on a higher plane and see further ahead. We should be on the roof and cannot stay in the basement.

Commercial work deals with people every day, providing food, clothing, daily necessities, oil, salt, fuel and rice. Do not look down on these things; these are important matters of the people. Our Communist Party must be concerned about the immediate interests of people every day. Man needs to eat, and he cannot live on eating Marxism-Leninism every day. His stomach makes loud noises if he doesn't eat for one day. The Yangtse River Bridge is great, its construction was very necessary, but we cannot say that commerce that concerns the daily lives of 600 million people is a small matter or unimportant.

It is better to be criticized every day if we make mistakes. If we do not criticize at the ordinary times, there always will be one day coming with a big criticism. Stalin had 70 percent contribution and 30 percent shortcomings. While he was alive, nothing was said, but once the criticism started, even his portrait was no longer seen. This is no good.

When we do work, we should use more than 90 percent of our time to study the situation, and less than 10 percent on policymaking. All correct policies are obtained on the basis of scientific analysis of the actual situation. Some comrades are the opposite:

---

a) The rail line built between Baoji, Shaanxi, and Chengdu, Sichuan, completed in 1956. This was the first line connecting Sichuan, China's most populous province, with the rest of China. — Eds.

they are busy at deciding this or that, but they very rarely
study and investigate the actual situation. This method of work
must be changed. We should see that one-sidedness always results from being busy at making policy instead of studying the
actual situation.

4

MANAGE COMMERCIAL WORK WELL
(November 1956)

This meeting of the department and bureau heads and directors of each province and city, convened by the Ministry of Commerce, the Ministry for the Purchase of Agricultural Products,[a] and the Federation of Supply and Marketing Cooperatives, has raised many questions. Now I will give several opinions for your consideration.

I. THE PROBLEM OF COMMODITY SUPPLY SHORTAGE

The commodity supply shortage this year reflects, in the field of commerce, problems existing in our economic construction work.

This year, industrial production is increasing. Agricultural production is also increasing, capital construction is developing. Achievements in our economic construction work predominate. For example, steel production has exceeded its original planned target. Though agricultural production suffered disasters, production still exceeds that of last year. The shortcoming is that the expenditures exceeded the financial budget by 2 to 3 billion yuan. Among the over budget expenditures, capital construction investment was 1.5 billion in excess, schools recruited an excessive number of students, and some places overspent for increasing salaries and promotion in salary grades. Furthermore, agricultural loans increased by 2.5 billion yuan. The great majority of this is necessary since agricultural cooperativization would meet very great difficulty if the state did not provide some support. The state's provision of more loans guaranteed that there was no chaos during the high tide of agricultural cooperativization. This is,

---

a) This ministry had only a brief existence from July 1955 through November 1956. — Eds.

necessary. But in some places the loans were excessive, and some loans were inappropriate. The above is the basic cause of market shortage. Of course, there are many shortcomings in the work of commercial departments.

It is not difficult to balance revenue and expenditure in the fiscal budget. The problem is that the money we put into circulation has to be balanced by tapping out the goods and materials from storehouses, and by selling commodities. Thus in this year state reserves and the stored goods and materials of the Ministry of Commerce will be decreased by 20 to 25 billion yuan. The stores of the five metals company will be greatly reduced and the cotton yarn company will also sell 20 million bolts of cotton cloth more. There is actually a deficit in the fiscal budget this year, and the cash income and expenses are actually imbalanced. Therefore, we should not observe the tense commodity supply situation this year only in terms of commerce, but instead, we should observe the whole situation of fiscal balance of revenue and expenditure and economic construction. The comrades of the commercial departments should be ideologically prepared for continued shortages of commodities during the period of the Second and Third Five-Year Plans. This kind of shortage is determined by the economic condition of our country. It is a very arduous task, for an economically backward country like ours, to basically complete national industrialization within a relatively short period. Therefore, we will have to spend some more money in the industrial construction field. It is impossible to realize industrialization and to use modern technology to change agriculture if we do not develop heavy industry. Of course, agriculture and light industry also need to be developed, and we need to spend some money as well. Owing to the development of national economic construction and the increase in social purchasing power, the demand for food and clothing by the people will increase, but the speed of development of agricultural production is relatively slow. Therefore, during the large-scale state construction, we should consider the needs of people. It is not easy to balance both commodity supplies and the distribution of goods and materials. Our work is to prevent this tight balance from breaking down.

This year the degree of shortage of commodity supply is unusual. In this year, we have used up 2 or 3 hundred thousand tons of iron and steel which we had accumulated since 1951. This will effect the iron and steel distribution of 1957 and 1958. Anyhow, it will take two or three years for this situation to ease. Next year, it will not be as serious as in this year, although the supply of some goods and materials still will be short.

Comrades will ask why we were rash this year. It should be pointed out that we are not totally inexperienced; however, it is not easy to absorb lessons and experiences. Taking commercial work as an example, since we had shortages of cotton cloth supply in 1954, we carried out planned supply. In the first half of this year it was said that there was more cotton cloth in some areas, so we increased supply. Now there is a shortage again.

Comrades who do commercial work cannot simply notice the commercial problems such as price and profit, they should also notice the problem of balance between the scale of state construction and the needs of the people's livelihood. Many mistakes have been made on this problem, and they have been quite significant.

II. METHODS TO IMPROVE COMMERCIAL WORK

Commercial work should be changed to some extent after the high tide of socialist transformation How should it change?

First, we used the method of utilizing, limiting, and transforming privately owned industrial and commercial enterprises in the past seven years. Now the capitalistic industrial and commercial enterprises all have come under joint state-private management, and small retailers also have been basically cooperativized. This is a radical change. Along with this, commercial work also needs change in order to fit this new condition.

We should change the purchase-sale relation. We should not rely entirely on unified procurement and exclusive selling. We should adopt some flexible methods. For example, we can practice selective purchase in the buying and selling relations of either industry or handicraft industry with commercial departments. The commercial departments should also change the past practice of forcibly assigning commodities from the top to bottom

We should change the method of market management. Now, under the leadership of the state, free markets have already opened gradually. Tentative opinions were already given on what should be opened, what should not be opened, and how to manage at the ten-province rural free market report meeting held by the State Council in October. We are planning to convene again a national market meeting next January, and we will have further studies and set up the rules.

We should change the organizational structure. The commercial
structure should have elaborate division at the top level. Should
lower levels also be divided elaborately? How should things be
done in economically developed areas? How should things be done
in economically backward areas? All of these need to be studied.

We should reform the work system. Now the goods selling system in department stores is very complicated. The shop assistants
have to take stock once a week or even every day. There are too
many tables and reports, and completing them is an extreme
scourge. They should be simplified. The accounting system is
also very complicated. Of course it will not work if there is only
one current account. It will not do to not have a system. However,
it should be simple, clear, and practical. I suggest that the cadres
at the department and bureau level in each province and city commercial department, within three months, personally spend three
to five days at one basic unit and do investigation and research.
They should sum up each kind of working system and put forward
methods for improvement, and submit a report to the Fifth Office
of the State Council[a] by the end of next February.

Second, in commercial work there is a tendency to be divorced
from the masses. This tendency was not notable when the state-
owned commerce, cooperative commerce, and privately owned
commerce coexisted. Now the whole market has been unified, and
the purchase and sale of commodities is under the monopolist
management of socialist commerce. If we do not improve working
methods and we do not work well, then the danger of becoming
seriously divorced from the masses arises.

Mostly, the phenomenon of being divorced from the masses exists in the purchase of agricultural products. The regional price
differentials of some products are unreasonable, such as the purchasing price for live pigs. The quality price differentials for
some products are unreasonable, and in many places the grade and
price are lowered when the agricultural and subsidiary products
are purchased. We are "both officials and merchants," so it is
very difficult for common people to deal with us. From now on, to
evaluate the grades of agricultural and subsidiary products, we
should use the method of democratic evaluation by members of

---

a) The State Council in the 1950s had numbered staff offices, each in charge
of a group of related ministries. The Fifth Staff Office was headed by Li Xiannian and took charge of finance, trade, and food. — Eds.

agricultural cooperatives. In some places, for some agricultural and subsidiary products which are produced and sold within the same place, people are unhappy with the large differential between the purchase and the sale price. This is caused by multiple managerial links, great expenditure, and great profits. It is also related to high tax rates. From now on, we should consider that for certain native and subsidiary products that are produced but not in quantity sufficient for sale and that need to be transfered in, we will only sell but not purchase, and only give a sale price but not a purchase price. In some places, peasants feel discontent because they are not allowed to retain any portion or an adequate portion of the products that are subject to either unified state procurement or designated state procurement. There is also a similar situation in regard to the purchase of cotton, peanuts, and live pigs. In some places, the commercial organs only have an intermediary function: they make money without touching goods. For example, in the management of aquatic products and forests, there is this kind of "taking a share of the spoils without participating."

Third, with regard to the relation between the Center and the localities, there exists a situation whereby the Center is over-centralized. In the early period after the founding of the People's Republic, it was necessary to have a relatively strong centralization for finance and economy, because only in this way could we struggle against private merchants and carry out economic planning. Centralization is still necessary in the future. However, in the commercial field centralization in the past few years has been excessive. The chief attributes of commercial work are its dispersed, local, and mass character and its direct relation with the masses. Commercial work has also an important policy character. If the policy is right, the masses will support it; if the policy is wrong, the masses will be unhappy. The policies made by the top are not necessarily right, and even if they are right, they are not necessarily suitable to the conditions in each area. In the commercial system, there are many comrades who like vertical leadership. This line is just like the thread used for making clothes. It breaks easily and policy can't be carried out easily. At the province level, there is at least an office of finance, grain and commerce, and it takes charge of this line. The weakest point is at the county level. There should be an assistant secretary of the county Party committee specially managing commercial work, and the county Party committee should discuss commercial work frequently. Thus, we should give a certain authority to the county level to make them have initiative. We should provide this item in the commercial system in the future.

Fourth, there are 2.5 million workers in the commercial system. There are two different kinds of attitudes toward these people. One is to take them as abacus beads. They only move when you touch them, and you do not let them express their opinions. This is the bureaucratic method of leadership. We should understand that we cannot only rely on the minister and directors of departments and bureaus to do our work. The other attitude is to fully mobilize these 2.5 million workers, to heighten their consciousness, then to make them take commercial work as a part of a revolutionary course and fulfill it enthusiastically. This is the leadership method of the mass line. We should organize a management committee in every basic unit. For small units, we should organize a management small group, and for smaller units, we will call it a management conference. The management committee has the power, in regard to appointing and removing the manager, to make recommendations to its upper level.

The Communist Party should rely on the masses. It does so when it commands a war as well as when it deals with commercial work. This is the method that combines leaders and the masses, and this is the mass line. If we use this method, the workers could give many opinions, and it could be difficult for the minister, bureau and department directors and managers to be on their posts. Maybe the opinions of workers are not comprehensive, but we should believe that the opinions of most people should be correct. If we don't rely on everybody's efforts, and only rely on a few people, we will not get many ideas. We should train and improve the 2.5 million workers. We should encourage people to give ideas and methods through the management committee, the management small group, and the management conference. The cadres at each level should often sum up their own work. Thus in several years, we will be able to establish a solid commerce rank.

The several points above explain the relation between commercial work and each aspect. What is called policy is nothing more than handling these relations correctly. As long as we handle the relations with each aspect well, our work can be done well.

III. THE PROBLEM OF "GETTING SCOLDED EVERY DAY"

How do we evaluate the commerce work in the past seven years?

I think that there are achievements as well as shortcomings and mistakes, but achievements predominate. There are objective causes as well as subjective causes for making mistakes. Some mistakes are made by objective causes, but many mistakes are made by lack of subjective effort. Both the higher and lower levels have shortcomings and mistakes. However, the main responsibility belongs to the higher level, because it is the higher leading organs who decide all the general and specific policies, the price schemes, the profit targets, and so on. The department director has responsibility, but it is not as big as the ministers. I will be the first one who is responsible if there is anything wrong in commercial work.

The cadres in commercial work often get scolded. This shows that there are many shortcomings and mistakes in commercial work, and it shows that the relation of commercial work with the people's livelihood is immediate. The broad masses of people are concerned with their own lives. The first seven so-called things to do after the door is opened are: firewood, rice, oil, salt, sauce, vinegar, and tea. They are all related to commercial work. Therefore, good or bad commercial work has an extremely broad and deep immediate connection with the people. This shows that commercial work is an indispensible part of revolutionary work, and it is extremely important work. For example, it is very important to manage pigs. Because if you manage pigs well, you can improve poeple's lives, and it is beneficial to socialist construction. Some comrades do not want to engage in commercial work. This idea is not right.

Is it good to be scolded every day? I do not think that there is anything bad. I am not advocating making mistakes every day. I am saying that it can increase our cautiousness after we are scolded; thus we can find out mistakes in our work and correct them. What is bad about this? We should welcome more opinions; opinions are the evaluation of our work. We are not ordinary merchants, or small retailers. We are ones who make revolution. We should not mind whether or not we are scolded; we should watch whether our work is done well. It can prevent us from becoming divorced from the masses if they blame us a lot. We should report people's criticism and opinions about us, the more the better, and the faster the better. Even if we get scolded a lot, all that is necessary is that people justly evaluate our achievements and mistakes by saying the two sentences: We "have guaranteed market supply" and "have stabilized prices." It will be very disadvantageous for our course if people only report the good things in our work but not the shortcomings.

5

THE SCALE OF CONSTRUCTION SHOULD BE COMPATIBLE WITH NATIONAL STRENGTH
(January 1957)*

In regard to financial and economic matters, I will give several opinions. First, the fiscal and economic conditions for the year 1956. Second, how to solve the fiscal and economic problems at the present time. Third, the construction scale should be suited to national financial capacity. Fourth, we should pay attention to the study of the proportional relation of the national economy.

THE FISCAL AND ECONOMIC CONDITIONS OF 1956

In 1956, our country gained great achievements both in socialist transformation and in socialist construction. The socialist transformation of agriculture, handicraft industry, and capitalist industry and commerce achieved a complete victory. During the high tide of socialist transformation and construction, the workers, peasants, and public school personnel in the whole nation greatly heightened their initiative and launched broad working competition; and there emerged large numbers of model workers. The intellectuals joined various kinds of planning work in science, advanced in science, and showed great enthusiasm. In the countryside, since the peasants worked harder after cooperativization, the output of grains and other crops (except cotton) still exceeded the output of 1955, which was a bumper harvest, although the natural disasters were worse than those of 1955. The gross value of industrial output and the completed amount of capital construction also increased very greatly. The target for the gross value of industrial production in the First Five-Year Plan has been fulfilled a year in advance. Cumulatively, in four years of capital construction, the gross amount of investment of the Five-Year Plan has been more

---

*This is a speech of Comrade Chen Yun at the nationwide meeting of the Party committee secretaries of each province, city, and autonomous region.

than 80 percent fulfilled. These situations show the major achievements in economic construction in 1956.

Some shortcomings and mistakes also occurred in the field of
finance work in 1956. The main ones were as follows:

1. We overspent nearly 3 billion yuan on finance and credit
loans. This 3 billion yuan includes the following three items:
(i) We overspent more than 1.5 billion yuan on capital construction
investment. Capital construction investment was mostly appropriate, but a part of the money used in each department of the central government and in each locality was inappropriate, and we
overspent. (ii) We overspent 600 or 700 million yuan on wages.
It was necessary to increase the wages in 1956, but the shortcoming was that wages increased too much. Compared to the original
plan of 840 thousand we recruited more than one million personnel
in various fields. This does not include over recruiting of personnel for colleges and universities, technical secondary schools,
technical schools and skilled worker training classes. The wages
of some personnel were increased too much, and the promotion
range of office and enterprise personnel was enlarged. Also,
some bonus systems were not appropriate. These three items of
money and the additional salary amount to about 600 or 700
million yuan. (iii) Credit was somewhat excessive. We overspent
more than 500 million yuan on agricultural loans and other loans.
The above three items of capital construction, wages, and loans
totaled nearly 3 billion yuan that was overspent.

2. The supplies of both producer and consumer goods were
tight. There were serious shortages of raw materials necessary
for capital construction and production, such as steel products,
wood, bamboo, coal, and so on, and of many consumer goods necessary for the livelihood of the people. Iron and steel are important
materials for capital construction and industrial production. Last
year, we used up 700,000 tons of reserves (of this 200,000 tons
were used on just two-wheeled double-shared plows[a] and portable
steam engines), so people engaged in bartering in some places.
Because of the lack of raw materials, the handicraftsmen raised
prices and rushed to purchase waste iron and steel everywhere.
In some places, there were even cases of handicraftsmen snatching
bamboo from supply and marketing cooperatives. Shortages
of daily conumer goods were also relatively widespread, and

---

a) A new type of plow whose use Mao Zedong strongly encouraged. — Eds.

speculative "oxen"* appeared for some particular commodities (such as bicycles). It seems that there must be a certain amount of social circulation guaranteed for any kind of goods or material. If there is less than this amount, there will be a shortage of supply and even black markets, hoarding and speculation.

We know that paper money is a measure of goods and materials. To issue paper money, we must have goods and materials to balance. The amount of goods and materials did increase between 1955 and 1956, but a situation of short supply arose. The cause was that nearly 3 billion yuan was overspent on finance and credit loans.

Thus it can be said economic construction work of 1956 was a major achievement but shortcomings and mistakes do exist. Experience cannot be accumulated in one morning or one night. We had shortcomings and mistakes in the past, and we can hardly avoid them in the future. We spent more than twenty years finding our revolutionary principles. We will have to spend a period of two or three five-year plans in order to accumulate construction experience. Our shortcomings and mistakes appeared on the path of advance, and they will be easily corrected. There is a short supply of some goods and materials at the present time, and we only supply limited quantities of a few goods and materials. In regard to the overall situation, the market is still stable, and there are not many black markets and "oxen." We believe that grain, vegetable oil, and cloth will be in short supply for a quite long period. As to other goods and materials, the situation of shortages will ease, as long as there are no great natural disasters within the next two years and we adopt proper measures. According to plan, we should slow down the rate of increase of social purchasing power, to make it slower than the rate of increase of consumer goods. We will fill the gap between supply and demand within two years, and basically balance purchasing power with the supply of goods and materials.

HOW TO SOLVE CURRENT FISCAL AND ECONOMIC PROBLEMS

There are three main ways to solve the problems occurring in fiscal and economic fields.

---

*"Oxen" refers to speculators who buy and resell.

1. Start a movement to increase production and practice economy. In the field of increasing production, we should greatly increase the production of agricultural products and subsidiary products which have good markets. We should also increase as much as possible the production of industrial and handicraft products, for which there are raw materials and markets. In the field of practicing economy, except for the necessary expenditure that we guarantee, we should economize on all expenses that can be saved, whether in capital construction or production; whether in enterprises and institutions or in offices, organizations and schools, and whether in the Central or local governments.

2. Properly cut down the amount of capital construction investment. The purpose is to suit the scale of capital construction in 1957 to the availability of national financial and material capacity. Thus, the amount of capital construction work and fiscal expenditures will be reduced below the control numbers issued originally. The amount of the reductions will depend on the available financial revenues and the supply of steel products, wood, and other raw and processed materials. After the amount of investment is reduced, we should analyze whether to cut down the major items or the minor items. If we do not postpone some of the major items, like cutting just "meat" but not the "bone," and if we let it go like this, shortages will still occur in the future.

3. Control the rate of increase of social purchasing power in a planned way. The total wage bill can increase only slightly within the next two years. Purchase prices of agricultural products, except those that can damage production if they are too low, generally cannot be increased. In this way purchasing power will increase under the control of the plan. In labor and wage work, we should ensure that no department, except for the assignment of college graduates, increase their personnel and that any units that must increase their personnel do so by internal readjustment within their own vertical system. Generally, increasing wages through rank promotion will be stopped for two years. In the meantime, we will still increase the production of consumer goods, sell government bonds, and encourage saving. Through these methods supply of consumer goods will return to balance with social purchasing power.

We will use the three measures mentioned above in order to guarantee a certain scale of economic construction, as well as to gradually ease shortages of raw and processed materials, and of consumer goods. That is to say, we will fulfill the construction tasks of the First Five-Year Plan, as well as guarantee market stability. In doing so, doubtlessly, we will face many difficulties. For example, we will have to handle affairs properly after some construction items are postponed, and make arrangements for the surplus workers. We should also handle well the work of middle school students who cannot enter the higher schools and who cannot get jobs.

THE SCALE OF CONSTRUCTION SHOULD BE SUITED TO THE NATIONAL FINANCIAL CAPACITY

The scale of construction must be suited to the national financial and material capacity. Whether it is suited or not determines whether there is economic stability or instability. Economic stability is extremely important for a big country, like ours, which has a population of 600 million people. There will be rashness and economic chaos if the scale of construction exceeds the national financial and material capacity. If the two suit each other, the economy will be stable. It is not good either, of course, if we are conservative and thus obstruct the speed of construction that we should have. However, it is easier to correct conservativeness than to correct a rash advance because it is easier to increase construction when there are more goods and materials. It is not that easy when financial and material capacity is not sufficient to cut down an enlarged scale of construction. This can cause serious waste. In his speech at the Eighth National Congress of the Communist Party, Comrade Bo Yibo[a] talked about three kinds of proportional relations: national income and accumulation, national income and national budgetary revenue, and national budgetary expenditure and capital construction investment. I much agree with his study. There could be a little discrepancy in the proportional figures that he gave, but it is completely necessary to find out these proportional relations. Now, I would like to try to find out some restrictive methods from another perspective, to prevent the danger of the scale of economic construction exceeding the national capacity. I think that each of the following points should be considered.

_____
a) Chairman of the State Economic Commission and head of the Third Staff Office of the State Council, which had responsibility for heavy industry and construction work. — Eds.

1. Financial revenue and expenditure and the bank credit loans must all be balanced, and we should have a small surplus. Generally, there will be a balance between social purchasing power and the supply of goods and materials only if the revenue and expenditure and credit loans are balanced. The balance of financial revenue and expenditure and the balance of demand and supply of goods and materials from 1950 to 1955 positively proves this point. In 1956, owing to fiscal deficit, the supply and demand of goods and materials was unbalanced, which proves this point from a negative side. This is an extremely important issue. Meanwhile, it should be pointed out that it is necessary to have a slight surplus between revenue and expenditure. Because the scale of economic construction of our country is expanding every day, we need to increase the amount of goods and materials in circulation every year, namely, to increase properly the amount of reserves. What is called fiscal surplus does not mean saving paper money, but saving relevant goods and materials. Of course, it does not mean that a part of the fiscal surplus may not be used. If the necessary amount of circulation and reserves is guaranteed, it may be used. The problems arose because too much was used in 1956.

2. There should be a sequence for the distribution of supplies of iron and steel, wood, and other raw and processed materials. When the supply of raw and processed materials is sufficient, there is no problem. But when there is a shortage there must be a sequence for their distribution. When there is a shortage of the supply of raw and processed materials, we should first guarantee the minimal needs of the production departments producing daily necessities, and next, guarantee the needs for production of producer goods. The remaining part can be used for capital construction. The necessity of this kind of lining up, guaranteeing production first and capital construction second, is mainly to maintain the minimum supply of the daily necessities for the people, to prevent purposelessly expanding the scale of capital construction, and to prevent production which takes away from daily necessities. As to the supply of financial and material resources, the requirements for producing daily necessities must be placed ahead of capital construction. This is the issue of properly handling the relation between people's livelihood and construction. We should know that the amount of capital construction depends on how much raw and processed materials there is, not how much paper money there is. In regard to the production of daily necessities for the people, the

reason I say that we should guarantee their minimal needs for raw
and processed materials is that the production target for this year
cannot be increased much on a base which was already very high
last year. Owing to the poor harvest of last year, light industrial
production, like cotton textiles, cannot be unlimited this year. We
must know that today we limit the supply of raw and processed
materials to the minimal production needs to try to find some resources for capital construction, in order to develop production in
the future.

3. The purchasing power of people should be increased to some
extent, but the rate of increase must be suited to supplies of consumer goods. The main components of purchasing power are the
wages of workers and staff, the income of peasants derived from
the sale of agricultural and subsidiary products, and the income
of other people. The excessively rapid increase of purchasing
power at present is due to the increase of the total wage bill and
increased prices for agricultural products. The increase in purchasing power that results from increased output of agricultural
products, however, should not be feared but actually regarded as
a positive development. What we should pay attention to is the
issue of increased prices for agricultural products. Price increases should be limited to those agricultural products whose purchasing prices are too low so that the development of production
will be stimulated. This is a principle which we must take seriously.
When prices of industrial crops are raised, we must consider the
price parity of grain and industrial crops in order to prevent excessive price increases for industrial crops which could squeeze
grain, even to the point that we would be forced to raise the grain
price again. That would bring the danger of successive price increases that would raise the overall price level. If price increases
for agricultural products were excessive we would have to reduce
construction investment, and at the same time it would produce more
difficulties for market supply and withdrawal of currency from circulation. We must be very careful in regard to this aspect.

The sources of raw and processed materials for producing consumer goods are first agricultural and subsidiary products; second
raw materials received in exchange for exported agricultural products; and third the raw and processed materials produced by heavy
industry. These three resources are all limited to a certain extent. The rate of increase of purchasing power of the people must
be balanced with the rate of increase of consumer goods.

4. As to the balance between the scale of capital construction and financial and material capacity, we should not only consider the current year, but also we must consider the past and the future. Financial strength and materials point to four things: investment, machinery equipment, raw and processed materials, consumer goods and materials, and foreign exchange. In 1956, when we planned capital construction, we only barely balanced it with the financial and material capacity of that year, and we did not consider the past or the future. As a result, the capital construction investment was increased vigorously, and we had to cut down in 1957. This is one of the important lessons of the execution of the 1956 plan. The State Economic Commission has trial-calculated that if the capital construction investment in 1957 were 12.6 billion yuan (new prices), the investment of 1958 would be 16.2 to 18.1 billion yuan. The fiscal expenditure of that year cannot withstand that large a burden. Let us also look at the situation in capital construction investment in the past few years: it was 6.5 billion yuan in 1953, 7.5 billion yuan in 1954, 8.6 billion yuan in 1955, but in 1956, it was suddenly increased to 14.0 billion yuan; 1956 was the fourth year of the First Five-Year Plan, and the import of equipment and the installation of machinery for many construction items were concentrated in that year and the following year. Therefore, the capital construction investment has increased somewhat more than in past years. But it was too much to suddenly increase it by 5.4 billion yuan. As a result, we could not balance either financial or material resources. Judging from this, even to make an annual plan, we must consider the past and the future, and connect the past and future. We must avoid sudden increases and declines that cause damage.

5. Our country's agriculture poses a very great constraining force on the scale of economic construction. The agricultural share of the economy is very large, and the relation between agricultural products and fiscal revenue is very immediate. According to calculations by the State Economic Commission, about 45 percent of national fiscal revenue is related to agriculture. Of course, industrial products based on agricultural raw materials have value created by workers. Therefore, we cannot say that payments of peasants to the state amount to 45 percent of national fiscal revenue. It just means that there is an immediate relation between national income and agriculture. In our country, since the agricultural population is large and the area of cultivation small, the rate of increase in agricultural production is not high. The gross value of

agricultural and sideline production in 1956 was 58.3 billion yuan.
If we calculate the rate of increase as 5 percent, the increase is
only 2.9 billion yuan. However if we calculate the rate of increase
of the rural population at 2 percent, there will be an increase of
10 million people each year. If each person spends 60 yuan each
year, we need to spend 600 million yuan each year, and the surplus
would be only 2.3 billion yuan. Although industrial processing of
increased output of economic crops will raise national income,
this increased production of economic crops is only a small proportion of agricultural production. We depend on this 2 billion-odd
yuan of agricultural products for a large part of newly increased
purchasing power and for increased export. Within the national
economy of our country, the proportion of industry will increase.
Agriculture also will develop. However, for quite a long period in
the future, agriculture will pose a very great constraining force
on the scale of economic construction. This point is sufficiently
proved by the fact that the poor agricultural harvests of 1954 and
1956 reduced industrial production, fiscal revenue, and capital construction investment in the following year.

WE SHOULD PAY ATTENTION TO THE STUDY
OF THE PROPORTIONAL RELATIONS OF THE
NATIONAL ECONOMY

The construction of the Second Five-Year Plan should differ
to some extent from that of the First Five-Year Plan. The
standard of the planning work should be raised to some extent.
When we drew up the First Five-Year Plan, we first focused on
how many new items of capital construction there should be, and
we only balanced new construction and financial resources. Present
circumstances are quite different. The items that have been completed or are being completed have vastly increased. If we do not
carefully study the proportional relations of the national economy,
we will inevitably produce an unbalanced and chaotic situation.
Nevertheless, to properly study the proportional relations, we
absolutely cannot rely on the books and mechanically copy or apply
them. We must find it out from the economic condition of our country and our past experiences. We should study those already developed proportional relations which are rational, but more importantly, we should study the exposed contradictions. I am still
not knowledgeable in this field, and we must work together with the
comrades of the appropriate departments. Now I will give some

views on the contradictions that are already evident.

1. As to the investment proportions of heavy industry, light industry, and agriculture, we should make arrangements according to the policy set forth in "On the Ten Major Relationships"[a] by Chairman Mao. Though the major share is still to be allocated to investment in heavy industry, we should increase the proportion of investment in light industry and agriculture. We should also increase investment in heavy industry that serves the production of light industry and agriculture. Thus, the speed of industrial construction may seem to slow down temporarily, but actually it will not be slow and it may increase.

2. In the advanced industrial departments such as coal, electric power, transportation, and so on, the problem of insufficient investment in the past has been exposed. The advanced becomes the backward. This situation must be changed very quickly; otherwise it will be very disadvantageous for the whole national economy.

3. Some contradictions are also evident in the relation between the iron and steel industry and the machinery industry in regard to the issue of the sequence of development and the amount of investment. These need to be studied and solved, to make the two coordinate with each other and help each other forward.

4. We should handle well the relation between civilian industry and military industry. It is completely necessary to develop military industry, and there needs to be some factories devoted to the production of military supplies. But we cannot develop military industry alone; it must be built on a base of powerful and large civilian industry.

5. About the problems of large and small factories, and the advanced and the backward. People like to build large factories and to master advanced technology. However, according to the real circumstances of our country at the present time, we should consider first whether we should have factories or not, and then consider whether they are to be advanced or backward. There should be large factories in the iron and steel industry, but there should be more medium and small-sized factories. In that way we can have rapid development and many varieties and meet the needs in each

---

a) Also frequently translated as "On the Ten Great Relationships," this was a major address given by Mao Zedong on April 25, 1956, to a Conference of Secretaries of Provincial and Municipal Party Committees. The (evidently somewhat revised) text of this speech was released by China only twenty years later: "On the Ten Major Relationships," Selected Works of Mao Tsetung (Beijing: Foreign Language Press, 1977), vol. V, pp 284-306. — Eds.

area. In the coal industry, it takes less time to build inclined shafts and small straight shafts than to build large straight shafts and they give quick returns and can meet urgent needs. We must build a certain number of large factories. But since we do not have sufficient foreign exchange, we cannot rely completely on imports for equipment; we must mainly rely on self-reliance.

6. We should correctly handle the relation between "bone" and "meat" in construction. In the past, we did not have the experience to handle this relation, and we paid attention to the "bone," and ignored the "meat." We also underestimated the degree of difficulty and the amount of investment required to construct industrial cities and industrial bases. We should pay attention to these problems before it is too late and get them solved properly.

7. The joint state-private enterprises must stop merging. Mergers that are not proper should be reversed. We should break the blind faith that a "large factory is proper" under all circumstances. It is not necessarily proper to forcibly merge small factories that originally have independent accounting, and to practice unified accounting. In our country, there are many old factories. In terms of organizational form it is not proper to have large mergers within such an industrial base.

6

RESPONSES TO A XINHUA CORRESPONDENT'S QUESTIONS ON PROBLEMS OF MARKET PRICES OF COMMODITIES
(April 1957)

Q: What is the recent condition of market price changes?

A: In the last few months, the prices of some commodities in the market went up. We can divide these commodities into four kinds: (1) The price of table salt, pork, some cooking oil (such as vegetable oil, sesame oil, tea oil, and soya-bean oil), tung oil, and several kinds of tea went up. Along with the price rise of pork and some oils, the prices of meat products, some pastries, and other items also went up. (2) The prices of high-quality cigarettes and woolen goods were raised, and so were the prices of hats and shoes for which the woolen goods are raw materials. (3) The prices of some handicraft products were raised, those for which iron, steel, bamboo, and wood are raw materials. (4) In the free market for small local products, the prices of some nonstaple foods, vegetables, and medicinal materials were raised. However, the commodities whose prices were raised are only a small part of the total commodities. The prices of most commodities, including grains, cotton cloth, coal, knit goods, and the important daily use articles of basic consumer goods that are essential for the people's livelihood, are stable.

Q: Why did the government raise the prices of pork, table salt, cooking oil, woolen goods, and high-quality cigarettes?

A: We all know that recently the government significantly raised the purchasing prices of pigs and certain vegetable oil materials. Since the purchasing prices of pigs and certain oil materials were rather low, the output of pork in the past two years had decreased, and the farming area of oil materials had not been increased. If we do not increase the purchasing prices, not only can we not increase the output, but also it will even be difficult to maintain the present amount of insufficient supply in the cities. In order to increase output, it is necessary to increase these pur-

chasing prices. We have to raise the selling prices, since the
purchasing prices were raised. However, the purchasing prices
were raised more. For example, the purchase price of pigs rose
13 percent, while the selling price only rose 7 percent. Can we
just raise the purchasing prices but not the selling prices? No.
Because if we do so, the government will lose a great deal of
money, it will produce difficulties for balancing fiscal revenue and
expenditure this year, and it will produce difficulties for balancing
purchasing power with the supply of commodities.

We all know that last year the number of workers and employees
increased two million and several hundred thousand; we also increased the wages of ordinary personnel of public schools and
enterprise workers. This greatly increased social purchasing
power. On the other hand, the gross product of consumer goods
this year did not increase as much as it did last year. The production of cotton cloth even decreased. Additionally, this year we
cannot tap reserves of commodities to supply the market. Thus,
this year, there is still an imbalance between social purchasing
power and the supply of commodities. In order to obtain a
balance between the two, the government decided to reduce the
expenses of government offices, the army, organizations, schools,
and so on as much as possible, and reduce collective purchasing power as much as possible, so that people in cities and
countryside will be able to buy the necessary commodities. We
should understand that the prices will rise chaotically and the market will be in chaos if we do not have a balance between fiscal
revenue and expenditure and between social purchasing power and
the supply of commodities. This will be very disadvantageous
for economic development and the stability of people's livelihood. Now, on our own initiative and in a planned way, we
raised the selling prices of pork and a part of cooking oil,
raised the rate of table salt (now the tax and price of salt are still
lower than before the war), and raised the prices of woolen goods, and
high-quality cigarettes. All of these are to balance fiscal revenue
and expenditure, and to balance social purchasing power and the
supply of commodities. Of course, there are many ways to
strive for these two balances. The present movements, which are
for increasing production and practicing economy and for striving
for a great bumper harvest in agriculture, and which we are launching vigorously all over the country, are the main methods to realize the two balances mentioned above. Nevertheless, to raise the

prices of certain commodities, in a planned way, is also an effective method. By using this method, we can raise the prices of
commodities whose prices should rise, keep down the prices of
commodities whose prices should not rise, and maintain the basic
stability of market prices. This is necessary for ensuring the
construction of the state and the people's livelihood.

Only a minority of people increased their expenditures owing to
the higher price of woolen goods and high-quality cigarettes. The
basic starting point of price policy of the government has always
been to first ensure the price stability of the commodities that are
necessities for people because these commodities are regularly
needed in large quantities by the whole country, and they are the main
part of family expenses. As for those most essential commodities
such as grains, the government has even used the methods of long-
distance transportation and subsidizing freight in order to ensure
the supply for cities. If the government did not use the subsidizing
method, the grain prices in the cities would be much higher. To
subsidize the main commodities which have a very important relation with the lives of people, while raising the prices of woolen
goods, high-quality cigarettes, and similar high quality consumer
goods to some extent and at certain times, is really an important
measure to ensure the stability of the livelihood of the people of the
whole country.

Q: What caused the price increases for some handicrafts, industrial products, vegetables, and small local products?

A: The reason the prices of some handicraft industrial products
rose was owing to the insufficient supply of waste iron and steel
materials, bamboo, wood, and so on, owing to price rises, and
owing to the wage raises of handicraft industrial workers. This
increased the production costs of the handicraft industry. For
some handicraft industrial products, the demand exceeded supply,
and people all rushed to buy them. This was also a cause of the
price rise. Why was the supply of raw and processed materials for
handicraft industry insufficient? This is because we invested more
on national capital construction last year. Of this, a part we should
have used for raw and processed materials for handicraft industrial
production was used for capital construction. Meanwhile, after the
formation of agricultural cooperatives last year, more steel, iron,
wood, and bamboo was used for rural capital construction. This is
also a cause of the shortage of raw and processed materials. Since
the movement for increasing production and practicing economy

was launched, the shortage situation of part of raw and processed material supply for handicraft industry has already begun to relax, but some of them cannot be solved within a short period. Therefore, the supply this year will still be tight. The government at each level and the departments concerned should vigorously encourage the development of the handicraft industry and help solve the difficulties of raw and processed materials. The handicraft industry cooperatives, small cooperative groups, and handicraftsmen should also try hard to save raw and processed materials and reduce costs.

The price rise of vegetables has a greater effect on the people's livelihood. There are two aspects to the increased price of vegetables. One is the seasonal price differential, namely, the price falls in the peak seasons and rises in the off seasons. This is inevitable as well as necessary. If it were not so, nobody would reserve vegetables to supply needs in the off seasons. Another kind of price rise occurs when the price is higher than the price in the same period the year before. The present price rise for vegetables contains both of the elements mentioned above. Why has this situation arisen? This is owing to the rapid increase of the population in some cities, while we did not accordingly enlarge the vegetable sown area. Though the sown area was enlarged appropriately in some cities, because the frost came early last fall, autumn vegetable production decreased; and the cold spring has been relatively long this year, so the growth of spring vegetables has been affected. The experience of these years has proved that we should not only enlarge the sown area of vegetables in proportion to the increase of urban population, but also, the enlargement should be greater than the increase of urban population in order to have certain reserves, because vegetable production is affected easily by natural disasters. As long as each local government really pays attention to properly enlarging the vegetable sown area around the cities, and improves the management of vegetables, it is possible to prevent improper price increases for vegetables. Natural disasters such as frost and a cold spring are inevitable, but the leading departments should redistribute vegetables among the areas.

The price rise of some small local products is because production lags behind demand. The free market has not yet been opened for a half year, and for most small local products it is still impossible to increase production greatly. The price will be naturally

stabilized when we increase production and balance supply and
demand. The leadership of the free market should be strengthened
in each place in order to encourage normal development.

Q: Certain commodity prices were raised in the past few
months. How much will it really affect the people's livelihood?

A: First, since we raised the purchasing prices of some agricultural products, and the free market prices of some nonstaple
food, small local products and the raw and processed materials of
handicraft industry also rose, the peasants increased their income.
Only a portion of the commodity price increases caused peasants
to increase their expenditure, but comparatively, peasants increased income more than the increase in expenditure. As to city
dwellers, they are affected to varying degree by the price rises
of some commodities. The expenditures of families with higher
purchasing power increased considerably more, and the expenditures of families with lower purchasing power increased considerably less. The situation of increased expenditures of people in
different cities is also different to some extent. Except for a tiny
minority, the income from increased wages exceeds the expenditures owing to increased prices.

It is a good thing that we greatly increased employment and increased wages. However, the ensuing problem is that many producer goods and consumer goods are still in short supply even after
their production has greatly increased. This amply demonstrates
that for a country like ours, a country which is economically backward and under construction, the living standard of people can
only be improved gradually on a base of production development.
We must make up our minds to struggle arduously for a long time.

Q: What will be the future trends of market prices?

A: Fiscal revenue and expenditures this year will be balanced,
and also the social purchasing power and the amount of commodity
supply will be roughly balanced, since the people of the country
vigorously join the movement for increasing production and practicing economy, since we have already properly cut down capital
construction investment, and since we raised the selling prices of
some commodities according to plans at the same time. Because
all the prices that should be regulated have already been regulated,
the government will adopt a policy of stabilizing the prices of commodities that are mainly managed by the state. Since the commodities
managed by the state amount to the greatest part of the total value of the
commodities in the whole nation, generally speaking, the prices will
remain stable in the future.

7

WE MUST SOLVE THE VEGETABLE
SUPPLY PROBLEM WELL
(July 1957)*

At present, the Party committees and governments of the big and medium-sized cities are faced with many important issues, one of which is vegetable supply. During the beginning of large-scale economic construction, it is all right to give more attention to industrial production and capital construction because the country needs industrialization. However, construction requires more workers and staff, and food must be supplied to the increased urban population. How could we give priority only to factory construction and overlook the food supply for the workers and staff? In the past, we paid attention to factory buildings and machines, to the neglect of the daily needs of the workers and staff, and supply of vegetables and other nonstaple food has not been handled effectively. I believe the supply of these things is of no less significance than the construction of factories, and it should be considered as important as factory construction. If we only pay attention to industrial construction and not to the solving of livelihood problems of the workers and staff, the workers may cause trouble, and these problems will have to be solved in any case. People should learn to draw lessons. The serious shortage of supply of vegetables last winter and this spring has taught us a profound lesson and forced us to convene meetings to solve this problem. Our Communist Party has led the revolution to success, and it is also capable of handling the socialist construction. What will have become of us if we cannot solve the vegetable problem?

The prerequisite for ensuring vegetable supply is to grow an adequate amount of vegetables. To accomplish this, sufficient growing acreage must be guaranteed, and a "safety coefficient" should be set.

*This is a part of Comrade Chen Yun's speech at a National Vegetable Conference.

63

In the suburbs of big and medium-sized cities, sufficient acreage
should be set aside for vegetable growing. First of all, the amount
of vegetables required should be calculated according to the size
of the population. Then the growing acreage should be figured out
according to the per mu output. Vegetable supply in each city
should mainly depend on its own suburbs. In order to enlarge the
vegetable growing area, instead of paying agricultural tax in grain,
peasants should be allowed to pay it in cash, and the quota of state-
purchased grain should also be reduced or exempted appropriately.
Grain production will not be affected much if the vegetable-growing
acreage is enlarged by 400 thousand mu in the whole country. If
we ask the peasants to grow vegetables while at the same time
asking them to pay their agricultural taxes in grain, all they can
do is to buy the grain — and that will not do.

In addition to relying on the suburbs for vegetables, the big and
medium-sized cities must also have vegetable-growing production
bases. They should depend mainly on suburban production and
make national allocation (of vegetables) subsidiary. They should
not neglect the suburban production and rely only on national allocation and transportation; neither should they have only suburban
production and go without vegetable-growing bases, as winter and
spring supplies could not be guaranteed. As I understand the vegetable supply network, Shanghai does not rely only on its suburbs
for vegetable supplies but also uses the adjacent several counties
in Songjiang and Suzhou prefectures, even Pinghu and Jiaxing
prefectures in Zhejiang Province, as its vegetable-growing bases.
The same is true in the north. Shandong Province is a base area
for growing Chinese cabbage. Tangshan and Baoding prefectures
of Hebei Province are vegetable-growing areas, too. Besides
maintaining and developing these bases which have come into being
over the years, new cities have to set up new bases to grow autumn
vegetables. In some of these base areas, experiments can be carried out this year on the application of more chemical fertilizer to
see exactly how much more vegetables can be harvested by applying an extra amount of chemical fertilizer. We have difficulties in
producing enough grain owing to inadequate cultivated land. If output of vegetables can be increased greatly by applying chemical
fertilizer on the several hundred thousand mu of vegetable growing
bases, that will solve a big problem. The experimental area doesn't
have to be too big as there is not enough chemical fertilizer
this year. If good results are obtained, some chemical fertilizer

can be imported next year specially for growing vegetables.

There must be a safety coefficient in the area sown to vege-tables, that is to say, some margin should be left in case natural disasters occur. Agricultural production is greatly affected by natural conditions. Every year, there are many calamity-stricken areas where grain output and vegetable output are reduced. If no margin is left in the acreage planted, there won't be enough vege-tables in reserve. Without enough reserves, supplies cannot be guaranteed in case of calamities.

We must ensure that peasants can make profits with enlarged vegetable-growing areas. Reasonable prices should be set. We should not sell vegetables at over-low prices at the expense of the peasants. It won't do if the peasants have no profits to make or even have to suffer losses. It is not good if the income from vege-table growing is too much higher than that from grain growing. But it is even worse if the former is lower than the latter. A care-ful calculation is needed in the various areas on what exactly is a reasonable amount of income for the vegetable-growers.

With a safety coefficient being set and with more vegetables be-ing grown, it is unavoidable that some vegetables will rot. Such things would happen even if no safety coefficient were set. But with a safety coefficient more vegetables will be wasted. Now we are faced with two problems. One is that people will curse the fact that there is short supply of vegetables every year. The other is that it is hard to avoid more waste if more vegetables are grown. Between the two choices, I prefer growing more than growing less. Should losses occur, they should be covered by the state, not by the common people. There are always ways of disposing surplus vege-tables. For example, pigs are now raised in all the big and me-dium-sized cities. The surplus vegetables can become pig feed. With more greenfeed, pigs will consume less grain. Actually, it is not certain that there will be a lot of surplus vegetables every year. Taking the country as a whole, if these areas are not stricken by calamities, those areas are; if there is surplus in these places, there is a shortage in those places. In the overall calcu-lation, there is not necessarily a great amount of surplus. Of course, efforts should be exerted to improve management and ad-ministration to alleviate the losses caused by the waste of vege-tables. Losses owing to poor management and administration should not be attributed to the setting of a safety coefficient.

The storage of vegetables is a problem which also needs to be conscientiously solved. Who should take the job? First of all, it should be the peasants who store the vegetables. For the peasants to do it, it should be ensured that they can profit from it. This could be done either by paying them storage fees or be seasonal price differentials. Short of these, they are unwilling to store vegetables. Second, the catering offices of the government organizations, army units, and schools can themselves store vegetables. For instance, in the north they would store vegetables which are enough for several months so that it is possible not to supply them with more vegetables in this period. Dispersed storage can reduce the amount the urban commercial departments must store. As a result, not as much investment will be required for capital construction. But attention should be paid to preventing rush purchasing for dispersed storage. Last, storage by the urban commercial departments is also indispensable.

To make pickles in peak periods is another method to solve the problem of vegetable supply in cities. The common people in many areas have the custom of making pickles. Government organizations, army units, and schools can also have a try. This should also be done step by step in accordance with the supply situation, equipment, and the necessary skills, and we cannot demand that this be completed this year.

In sum, vegetable supply in cities is an important matter. We must try every possible means to solve this problem properly.

8

PAY ATTENTION TO GRAIN WORK
(September 1957)*

I. THIS YEAR'S HARVEST AND OUR POLICY

The disaster condition in certain provinces is serious this
year, and the harvest in the Northeast and Inner Mongolia areas
cannot yet be determined. But looking at the whole situation, it
probably will be an average year tending toward a bumper harvest.
According to this estimate, our policy should be to grasp the opportunity to ensure normal grain procurement and to practice little
sale,[a] in order to use bumper harvests to make up for good harvests.
The so-called opportunity arises because, first, this is an average
year tending toward a bumper harvest, and, second, we are having
a socialist education movement in the countryside. So-called
normal procurement means we must ensure that we can maintain
the amount of procurement at a level above 85 billion jin.[b]

Many provinces and regions want to have low procurement and
high sales. In regard to one province or one region, this opinion
may have a certain rationale. But considering this from the perspective of the whole country, it would be unthinkable to manage it
according to the figures given by many comrades so that the state
would use 2 or 3 billion jin of reserve grain from 1957 to 1958.[c]
We think that under the circumstance of an average year tending
toward a bumper harvest and having a socialist education move-

---

*This is the main content of a concluding speech by Comrade Chen Yun at the
the nationwide meeting on grain work.

a) Procurement includes both the grain collected as tax and grain purchased
from the peasantry. Sales include both those to the urban population and to
rural households that lack grain. Rural sales are frequently referred to as
"resales." — Eds.

b) 42.5 million metric tons. One jin is equal to half a kilogram. — Eds.

c) This is a reference to the 1957-58 grain procurement year that began
July 1, 1957, and extends through June 30, 1958. — Eds.

ment, there is something definitely wrong if the state cannot add
4 or 5 billion jin of grain to state reserves, but instead uses 2 or
3 billion jin of reserve grain. The reason is that the nation will be
in a dangerous position if next year is a year of disasters and we
must cut down again and, as a result, the overall situation becomes
passive.

The present issue is that we must choose one of two policies:
either to ensure normal procurement and practice little sale, or
to have low procurement and large sales. We should choose the
former, not the latter, because the latter is a risky policy. The
comrades of Liaoning and Heilongjiang provinces said that the
provincial Party committees had made self-criticisms because they
did not pay close attention to grain procurement last year. We
must all make a self-criticism if we do not pay close attention to
grain procurement this year, and if the grain work goes wrong because of the disasters of next year.

Comrade Mao Zedong pointed out in "The Situation of the Summer
of 1957:

in the next few years, we must receive 35 billion jin in grain taxes and 50 billion jin of procured grain. They cannot be less. We can make adjustments to
some extent according to the year's harvest. In the countryside, because production increases every year and the families lacking grain decrease every
year, the sale of grain should be reduced gradually every year. In the places
where too much grain is sold in the cities, we should also reduce the sale of
grain by a certain amount. Thus, the state grain reserves can be increased
year by year in order to meet emergency needs.[a]

We do not say procure more and sell less, because it is easy to
misunderstand that as the more that is procured the better. Therefore, we only say ensure normal procurement and practice little
sale. We do not hope to purchase much; nor should we purchase
much. We overprocured grain in 1954, and the result was a shortage situation in 1955, and we had to adjust again the state unified
sale work. This mistake should not be repeated.

The experience of the past few years is that the difference between a good harvest and a bad harvest is only 2 or 3 billion jin in

---

a) A statement by Mao distributed to delegates to a conference of the secretaries of provincial and municipal Party committees held in Qingdao in July
1957. See Selected Works of Mao Tsetung (Beijing: Foreign Language Press,
1977), vol V, pp 473-482, for the full text. The passage cited here appears
on page 476. — Eds.

grain procurement but a very large difference in the amount of grain sold. The sales volume of grain last year was 85.1 billion jin. We faced disasters that year and had just completed cooperativization. There would have been fewer problems if we had sold less. The problem was we oversold more than 4 billion jin. We had good harvests in 1955, and the sales volume of grain was only 72.2 billion jin. Comparing this with 1956, when we suffered disasters, the difference in sales volume was 12.9 billion jin. Of course we should procure a little bit more in a good harvest year, but the real work is mainly to sell less. In general, to grasp the opportunity does not mean procuring more, but ensuring normal procurement. We hope that we will take the objective of less sales as the keypoint of our work, because people will not starve to death if we sell a little bit less in a good harvest area or in a good harvest year.

II. ON THE PROCUREMENT ISSUE

We should procure 85 billion jin of grain from the peasantry. This must be confirmed; otherwise we cannot ensure the smooth progress of national construction. Of course, we need to make certain adjustments for a good or bad harvest.

If production increases, we properly should procure some more. This is necessary for making up a bad harvest with a good one. If we do not procure more when production increases, we will have a hard time in a bad harvest year or in a poor harvest area. The amount of increased procurement usually should be at least 40 percent of the amount of increased production. Under special circumstances, procurement should be even a little more than this. So-called "special" means the serious disequilibrium between good and bad harvest in the areas in a province, between the provinces, and between two years. But we cannot procure too much either. After a bumper harvest, the cooperatives should save a little bit more, and peasants should also eat little bit more in order to give them an incentive for production initiative.

We should do the work of grain purchasing well, request peasants to turn in the exact amount, and guarantee the quality. We should correct the situation of delay or debts of public grains, and should continue to maintain the good tradition of turning in good-quality grain to the state. Cooperatives that lack grain can turn in money as a substitute. The grain purchasing and the burden to the state of peasants engaged in individual farming should follow the rules strictly. Cooperatives must manage this matter well.

III. ON THE ISSUE OF UNIFIED SALE

The grain ration of peasants can be fixed according to the ration per person. Each province can decide the number of ration categories and the size of the difference between the categories. However, the total amount of ration should not exceed the unified sales target fixed by the state.

We allow cooperatives to manage oil presses, bean-curd plants, and noodle plants, but there should not be too many, and they must be controlled appropriately. We should prohibit cooperatives from willfully using grain to produce prepared food.

Do not overlook the work of unified sales in medium and small disaster areas within bumper harvest areas and within poor harvest areas. In the past, we often ignored small disaster areas enclosed within regions of bumper harvests, and therefore problems arose. From now on, we should make proper arrangements in the work of unified sales.

We must also firmly grasp unified sales work in cities and towns. The ration standard of city or town dwellers, what can be lowered or should be lowered, will be lowered appropriately. A certain proportion of the grain ration can be supplied in sweet potatoes.

The amount of grain used by collective food units should be regulated strictly. Nobody is allowed to make a fraudulent application regarding the number of people in order to receive more grain. We should use food coupons for prepared food in disaster areas first, and we do not apply it in the whole nation at the present time. We should rectify the food coupon system. Just like paper money, there should be a fixed number of food coupons in circulation, but it will not be good if there are too many, because there will be panic purchasing as soon as there seems to be something unstable. The purpose of rectification is to reduce loopholes that can be exploited and to prevent rash purchasing.

Here I must emphasize the issue of discipline in unified sales work. To ensure not selling too much, we must issue selling targets for each month and season. The State Council has been doing so since last September. But people do not pay attention to this in most areas, and the unified sales target has been exceeded every month. This is a very big loophole. Therefore, we will set up a discipline from now on: the unified sales target issued must be carried out by all localities and each department, and it may not be exceeded without consent.

IV. THE WHOLE PARTY SHOULD PAY
    ATTENTION TO GRAIN WORK

Grain work is very important, and it affects the immediate interests of people in the whole nation. We not only have to procure
surplus grain from 500 million peasants, but also supply grain to
100 million city and town dwellers, and to part of the rural population
lacking grain. That is, it concerns not only how much we purchase
from the 500 million peasants, but also the sale that meets the
needs of nearly 200 million people. In general, it affects the immediate personal interest of everybody in the whole country. This
is the first point. Second, there is a direct relation between grain
distribution and agricultural production. Unified procurement and
unified sale of grain are a kind of distribution of grain by the state.
If we do it well, it will encourage agricultural production. If not,
it will create a disadvantageous effect. The peasants pay attention
to production and distribution at the same time, and distribution
and production are immediately connected. In regard to grain distribution, we should consider the interest of both the state and the
peasants. If we only consider the needs of the state and ignore the
needs of the peasants, it will affect the initiative of the peasants
and be disadvantageous to agricultural production or even the development of the whole national economy. If we do not consider
the needs of the state and only emphasize the needs of the peasants,
it will affect the grain supply of city or town dwellers and obstruct
national construction. Third, grain is the most important material
for stabilizing the market and ensuring construction. Now there is
nothing more important than grain. When we talk about whether the
market is stable, what we mean is whether the situation of grain
and the grain price are stable. If the situation and the price of
grain are not stable, the prices of the whole market cannot be stable, and we cannot continue national construction. The above shows
that grain work is extremely important. It is not purely economic
work, but it is also important political work. The Party committees of each level must strengthen leadership and really solve the
problems. We thought in the past that after cooperativization the
grain work could be done somewhat more easily since more than
100 million peasant families became several hundred thousand cooperatives. Now it seems that this thinking was not correct; at
least it will not be true for a period of time. Therefore, the whole
Party still must put grain work in an important position.

In the past, we spent much time mobilizing the whole Party and making a great effort to engage in grain work. There is a reason for this. For our country, if we use grain economically, there will be enough for food and use. If we eat as much as we want, there will not be enough for both. If we do not firmly grasp distribution, too much grain will be eaten up after the harvest. The issue now is that we want to buy some of the grain that peasants do not need to eat. Actually, this is the contradiction between economizing and eating without control. This is the very symptom of the grain problem of our country at the present time and for some time in the future. On the one hand, we ask people not to eat and use without control. On the other hand, we should also guarantee that peasants can get basically enough to eat and use, in order to encourage peasants' production initiative. Under this circumstance, the grain work certainly will be broad and difficult mass work, and this kind of mass work will continue for a long time. Comrades of the whole Party, especially those who engage in financial and economic work, must understand this completely.

9

PROBLEMS WE MUST PAY ATTENTION TO
AFTER THE REFORM OF THE SYSTEM
(September 1957)*

1. We must strengthen the balancing work among various locales after certain powers of the central government are transfered to lower levels. It is absolutely necessary to expand the power of the locales. Generally speaking localities know their situation more clearly than the Center does. After the institutional structure is changed, local governments can better handle affairs based on local conditions. But we must strengthen the national balance work. Since economic units are scattered, there can be no planned economy without an overall, integrated balance. In the past, the central ministries probably overlooked local governments, but after central authority is transferred down, a tendency of overlooking the whole situation can occur as well. Therefore, there should be appropriate decentralization, on the one hand, and we simultaneously should strengthen synthesis, on the other. We think that balance work should be strengthened, instead of weakened, after decentralization. From now on, in all the places in the nation, there should be certain economic development, but we must pay attention lest we waste the nation's existing production equipment. For example, the productive equipment existing in coastal cities should not be left unused when interior provinces are industrializing. It is wrong to consider only coastal cities but not the interior. For instance, the manufacture of thermoses should be concentrated in coastal areas, for long distance transport and sale is inappropriate; but the demand of the interior to be self-sufficient in everything is wrong, because it necessarily leads to waste of existing facilities. Therefore the capital construction items in each locality must be examined and balanced by national planning organs.

---

*This is a part of a speech by Comrade Chen Yun on the issues of reform of the economic system at the Third Plenum of the Eighth Central Committee.

2. The localities should actually control the direction of financial investment. We believe that the main direction of financial
investment — the greater part of the money of the localities —
should be directed toward the development of agricultural production, such as the chemical fertilizer industry, water conservancy,
reclamation of reclaimable wastelands, etc.

3. Once the fiscal system is changed, we must establish an appropriate financial management system. After authority has been
decentralized from the Center to the provinces (cities), the provinces (cities) must also share their power with their districts and
counties. From now on, each locality and enterprise will have a
certain flexibility in financial resources, so that it is easier to
handle affairs; but it could be worse without good management. It
is hard to avoid corruption and waste since there are several hundred thousand units. We must establish various management systems to avoid and reduce corruption and waste. For example, we
must establish an accounting system. There must be account books,
and the items and categories of expenditures to be used in every
unit must be specified. The use of funds may not be approved by
one person, but must go through a specified organization. We must
have a report system: all of the income and expenditure of each
locality must be entered in the work report of that governmental
level; the financial affairs of an enterprise should be listed in its
annual report. We must have an inspection system. The Ministry
of Finance, the Ministry of Supervision,[a] and the government at
each level should determine the method of inspection.

4. The system of revenue sharing between the Center and the
localities will be basically unchanged for three years; however,
after one year of implementation, there should be a partial adjustment if there is anything inappropriate. There should be a limit on
revenue sharing. Within three years, local revenue sharing should
not exceed 3 to 3.6 billion yuan, and retained foreign exchange
should not exceed 45 to 50 million U.S. dollars. These two figures
are necessary as well as possible. If these items are too large,
it will influence national key point construction. We estimate that
within three years, local retained revenue will expand from a small

---

a) This ministry was established in September 1954 and abolished in April
1959. According to H. Franz Schurmann (Ideology and Organization in Communist
China, Berkeley: University of California Press, 1966, p. 328), it headed a nationwide system of accounting offices designed to enhance economic controls.
— Eds.

to a large amount and rich provinces (cities) will get more, poor
ones will get less. The situation of economic development has determined this. After one year of institutional improvement, we
should sum up the experience, and we might need a partial adjustment,
because 3 to 3.6 billion yuan retained by the localities in three
years is an estimate. Within these figures, there will be about 1
to 1.6 billion yuan of financial surplus, and 2 billion yuan of proportional sharing, but the result of implementation might be very
different. The difference between rich and poor areas might also
be very great. We can only discover the problems after one year
of experience. Therefore, we say that the system will be basically
unchanged for three years, and a necessary partial adjustment is
allowed after one year of implementation.

10

REGULATION ON THE IMPROVEMENT OF THE INDUSTRIAL MANAGEMENT SYSTEM
(November 1957)*

Our present industrial management system has two main short-comings. One is that some industrial enterprises suitable for local management are now still directly managed by the industrial departments of the central government; at the same time, local administrative organs enjoy too little authority over industrial management with regard to material distribution, financial control, and personnel management. The other shortcoming is that the person in charge of an industrial enterprise has too little authority over that enterprise, while the central industrial administrative department has too much control over the business in that enterprise. These two major shortcomings restrain the initiative and positiveness in work of local administrative organs and leading personnel in enterprises. Our country is a socialist country, and our country's construction is planned construction; the production and construction work of various enterprises in various places throughout the country must serve the unified state plan; they certainly cannot oppose the unified state plan. But with the unified state plan, it is completely necessary to empower local governments with a certain degree of authority to do what is suitable to local circumstances. This certain degree of flexible power to be enjoyed by local governments and industrial enterprises within the scope of the unified state plan is precisely to fulfill the unified state plan in the manner most suitable to local circumstances, and is what the unified state plan needs. In order to appropriately enlarge the authority of local governments and industrial enterprises in industrial management, the State Council lays down the following regulations.

*This is a State Council document drafted under the direction of Comrade Chen Yun. [This translation is adapted from the translation of the final text released in 1958 which appeared in Union Research Service, Volume 9, pp. 276-282.]

FIRST, APPROPRIATELY ENLARGE THE AUTHORITY
OF PROVINCES, AUTONOMOUS REGIONS, AND
MUNICIPALITIES DIRECTLY UNDER THE CENTRAL
GOVERNMENT IN INDUSTRIAL MANAGEMENT

1. Readjust the present control of enterprises, and let provinces, autonomous regions, and municipalities directly under the central government take over some of the enterprises now under direct control of the central government.

Most of the enterprises now subordinate to the Ministry of Light Industry and the Ministry of Food Industry, with the exception of certain enterprises that must be controlled by the central authority, are to be devolved to the provinces, autonomous regions, and municipalities directly under the central government. In the textile industry, for the present, only a small number of enterprises are to be devolved, and further steps will be decided upon according to concrete conditions in the future.

As to enterprises belonging to the various departments of heavy industry, all large-scale mines, large-scale metallurgical enterprises, large-scale chemical industrial enterprises, important coal bases, large power stations and electricity networks, oil refineries, factories manufacturing large and precision machines, factories manufacturing electric motors and instruments, the military industry, and other industries that need complex skills are still to be controlled by the various industrial departments of the central government. Apart from these, all other factories suitable for local administration are to be devolved step by step according to actual conditions.

All enterprises under the Ministry of Forestry, except a few units that require direct control from the ministry, are to be devolved.

A number of ports and enterprises under the Ministry of Communications are to be devolved.

In the field of construction, earth construction works in many districts are to be gradually devolved and put under the unified management of local authorities.

Each industrial and communication department of the central government, based on the above-mentioned principles, should consult with local governments, draw up lists of enterprises to be devolved, and, after the lists are submitted for approval to the State Council, start the transfer of power to lower levels.

In all enterprises still under the jurisdiction of various depart-

ments of the central government, the central-local dual leadership
system — with the central authority as the main — is to be followed, and the leadership and supervision exercised by local authorities over these enterprises are to be strengthened.

2. Increase the authority of provinces, autonomous regions, and
municipalities directly under the central government, in the distribution of materials.

Materials needed by enterprises under various departments of
the central government, by enterprises under local authorities
(including state-private jointly operated enterprises under local
authorities), and by the commercial system, no matter whether they
are materials to be distributed in a unified manner in the whole
country by the State Economic Commission (hereafter called unified-distribution materials) or those to be distributed in a unified
manner by various departments of the central government (hereafter called ministry-controlled materials), are still to be applied
for and distributed according to the original system. Materials
needed by local state-operated and local state-private jointly operated enterprises are to be applied for and distributed in a unified
manner by provinces, autonomous regions, and municipalities directly under the central government. However, under the condition of guaranteeing the fulfillment of the state plan, people's
councils in provinces, autonomous regions, and municipalities directly under the central government have the authority, based upon
local conditions and the urgency of requirements, to adjust the
quantities, varieties, and time of use of materials applied for and
received — for their own use — by central enterprises, local enterprises, and local commercial organs located within the jurisdiction
of the respective provinces, autonomous regions, and municipalities, and the enterprises concerned should conform to such adjustments.

Generally, provinces, autonomous regions, and municipalities
directly under the central government may not allocate and use
materials belonging to various departments of the central government, no matter whether such materials are stored in certain
enterprises or in warehouses. If the local government wants to
make an allocation it must get permission from the central departments concerned. When local governments want to use special
raw materials for the manufacture of military products, they must
also get permission from the central departments concerned.

If the quantities of unified-distribution materials and ministry-

controlled materials produced by enterprises under the management of a province, an autonomous region or a municipality directly
under the central authority are more than the quotas fixed in state
plans, the local government may take a certain percentage of the
over-quota portion for its own distribution and use; but it may not
alter the assortment plan. Overplan production of enterprises under
various ministries of the central government — with the exception
of a few enterprises and a few products designated by the central
government — generally can be shared in a fixed proportion with
local governments.

When various provinces, autonomous regions, and municipalities
directly under the central authority ask machinery-manufacturing
enterprises under various central ministries to produce certain
items over and above originally fixed quotas, if the items in question come under the unified distribution of the State Economic Commission or the control of any of the central ministries, approval
must be obtained from the relevant machine-building department
of the central government in order to avoid any blind increase in
production.

3. Of the profits of enterprises that were formerly under the
control of various central ministries but are now devolved and put
under the management of local governments, 20 percent goes to local
authorities and 80 percent goes to the central government.

Local governments are not entitled to share the profits gained by
enterprises belonging to the Second Ministry of Machine Building,
the Third Ministry of Machine Building, the Ministry of Post and
Telecommunications, the Ministry of Railways, the foreign sale
section of the Ministry of Foreign Trade, and the Civil Aviation
Bureau; or to those gained by large-scale mines, large-scale metallurgical plants, large-scale chemical industries, large-scale coal
mines, large electricity networks, oil refineries, and large factories manufacturing machinery and electric motors; or to those
gained by inter-provincial marine transport enterprises along the
Changjiang [Yangtze River] and the seacoast. Except these, local
governments may receive 20 percent of the total profits gained by
other enterprises, such as textile enterprises, that are still under
the management of the central ministries.

This fixed 2 to 8 ratio of profits shall remain unchanged for three
years in all enterprises in which local governments are entitled to
share profits.

The profits of enterprises that have been under local management from the very beginning still go entirely to local governments.

4. Increase the power of local authorities in personnel manage-ment. In all of the enterprises that have been devolved to local government management, except that the local government share of profits is limited to 20 percent, personnel management and other matters are to be handled as in local enterprises. Under the con-dition of not weakening the staff of major factories and mines, the provinces, autonomous regions, and municipalities may adjust ap-propriately the cadres in enterprises remaining under the control of various central ministries. But when transferring cadres under the jurisdiction of the State Council, local authorities should get approval from the State Council; local authorities also should con-sult with the relevant industrial departments when transfering cadres under the jurisdiction of various industrial departments. When transferring cadres, particularly when transferring high-level technical cadres, attention should be paid to the cadres' orig-inal profession, and consideration should be given to enabling these cadres to remain at their working posts for a definite period.

Enterprises belonging to various central ministries, together with their management organs stationed at various places, should accept the leadership and supervision of local people's councils concerning their staff arrangements.

SECOND, APPROPRIATELY ENLARGE THE AUTHORITY OF PERSONS IN CHARGE OF ENTERPRISES IN THE INTERNAL MANAGEMENT OF THE ENTERPRISES

1. In controlling a plan, fewer targets should be fixed as orders, and more responsibility should be entrusted to persons in charge of the enterprises.

In production plans, formerly there were twelve compulsory tar-gets which were fixed by the State Council and could not be changed without approval of the State Council; they were: the gross value of output, quantities of important products, new varieties of products to be trial manufactured, important technical economic quotas, the rate of reduction of cost, the amount of reduction of cost, the total number of staff and workers, the number of workers at the end of the year, the total wage bill, the average wage, labor productivity, and profit. Now the number of targets fixed by the State Council are to be reduced to four, namely: (1) quantities of important products, (2) the total number of staff and workers, (3) the total wage bill, and (4) profit. The other eight, in general, are to be considered nonbinding targets. When transmitting the plan downward or submitting the plan upward, these nonbinding targets should still be included, together with the four binding targets, as basis for calculation; when putting the plan into implementation, however, enterprises concerned may make some amendments based on concrete conditions. The amended nonbinding targets should be reported to relevant ministries and bureaus for recording.

Apart from the four binding targets laid down by the State Council, each industrial ministry may, based on particular requirements of various enterprises, fix some additional binding targets, such as those for the trial manufacture of new products, for important technical economic quota, and for the rate of reduction of cost. According to local conditions, people's councils in various provinces, autonomous regions, and municipalities directly under the central government also may set additional binding targets for enterprises under their jurisdiction, such as fixing the quantities of certain products the supplies of which are to be balanced in the respective provinces, autonomous regions, and municipalities.

In capital construction plans, binding targets fixed by the State Council for the year 1957 are four in number, namely: (1) total amount of investment, (2) above-norm items, (3) mobilization of productive power, and (4) amount of construction and installation work. From now on these four targets are still to be carried out. Targets for labor and wages in construction and installation departments are to be handled as in the past. When spending the investment in local capital construction, under the premise of guaranteeing the fulfillment of the above-mentioned binding targets, and within the total amount of local investment fixed by the State Council, each province, autonomous region, and municipality directly under the central government may readjust construction items and construction steps.

A state plan fixes yearly targets only. Concerning quarterly and monthly plans, each department in charge should, according to concrete conditions, decide on which enterprises should have their plans drawn up by the ministries and bureaus in charge, and which should be allowed to draw up their own plans.

The procedure of drawing up and fixing the plan is to be simplified. The present procedure of transmitting downward twice and submitting upward twice is to be changed to transmitting downward twice and submitting upward once only. In other words, first

the higher authority is to transmit the control figures downward,
where the plan is drafted, then the draft is sent back for approval;
and then the higher authority distributes the approved plan downward. Efforts should be made to have a yearly plan generally
fixed by November of the previous year; after the approved plan
is transmitted downward, in general it will not be amended. Existing tables and reports should be resolutely simplified.

2. Profits are to be divided between the state and the enterprise, and the financial management system of the enterprise is to
be improved. The total profit gained by an enterprise is to be
shared according to a certain proportion between the state and that
enterprise. This proportion is to be fixed in the following way.
Take (1) the four-item expenditure (expenditure on technical and
organizational measures, on trial manufacture of new products, on
labor insurance and protection, and on miscellaneous purchases)
that an industrial department received from the state during the
First Five-Year Plan period, (2) the enterprise reward fund, and
(3) 40 percent of overplan profit, and add the three together; then
calculate the ratio by comparing this sum with the total profit
handed over by that industrial department to the state during the
same five-year period. In other words, express the total amount
of funds received by an industrial department from these three
sources as a percent of the total profits it handed over to the state,
and use this percentage as the fixed share of profit that particular
industrial department is to receive from now on. Hereafter in the
annual budget, the state will discontinue appropriating the four-
item expenditure and the enterprise reward fund; expenses for
these will be covered from the fixed share of profit. After this
percentage of profit is fixed, it will not be changed for three years,
and each year the actual amount will be calculated according to the
actual amount of profit. Each industrial ministry should, based
on the above-mentioned principle and also on concrete conditions,
fix different shares for each enterprise under their respective
jurisdiction, so as to realize sharing of profits between the state
and the enterprise. However, each industrial ministry may centralize a portion of the profits received by enterprises directly
under them, to use as an adjustment fund among enterprises. Industrial management departments of each province, autonomous
region, and municipality directly under the central government also
may take out a portion of profits received by enterprises directly
under them (including enterprises decentralized by the central

authority), and use this as an adjustment fund among local enter-prises.

Expenses for trial manufacture of new products in national de-fense enterprises will be separately funded by the departments in charge.

Since in the past there were no such regulations concerning the four-items expenditure, the enterprise reward fund, and the shar-ing of excess profits in state-private jointly operated enterprises as there were for state enterprises; and since most of the state-private jointly operated enterprises are medium and small in scale, when implementing this profit-sharing principle special in-vestigations should be conducted and proper methods stipulated in fixing the percentage of profits to be received by state-private jointly operated enterprises.

When spending their profits, enterprises must use the larger portion of the money in productive undertakings and, at the same time, give appropriate consideration to the welfare of the staff and workers.

Certain unreasonable regulations in existence, such as that for-bidding "the alteration of form" and "the increase of value" after a big overhaul, are to be abolished. As long as the plan is not af-fected, an enterprise may adjust its various items of administrative expenses within the budget. Within the authority granted by the superior organ, an enterprise may increase or decrease its fixed assets, or report assets as obsolete.

3. The staff management system of enterprises is to be im-proved. With the exception of leading and responsible personnel (factory directors, deputy directors, managers, and assistant managers), as well as important technical personnel, all other staff and workers are to be managed by the enterprises themselves.

So long as they do not increase the total number of the staff and workers, enterprises have the authority to readjust their own or-ganizations and personnel.

11

REGULATION ON THE IMPROVEMENT OF
THE COMMERCIAL MANAGEMENT SYSTEM
(November 1957)*

First, the establishment of local (provincial, autonomous region, municipal, and county) commercial organs is to be decided by the people's councils of each province, autonomous region, and municipality directly under the central government, in accordance with local conditions. When two or more commercial departments or bureaus are merged, from the financial point of view it is proper for them to abandon their original system of independent calculation and implement a new system of unified calculation. But they must still accept guidance on administrative principles and policies from commercial departments to which they were formerly subordinated. In principle, local commercial administrative organizations and enterprise organizations should be merged. For example, commercial departments and bureaus are to be changed into organizations taking charge of both administrative affairs and enterprise management, and the existing local specialized commercial companies are to be abolished and become a bureau or office within a commercial department or bureau. In certain large cities or districts, merging is not necessary if a careful study shows that it is impracticable.

Second, dual leadership, with relevant central commercial departments as the principal and local authorities as the auxiliary, is to be implemented over purchase and supply stations (first class wholesale depots, large-scale cold storage, and warehouses) established by various central commercial departments in cities or ports where production is concentrated. Purchase and supply stations (second class wholesale depots) established by the com-

---

*This is a State Council document drafted under the direction of Comrade Chen Yun. [This translation is adapted from the translation of the final text released in 1958 which appeared in Union Research Service, Volume 9, pp. 282-285.]

mercial department or bureau of a province, autonomous region, or municipality directly under the central government are to be placed under dual leadership with the commercial department or bureau of that province, autonomous region, or municipality as the principal, and the local government as the auxiliary.

Third, with the exception of certain large-scale enterprises that local authorities consider difficult to manage, all processing enterprises under various commercial departments of the central government are to be handed over to local authorities and put under the direct management of local commercial organs. However, in processing enterprises that are so devolved, regulations concerning production tasks, product specifications and standards, readjustments of installed productive capacity, and processing expenses are still to be managed in a unified manner by various central commercial departments in order to balance the whole nation's production.

Fourth, the State Council promulgates only four targets for the commercial plan each year; they are (1) the purchase plan, (2) the sale plan, (3) the total number of staff and workers, and (4) the profit target. At the same time, local authorities are allowed 5 percent flexibility above and below the targets when putting the purchase plan and the sales plan into effect. However, alterations of the figures of planned commodities under the control of various central commercial departments can be made only after approval is obtained from the central departments concerned. If commercial departments are required to purchase the products that local industries produce over and above the production plan, they may do so after obtaining approval from superior commercial organs. Any alteration of the purchase figures or sales figures or items under state planned purchase — such as grain, oil and fat, and cotton — must be approved by the State Council. Under extraordinary conditions, the people's council of a province, an autonomous region, or a municipality directly under the central authority may make the alteration first and then report to the State Council for the record. Hereafter the profit target will be transmitted downward only to the level of the province, autonomous region, and municipality directly under the central government, and will not be transmitted to the basic-level enterprises, in order to prevent basic-level shops from engaging in activities in violation of commercial policies while trying to fulfil the profit target. Each central commercial department, however, should lay down measures ensuring that the basic-level enterprises do not lower their profits by themselves. Since this measure of transmitting the profit targets only to the level of the province, autonomous region, and municipality directly under the central government, and not further downward to the basic-level enterprises, is a great and important change, it should not be carried out in the whole country all at once, but must be implemented on a trial basis in one or two provinces and regions by various central commercial departments, and popularized only after effective results have been obtained.

Fifth, the total profits of enterprises of various central commercial departments are to be shared with local authorities. Provinces, autonomous regions and municipalities directly under the central government are not entitled to any share of profits obtained from grain transactions and the external sale portion of foreign trade, but are entitled to those obtained from the internal sale portion of foreign trade. The methods used by supply and marketing cooperatives to divide bonuses among cooperative members and put aside public accumulation and other funds are to remain the same. Revenue from foods and beverages and from service trades are still to be collected by local authorities as before. Apart from items mentioned above, all enterprise profits of central commercial departments are to be shared with local authorities at the ratio of 2 to 8 — 20 percent goes to local authorities, and 80 percent goes to the central authority.

When commercial departments are required to make purchases or sales at a loss in order to encourage production to relieve famine, people's councils of provinces, autonomous regions, and municipalities directly under the central government are authorized to see that local commercial departments handle the matter well. Any eventual loss may be listed as enterprise loss and met by enterprise profit.

Sixth, a division of labor is to be implemented in the control of commodity prices. Both the purchase prices and sales prices of agricultural and agricultural subsidiary products under planned purchase and unified purchase are to be fixed in a unified manner by various commercial departments of the central government; in secondary areas of production, however, local governments are to be entrusted to control the prices according to price levels fixed by central commercial departments. This method is also to apply to purchase prices of scrap copper, scrap tin, and scrap iron and steel, which items are under unified purchase. Prices of category three commodities such as small native products and

commodities that local authorities have fixed to be locally purchased in the unified manner are to be controlled by local governments; but the price levels under the control of central commercial
departments should be taken as reference. A price fluctuation
limit should be laid down by the central authority once every year.

With regard to industrial products, purchase prices of commodities under the unified allocation of the State Economic Commission or distributed in a unified manner by various central industrial ministries are to be controlled according to the allocation
prices fixed by the state. Apart from these, purchase prices of all
other industrial products are to be controlled by the provinces,
autonomous regions, and municipalities directly under the central
government, according to the principle laid down by various central
commercial departments. The selling price of industrial articles
in the market, in major markets, and for important articles are
to be fixed by central commercial departments, while in secondary
markets, and for secondary articles the prices are to be fixed by
various provinces, autonomous regions, and municipalities directly
under the central government according to the price-fixing principle laid down by central commercial departments and in consultation with neighboring regions. The central government and local
authorities are to establish unified price-control organs at various
levels, and the central government is to convene a price conference
each year to fix the price level for the whole year.

Seventh, foreign exchange is to be shared between the central
government and local authorities. With a view to encouraging local
authorities to positively fulfill the state's export plans and strive
to overfulfill the export quotas of certain industrial and agricultural products, the central government will give local authorities
a fixed percentage of the foreign exchange obtained. Detailed
measures are to be found in a separate notification.

12

SEVERAL MAJOR ISSUES IN
CURRENT CAPITAL CONSTRUCTION WORK
(March 1959)

The year 1958 witnessed great advances, not only in agriculture and industry but also in capital construction, thanks to a great display of revolutionary vigor on the part of the people all over the country under the Party's leadership. Capital construction on an even larger scale will get under way in 1959. This is an arduous task. Nevertheless, we now have more materials and facilities, greater mineral and hydraulic resources available, greater technical abilities for prospecting, designing and building operations, and experience in organizing the great masses of people in capital construction as well as the high enthusiasm of the whole Party and the whole people to speed up our socialist construction. We shall surely be able to overcome all difficulties on the road ahead and victoriously complete this task so long as we firmly implement the Party's general line of going all out, aiming high and achieving greater, faster, better, and more economical results in building socialism and the comprehensive policies to this effect and do better and more meticulous work as we go along. I am here advancing some opinions concerning some of the major issues in current capital construction work in industry and communications.

I. THE DISTRIBUTION OF INDUSTRIES

Distribution of industries is a most important issue in capital construction. A rational distribution of industries will develop the industry with greater, faster, better, and more economical results by more fully utilizing our favorable conditions of a vast territory, rich resources, good climate, and large population. It will also help to change step by step the now irrational distribution of industrial productive forces in our country and establish at a relatively fast pace a comprehensive industrial system so as to promote better integration of industry and agriculture and of cities and rural

areas. Therefore, a nationwide, rational distribution of industrial
productive forces in a planned way is an issue of far-reaching and
all-round significance and an issue of strategic significance in capital construction. A problem of such nature cannot be solved well
in a piecemeal manner with only present convenience in mind and
without a long-term plan and overall arrangement. In deciding the
location of industries, we should use the spirit of "the whole nation
is a single chessboard" so as to integrate both immediate interests
and future interests, the interests of a section and those of the
whole.

Many questions have to be solved in order to meet the above-
mentioned demands. There are three main issues that people currently are most concerned about: First, in establishing a fairly
comprehensive industrial system, should we begin on a nationwide
level, or begin with the cooperative regions, provinces, and autonomous regions? Second, should the industrial enterprises be more
concentrated or more dispersed? Third, should most new enterprises be large scale or medium and small scale?

Let me begin with the first question.

Our country's territory is big and its people numerous. Out of
all the provinces, municipalities and autonomous regions, only the
five provinces and autonomous regions of Neimeng, Ningxia, Qing-
hai, Xinjiang, and Xizang and the two cities of Beijing and Tianjin
have a population of several million. The rest of the provinces,
cities, and regions have at the most 60-70 million people and at the
least more than 10 million. However, only a few provinces and cities possess strong industrial bases, while most provinces and (autonomous) regions are weak or very weak in this respect. In the
course of the construction of the First Five-Year Plan, there was
substantial development of our industry, and the unbalanced concentration of industry along the coastal areas was somewhat remedied,
though there has not yet been any fundamental change. Relatively
long-term efforts are needed to bring about fundamental changes
in the weak foundation and irrational distribution of our industries.
In order to establish a comprehensive industrial system, we have
to have coordination among the various ministries of heavy industry, light industry and transportation, especially coordination
among the various ministries of heavy industry; we must guarantee
that the fuel and power industry, the raw materials industry, and
the machine-building industry can meet the needs of expanding reproduction; and we must have agriculture able to supply relatively

ample surplus produce. These are obviously not things that can be resolved in a short period of time.

This being the case, should we start to establish a comprehensive industrial system nationwide, or should we begin with provinces, autonomous regions, or cooperative regions? This issue cannot be decided correctly by subjective desire but rather must be decided based on objective needs and actual possibilities. Our industrial and agricultural production is developing rapidly, and our material and technical strength can increase to different degrees each year. Nevertheless, we must be well aware of the fact that in the past several years our construction force and the supply of materials and equipment have been quite restricted and far from adequate to the needs of the huge task of construction. Under such circumstances, we can only build up the industrial system first on a nationwide basis, then consider the cooperative regions, and then (finally consider) some provinces and autonomous regions with appropriate conditions. Only by first establishing a national industrial system will it be possible to build up industrial systems in cooperative regions. By the same token, the establishment of industrial systems in provinces and autonomous regions will be possible only after those in the cooperative regions have been built. Otherwise, if we start in cooperative regions or in provinces and autonomous regions and projects are undertaken all at once throughout the country, the construction forces will inevitably be dispersed, construction speed retarded, and the overall arrangement hampered. This would be disadvantageous not only to national industrial construction but also to industrial construction in the provinces and autonomous regions.

To begin with the establishment of a nationwide industrial system will not hamper but rather will benefit the industrial systems in cooperative regions and some provinces and autonomous regions in the future when they are in earnest need and when conditions are ripe, since a national industrial system is made up of industries located in various cooperative regions, provinces, and autonomous regions. In the process of developing such a nationwide system, we must be able to build various numbers of new key enterprises in the different cooperative regions, provinces, and autonomous provinces. These key enterprises are both component parts of the national industrial system and important starting points for constructing industrial systems of the cooperative regions, provinces, and autonomous regions in the future. In laying out its plan for the national industrial system, the state should take into consideration both the conditions in cooperative regions, provinces, and autonomous regions for carrying out industrial construction at the present stage and the creation of favorable conditions to develop in the future their industrial systems at different levels and with their own peculiarities. Therefore, the need to establish a nationwide industrial system first and the need to develop industrial systems in cooperative regions, provinces, and autonomous regions are basically identical. This is one side of the coin. On the other side, it must be pointed out that owing to the limitations of objective conditions, in matters of assigning construction projects and allotting building materials and equipment, there is a contradiction between meeting the needs of the country and that of the localities. The principle for resolving this contradiction should be that the partial situation is subordinate to the overall situation and that parts are subordinate to the whole. Provinces and autonomous regions should proceed from the overall situation and correctly set their construction tasks in light of the requirements of national and regional industrial construction and of their own peculiarities. Of course, this does not mean at all that localities should not vigorously undertake industrial projects even if they possess the ability and the conditions. All along it has been the unswerving policy of our Party that under the guidance of the state plan, the enthusiasm of local authorities at various levels should be fully aroused and the strength of the masses mobilized to try every possible means to develop industrial construction. On the one hand, we must concentrate our efforts to ensure the key projects and establish a national industrial system as rapidly as possible. On the other hand, we should develop various local industries to the best of our abilities in accordance with the possibilities of different localities and step-by-step strengthen their industrial foundations so as to better meet the needs of the local people and people in other areas with regard to production and their daily life.

As mentioned before, the industrial systems constructed by the various cooperative regions, provinces, and autonomous regions will be at the different levels and have their own peculiarities. Modern industry is an extremely complex form of economy which carries with it extensive coordination among specialized departments. Therefore, there must be division of labor and coordination among various regions, departments, and enterprises and even among the various sections within a single enterprise. For instance, the production of thermo-electric power equipment of over 12,000 kilowatt capacity requires nationwide coordination of more than 80 large and medium-sized machine tool enterprises as well as coordination of heavy industries such as metallurgy, coal, electric power, and chemicals. It also requires coordination of light industries, such as papermaking, ceramics, and textiles. The production of a complex variety of things such as these, requiring a high degree of coordination and cooperation, is not possible in any one enterprise and is even difficult in any one province or autonomous region. It can be accomplished only by a rational division of production tasks and by organizing cooperation on an even larger scale. To strengthen coordination among regions, departments, and enterprises is an indispensable condition to ensure common development. This holds true not only for building a national industrial system at present but also for the future development of industrial systems in the cooperative regions, provinces, and autonomous regions.

It is unrealistic to establish in one province or autonomous region an all-comprehensive, fully equipped, fully competent independent industrial system. Everybody knows that in developing agriculture, different crops should be grown in accordance with different soil, climate, and other conditions. Violating this principle will keep agricultural production from increasing and even cause it to suffer great losses. Consideration should also be given to local natural resources when planning industrial development. To illustrate: a copper mine cannot be opened up where there is no copper ore. It is economically irrational not to put efforts into what is possible and in urgent need by the nation but instead to attempt vainly to do what is hardly possible, without giving a thought to the availability of local natural resources and to economic characteristics.

Now the second question. Should the enterprises be more concentrated or more dispersed?

Some comrades favor the concentrated construction of industrial enterprises in the existing big and medium-sized cities, arguing that this could be done quickly and with less investment. We think that enterprises should be located near the sources of supply of raw materials and fuel and close to the areas where their products will be consumed so as to secure the maximum economic results from a minimum investment. Of course, national security needs should also be taken into consideration. It is entirely necessary to set up or enlarge some enterprises in the big and medium-sized cities in accordance with possibilities and needs, taking advantage of the foundations already available. But most enterprises should be properly dispersed among medium-sized and small cities and towns or places with mineral resources.

Will it really take longer to build factories in medium-sized and small cities and towns and new mining areas than in big and medium-sized cities? No. Some people always approach this question from the standpoint of temporary convenience: availability of electric power, water supply, communications facilities, and availability of assistance from skilled labor in surrounding areas for construction and subsequent operation. But they have not given enough consideration to the fact that in many of the big and medium-sized cities, electric power, water, materials and transportation are already in short supply. If factories are increased in these cities, it will be necessary to build new power plants, enlarge the water supply and increase transport facilities, thereby not only not being faster, but often being slower than in medium-sized and small towns and new mining areas. As for whether technical assistance is available in the surrounding areas, this is a matter of proper organization and assignment of technical personnel. As long as we organize and arrange things well, construction of industrial bases in medium-sized and small towns and new mining areas should also have access to technical assistance. So, instead of a slower pace, it may even be somewhat faster to build factories in medium and smaller cities and in new mining areas.

Is it true that somewhat more investment is required to build factories in medium and smaller cities and in new mining areas? Not necessarily under normal circumstances, and in fact it may cost a little less. The cost of equipment is the same in medium and smaller cities and in big cities, and the cost of water supply, drainage works, power supply, communication, and transportation as well as urban public utilities is about the same. As for the investment in building materials, local materials can be utilized and more temporary workers can be employed in the medium and smaller cities and new mining areas so that the standards of the nonproductive buildings can be lowered and the nonproductive building areas can be reduced. Therefore, construction of factories of the same size requires less in medium to small cities than in medium to large cities.

In addition to the difference in construction speed and investment, when planning the location of enterprises consideration should also be given to the economic results after the enterprises go into operation. If enterprises are too concentrated in big and medium-sized cities, they will be separated from sources of supply of raw materials and fuels and their consumers, which will add to the difficulties in supply and transportation, increase the cost of production of the products, and thus result in long-term economic irrationalities. But if enterprises are appropriately dispersed among the medium and smaller cities and the new mining areas, they will get the support of the local people during construction, which will better resolve the difficulties in manpower and materials. Moreover, after the enterprises go into operation, production supply and marketing can be coordinated more closely and [thus] production will be organized more rationally, transportation distances will be shortened, and the cost of producing products will be reduced further. At the same time, the stronger contacts between enterprises and the producers of raw materials and consumers will help enterprises to improve management and turn out products with better quality and more variety. To derive these advantages, it is well worth while in the long run to spend a little more time and money in the establishment of the plant.

The matter of concentration or dispersal of enterprises is not a question for industry alone, but is also a question concerning relations between industry and agriculture and between urban and rural areas. In planning the locations of enterprises, we must give full attention to combining industry and agriculture and combining urban with rural areas. Engels has said, "Big industry should so far as possible be more evenly distributed throughout the nation so as to eliminate the conditions that tend to cause a split between city and country."* Under the socialist system, it is entirely possible to more evenly distribute large industries throughout the country, closely linking industry and agriculture and gradually changing agriculture from manual farming to mechanized production and gradually bringing culture to the uncultured agricultural population. The policies of the Party — that is, we should develop industry and agriculture simultaneously with priority on heavy industry, develop simultaneously heavy industry and light industry, central industry and local industry, large enterprises and medium and small enterprises, and use both foreign and native, modern, and simple meth-

---

*Anti-Dühring, Selected Works of Marx and Engels, vol. 3, p. 336.

ods — are long-term policies guiding our industrial construction. They are also policies to speed up the combination of industry and agriculture, urban and rural areas, The distribution of enterprises must conform with these policies. If we follow the above principles and appropriately distribute the enterprises throughout the country, it will benefit the acceleration of socialist construction.

Now let us discuss the third question: should the major part of the new enterprises consist of large units or of units of medium and small size?

The distribution of enterprises and their size are interrelated. The idea of some people to concentrate enterprises in big and medium-sized cities cannot be separated from the fact that they want more large enterprises and fewer medium and small ones. As we prefer to place most of the enterprises in medium-sized and small cities and in mining districts, we certainly hold that except for the necessary large enterprises, we should go all out to set up medium and small enterprises.

The policy that large, medium, and small enterprises should be built simultaneously with most being medium and small has been understood by more and more comrades and is being implemented progressively in practice. Some areas and departments have planned their construction in line with this policy and are ready to scale down some already planned large enterprises which should and can be reduced in size. However, the erroneous idea of establishing large and comprehensive enterprises still exists in some areas and departments.

We must build step by step a number of large modern enterprises as the mainstay of our industrial establishment, without which we could hardly turn our country into a powerful, modern, industrial country. This we have done in the past and must continue to do in the future. However, it takes a longer period of time to build large enterprises. A great iron and steel combine from its inception to its completion requires at least five or six years. The output of a medium or a small enterprise is smaller, but it is something we can design, build, equip, and put into operation in much less time; the cost is low and the technical requirements are relatively easy to meet. To increase speed and thereby better meet the nation's construction needs, we should first build more medium and small industrial plants. We should also try our best to build some large enterprises, starting from smaller sections and enlarging by stages, so that production can be started at an earlier date. By so

doing, we can also obtain experience in construction, cultivate
a technical force, and prepare conditions for future development.

II. ARRANGING THE ORDER OF
   CONSTRUCTION PROJECTS

If distribution of industries is considered as strategy in capital
construction, then to arrange every year's construction projects in
order of importance and urgency is a battle plan to implement the
strategy.

The scale and scope of our capital construction are constantly
growing. Taking the country as a whole, we have state-planned
projects with investment and materials allotted by the state. We
also have projects planned and financed by provinces, municipalities, autonomous regions, and various departments. Within a province, a region, and a department, there are province-, region-, or
department-planned projects, and there are also those of prefectures, counties, communes, and enterprises. We must arouse the
enthusiasm of various local authorities and departments to increase
construction whenever possible. With the development of our economy, we will have more and more construction projects, and our
construction task will become heavier. But the supply of major
building materials and equipment often fails to keep up with the
needs of development in terms of timely supply and variety. This
is a sharp contradiction. In order to solve this contradiction, we
must, in accordance with our country's financial and material resources and in the spirit of "taking the whole country as a single
chessboard," rank the construction projects in order of importance
and urgency and orient the enthusiasm of the local authorities and
departments into the orbit of the state plan so that our strength can
be concentrated on the main direction of the battle to ensure first
of all the fulfillment of the state plan, especially the construction
of the key projects. Construction needed by the locales and departments will be carried out next when there is energy to spare. We
must arrange the capital construction projects in a unified order
and avoid blindly adding construction projects and enlarging the
scale of construction. This is not only a problem to be solved with
special efforts this year, but a problem to pay attention to resolving
every ensuing year.

In scheduling the capital construction projects, we should have
the overall situation in mind, giving priority to key projects while
also considering the rest so as to keep capital construction in pace

with the development needs of the national economy.

The construction of key projects must be guaranteed. If all projects got started indiscriminately and edged ahead all at once, not only the construction of key projects could not be guaranteed, the rest could not be completed on schedule either. Nevertheless, under the premise that construction of key projects is completed, we must pay attention to overall balance and strive to eliminate weak links in order to enable key projects to link up with others so that the various economic departments can coordinate with one another and develop proportionately. To guarantee the key projects and to give allowance to the rest are the two aspects in arranging construction. Only looking at the overall situation to the neglect of key points is one kind of partiality; only paying attention to key points to the neglect of the overall situation is another kind of one-sidedness. And both of these should be avoided.

Is ensuring the completion of key projects the same thing as ensuring the completion only of large enterprises? There is no doubt that construction of large key projects should be guaranteed. But there are also a large number of medium and small-scale projects among the key projects. For instance, construction of medium and small mills for special steel, nonferrous metal plants and mines, and precision instrument factories plays a big role in the establishment of a relatively comprehensive industrial system. Therefore, to build more of these kinds of enterprises and put them into operation at an early date should also be considered as an important part of ensuring the completion of key projects. Attention should be given to these projects when allotting raw materials and equipment. In the past, often the medium and small enterprises that have an important role to play in the development of the national economy have been considered not as key projects but rather as minor points and have been pushed aside during the planning of construction. This practice is wrong.

Is ensuring the completion of important projects the same thing as ensuring the completion of heavy industry projects? Key projects consist mainly of heavy industry enterprises but there are also some light industry projects among them. Light industry projects that are essential to the needs of the people may be key points for certain localities at certain times. It is wrong to regard such projects as unimportant and, giving inadequate attention to them, push them aside when construction plans are drawn up.

Some enterprises which may not seem like key items from the

standpoint of a province, a municipality, or an autonomous region may be indispensable from the national standpoint, such as critical parts for some large enterprises and chemical factories producing special raw materials. Importance must be attached to these enterprises when arranging the order of construction projects. Special consideration must also be given to some special regional tasks. That is to say, localities should be aware of the needs of the whole country, and the various departments of the central government should keep local needs in mind, too. The one-sidedness of seeing only one side at the expense of the other side should be avoided.

The national economy is an organic whole. In the process of industrial construction, we must give consideration to all the links. Meanwhile, we should also consider the coordination of communication and transportation, commercial undertakings, urban construction, residence of workers and staff, as well as service industries. We should never pay attention to only one aspect and neglect other aspects. We must be more and more meticulous in our economic work and make concrete analysis of all the problems in our economic construction.

To arrange the capital construction projects in order of importance is a problem not only for the whole country but also for the various localities and departments; it is even a problem existing within single enterprises. One should not take all the workshops in all the key enterprises as important and all the workshops in ordinary enterprises as minor. For instance, an iron and steel mill is a key project, but certain of its subordinate workshops are not necessarily key points. We must not treat a relatively unimportant workshop as an important shop and thus delay construction of what is more urgent. That is to say, in arranging the order of construction projects, we should be aware of the fact that there are minor elements in important projects. To cite another example, some papermaking mills may not be very important in terms of their overall construction, but their workshops producing paper for industrial use should be considered as key points. That is to say, in arranging the order of construction projects, we should understand that there are key points in minor projects. Minor elements in important projects and important elements in minor projects is an objective reality. Only by making concrete analysis of concrete conditions can we make proper arrangements.

Moreover, at the tail end of a project, not much manpower and

material are needed, and there is not much work. Thus, it is easy
to overlook, postponing the time of handling over the completed
project, completing the project in a careless and rash way, and ignoring quality. This will in turn lead to the situation where enterprises cannot go into operation on schedule or, after operation
starts, production cannot proceed normally. Therefore, tail end
work deserves full attention in the planning of construction projects.

In order to arrange properly the order of construction projects,
we should first of all do a good job to straighten out the thinking of
our cadres. There are bound to be differences of opinion among
them concerning matters of priority, importance, loss, and gain.
Through ideological work, we should help people to adopt an overall
point of view and discard the view that only takes partial interests
into account and loses sight of the overall situation. We should also
urge them to exercise a communist spirit and oppose departmental-
ism. Otherwise, doing a good job in arranging the order of construction projects will become merely empty words. After the construction schedule has been adopted, then it is important to establish unified control of building materials, important equipment, and
a labor force for construction and installation work. In other
words, we should put all the building materials, major equipment,
and labor force under the unified control of the Center's relevant
departments, the provinces, municipalities, and autonomous regions
and dispatch and utilize them in accordance with the order of the
projects. Only by concentrating our manpower and material resources in this way can the fulfillment of the state construction plan
be ensured.

III. THE DESIGNING OF ENTERPRISES

Once decisions are made to execute certain construction projects, designing becomes the crux of the matter. The work of designing determines whether construction can be rapid, of assured
quality, economical in outlay, and whether maximum economic returns can be obtained when the construction is completed.

In the last few years, much progress has been made in the designing work of capital construction. We have now a great deal of
experience in designing, both successful and otherwise. We have
accumulated a wealth of design data and organized a force of
200,000 designers. However, progress in designing is not balanced.
In general, the designing of the civil engineering aspects of a project proceeds a little faster than that of the technical aspects. To

raise our designing work a step higher, attention needs to be directed to two problems, namely: first, how to make combined use of native and foreign methods; and second, how to get our designers to be both creative and realistic.

In the work of designing, we in this country have gone through the stage of copying foreign designs, then of making modifications in foreign designs, and now we are entering the stage of making our designs by ourselves. Of course, we should incorporate the advanced experience of foreign countries even when we are able to make our own designs. Then, what kind of designs can better meet the requirements of achieving greater, faster, better, and more economical results? To be specific, the design of some construction structures have quite high standards, and the designs of others have lower standards; in technical equipment, some have a high degree of mechanization and automation, some have a lower degree in this respect, and others may combine semimechanization with hand labor. Which should make up the major part? In our opinion, we sometimes need the first, sometimes the second, but to a large extent the native rather than the foreign standard of designing is advisable at present. To use a common expression, we need both foreign and native designs, but for the time being the major part should consist of native ones. Whether in the metallurgical, machine tool, or other industries, we should design and build a number of enterprises with modern equipment that are highly mechanized and automated, and make these indispensable key enterprises in raising the technical level of our industry. At the same time, we should also design and build numerous enterprises with a lower degree of mechanization and less advanced equipment.

Let me now explain this question by using as an example the iron and steel industrial departments. The Seamless Steel Pipe Mill of Anshan Iron and Steel Company is constructed according to very high technical standards and is entirely mechanized and automatic. It is designed for an annual output of 60,000 tons of seamless pipes. But it took a relatively long time to build it, three or four years. At present, our country needs over a million tons of seamless steel pipes annually, and to produce this quantity would require more than ten mills of this size. Even if the building of these mills were to begin at the same time, there would not be enough time to finish them to meet the demand. Moreover, it would be impossible for us to manufacture enough advanced equipment for them. Since we cannot wait, nor can we afford to rely completely on imports, what should be done? There is a Yongxin Seamless Steel Pipe Mill in Shanghai. It is housed in an old building, its equipment is comparatively simple, but it can produce 7,000-10,000 tons of seamless steel pipes a year. Furthermore, it took only several months to build the mill. The Designing Institute of the Ferrous Metal Smelting Industry of the Ministry of Metallurgical Industry has, taking the construction and equipment of this mill as reference and absorbing some usable new techniques from the Seamless Steel Pipe Mill of Anshan Iron and Steel Company, designed a seamless steel pipe mill with an annual production capacity of about 15,000 tons of seamless pipes of diameters up to 76 millimeters. If we make the best use of our time and do everything properly, it will only take about a year to complete this project. If we build several tens of small mills like this, a few at a time, and a few big mills of the size of the Seamless Steel Pipe Mill of Anshan Iron and Steel Company, it will be possible to meet the urgent needs of the present time and those of the near future.

Again let me take as an illustration the machine industry departments. During the period of the First Five-Year Plan, we constructed quite a few modern machine tool factories which have played an important role in expanding our machine industry. Meanwhile, we ourselves have also built a great number of simply equipped machine factories. Everyone knows that we need an immense amount of machines and equipment to furnish our various industries, but there is a gap between the production capacities of the existing machinery factories and our actual needs. If we were to build only the first type of factories, it would take a relatively long time and require a lot of investment. On the other hand, if we build some modern machine factories while at the same time building a large number of simply equipped ones, it would be possible, within a comparatively short time and with relatively small investment, to increase our capacity to produce machines and other equipment to generally meet the needs of the development of our construction. In developing the machine industry, we should not adopt the attitude that it is better to go without than to use simple means, and thus build only modern machine tool factories. On the contrary, we should build some modern factories for large or precision products and also many simple factories, in the conviction that it is better to use simple means than to go without, so as to make up the insufficiencies of the modern machine tool factories.

The practice of combining foreign and native methods should be followed not only within industrial departments but also within single enterprises. For instance, in designing an important workshop in a factory, designers may adopt high standards in accordance with its requirement, while for the subordinate workshops, lower standards may be reasonably adopted.

The terms modern/foreign and simple/native, as used in this article, are relevant to certain times, certain areas, and certain conditions of production and technical levels. What is called modern in one area may be considered simple in another area, and what is called simple here may be considered modern there. What is modern now may become simple in the future if it remains unimproved, and what is simple now may become modern if serious work is done to improve it. Therefore, the policy with reference to design work, i.e., to combine foreign and modern methods with native and simple methods, is a policy that should be carried out extensively over a long period of time. In a sense, there is the need at any time to combine foreign and modern methods with native and simple methods. The only difference is that, compared with the modern and simple methods now, those in the future will be at an advanced stage both in terms of content and form. Our task regarding the issue of modern/foreign and native/simple is to make arrangements for "using modern and foreign methods when they should be used" and relying on "simple and native methods whenever they can be used" to meet the diverse requirements of different times, different places, and dissimilar conditions. Meanwhile, we should, in light of needs and possibilities, improve both foreign/modern and native/simple methods and combine the two properly.

What types and how many modern methods do we need and what type and how many simple methods do we need? During what period, in what places, and under what circumstances do we need them? How should we improve the modern methods? How should we improve the simple ones? What should we do so as best to combine the two? In order to answer all these questions correctly, our designers have to follow the principle of seeking truth from facts and give play to their creative spirit.

The creative spirit we are advocating differs from conservatism on the one hand and from unrealistic and rash operations on the other. Those affected by conservatism always lag behind objective reality both in thought and in action and fail to cope with changed objective conditions. Those who do things rashly always ignore objective conditions, violate objective laws, take fantasy for truth,

handle affairs according to their wishful thinking, or try to advance
to the present what can be realized only in the future. People in
both instances do not seek truth from facts, and therefore neither
of them can possibly have any real creative spirit. Freedom is the
recognition of necessity. The more people seek truth from facts
and the more their thought and actions conform with realistic conditions and objective laws, the more they can give play to their creative spirit. Our design personnel should thoroughly implement the
Party's policy on construction, and in accordance with the needs of
economic development and principles in the natural sciences, ac-
quire a comprehensive understanding and make concrete analysis
of the geological conditions, resources and other natural conditions,
of the raw materials, production and supply of equipment, of the
current scientific and technical levels, of the labor conditions, and
of the living habits of the people. In this way, they can draw up designing plans which will conform to actual needs and thus keep our
capital construction work ever changing for the better and developing in all respects. To this end, our designers should always study
theory, study science, go deep into reality, link up with the masses,
and raise their political consciousness and technical level.

Let me talk a bit here about the relation between new and veteran
designers. In general, the youthful designers are open-minded,
venturesome, enterprising, and more enthusiastic about new things.
But they are short of experience and knowledge. The veteran designers possess more experience and knowledge, but are short of
zeal in forging ahead and not as sensitive to new things. It is our
hope that new and veteran designers will learn from and help each
other, unite, and join efforts in fulfilling the tasks of the Party and
the state.

IV. MANAGEMENT AND CONSTRUCTION

Whether capital construction projects can be completed in a
greater, faster, better, and more economical way still depends a
great deal on construction. It is an arduous and glorious task for
all the building workers and staff to be entrusted with seeing that
steady improvements are made in construction, quality of work-
manship is maintained, and that if possible, the completed job is
turned over ahead of time for the commendement of production
operations.

In the year 1958, staff and workers engaging in capital construction in numerous places around the country created a method to

"speed up construction." This has given expression to the desire
of the great masses of staff and workers to fulfill the country's task
of capital construction with greater, faster, better, and more economical results. It has also contributed to an increase in labor
productivity, a higher speed in construction, and a decrease in
costs.

Carrying out the "more, faster, better, and more economical"
construction method has posed many new demands on planning and
organizing construction, on producing structural components, and
on the leadership system.

In the past, it was customary to start on numerous projects in
one area at the same time. This extended the battle line, scattered
the construction force, and made impossible the concentrated use
of building materials and equipment. This caused delay of completion of many projects and retarded the speed of construction. The
new way calls for arranging construction projects in order of importance and urgency so as to concentrate the construction force,
building materials, and equipment. In this way, the battle line is
shortened, projects are started a few at a time, a new group is
started after another group is completed, and construction as a
whole is thus speeded up. Comrades in Beijing describe the old
way as "divide up the force to guard many passes, use the force in
a dispersed way, and fight a war of attrition." They advocate that
we discard the old method and adopt a new method, i.e., "Shorten
the battle line, concentrate forces, and fight a war of annihilation."
Their idea obviously is correct.

In the past, in organizing construction, the assembly line method
was adopted in a simple parallel way. That is to say, a number of
projects were started at the same time and workers doing different
jobs went from one construction site to another in a flow process.
In this way, the workers were shifted frequently from one work site
to another and too much time was wasted. At the same time, the
labor force was organized into specialized work groups and the division of labor was too fine, which often caused disconnections in
the working process and too long a disruption in the work. This is
a relatively slow and uneconomical operational method. The new
method is to concentrate the construction force on a few projects,
adopt assembly-line procedures in a parallel but grade-separated
way, and organize a composite working team suitable to such a
working procedure, which will include various kinds of jobs. This
makes it possible for each project, from beginning to end, to be

taken charge of by one working team. In the process of construction, the speed of the principal job may be accelerated first, thus opening up working areas for other jobs and enabling the whole project to start up full-scale. This permits work on various sections at the same time or in quick succession and close coordination of all jobs so that time and space may be utilized to the fullest extent and suspension of work reduced to the minimum. Thus, the entire construction process is expedited.

With regard to structural components, in the past most were prepared at the work site and only a few were prefabricated. Now, because of the introduction of new construction methods, not only most of the simple components, such as doors and windows, are pre-assembled, but many of the reinforced concrete components are prefabricated, too, and the production equipment, sewage, central heating, electric appliances, and sanitary equipment are also pre-assembled and delivered to the work site ready to be placed in position. Facts prove that the use of such prefabricated and pre-assembled components not only increases the speed of the construction but also helps ensure its quality. With the extensive use of prefabricated and pre-assembled components, the volume of hoisting is increased. This makes it necessary to appropriately increase the quantity of modern machinery and, at the same time, to continue to arouse the masses, carry out technical reform, improve working methods and working tools, and make native type or seminative and semiforeign machines.

With regard to the system of leadership, in the past each of the several construction units at one work site would advocate vertical lines of authority as primary and lacked unified leadership, making it very inconvenient to control the whole situation. There also existed for a long time a lack of coordination between the unit that owned the project and the unit building it. Now because we are carrying out centralized leadership by the Party committee of the work site or the Party committee of the locality over the owners of the projects and the building units, over the general contractors and the subcontractors, as well as over the Party, government, trade union and the Youth League, coordination of action of various forces has become possible. Thus, the lack of efficient control and coordination as existed in the past has been changed fundamentally and the spirit of coordination has developed.

These important changes following the introduction of the new construction method undoubtedly are favorable to the full implementation of the principle of achieving greater, faster, better, and more economical results in capital construction. But there are still leading personnel in a small number of construction units who take a one-sided view of this connection, thinking that the new method is aimed merely at speed. So they start work in a hurry without first examining the concrete conditions and making the necessary preparations. This has resulted in confusion at individual work sites, deterioration of work quality, waste of huge amounts of materials, as well as accidents and injuries. These comrades have failed to understand that the quicker they want to get the jobs done, the better they should make preparations and the more they should endeavor to guarantee the quality of work and ensure construction safety.

It is inevitable that certain shortcomings arise as the new method of construction is implemented. It is our task to explain correctly the contents of the new method and to popularize it step by step. With progress in capital construction, we should also sum up new experience so that the new construction can unceasingly approach perfection.

V. SPEED AND QUALITY

The general policy of the Party guiding socialist construction is to achieve greater, faster, better, and more economical results. This policy demands striving for high speed and ensuring good quality. The two are unified and inseparable. In the course of capital construction, whether it is the distribution of industry, arrangement of the order to construction projects, design of enterprises, or management of construction, this policy must be fully implemented so that we can expedite construction and ensure excellent quality in all the completed projects, thus obtaining the biggest possible returns on our investment.

Capital construction concerns the long-range interests of the state. It is true that we must have high speed, but there must be no negligence whatsoever in regard to quality. Because the work has to be done over again if its quality is poor, this leads to waste of manpower, material, and money. In some cases, it may even cause production to be irrational for long periods or affect the smooth production of commodities. These are all what we should always concentrate on avoiding in the process of construction. Neglect of quality will not expedite but retard construction, while reasonable attention to quality will enhance speed. Our current emphasis on paying attention to quality is completely in line with our demand for the high speed development of construction.

Where should we begin in order to ensure and constantly improve the quality of the construction projects? The answer is that in designing and construction, we must reasonably ensure the quality of the structural components, the building materials and equipment installation, and at the same time we should train technical personnel and strengthen technical management.

The structural work is extremely important. Whether a factory building is solid depends first of all on its structure. We must oppose the blind seeking of overly high standards or overemphasis on a big safety coefficient; we should also guard against inappropriately low structural standards and too small a safety coefficient. In capital construction, we must continue to practice strict economy and keep the cost as low as possible. But such economy should not be carried so far as to affect the quality of construction. In order to reasonably ensure quality of the structural work, we should take into consideration the different production techniques of various enterprises and different natural conditions of various areas and cautiously work out the different structural standards to suit individual projects and local conditions. Where steel structures should be used, reinforced concrete may not be substituted; where reinforced concrete structures should be used bricks and wood must not be substituted. Of course, where brick and wood structures are suitable, they should be used. The designs for one production technique under one kind of natural conditions should not be applied casually to another production technique under another kind of natural conditions. A standard design which has already been finalized after tests and approved after examination must not be revised without the agreement of the original designing department.

The quality of a project depends, to a very large extent, on the quality of the building materials used. The building materials must be selected in accordance with the design specifications of the project. We should oppose the tendency to put good or large materials to bad or petty use and to not use small materials and not use substitutes when possible, so that we can avoid waste and expedite construction. We also oppose the tendency to use carelessly materials that do not meet specifications in disregard of the reasonable requirements of the design, because the quality of the project cannot be ensured as it should be. In the course of construction, examination of the quality and standards of the materials must be strength-

ened and supervision should be imposed on the factories producing
building materials so as to make sure that the products manufactured are up to standard. Change of materials in the course of construction is allowable but must first be subject to serious calculation and testing. No change is allowed where there shouldn't be
any. Building-material industry departments should work hard to
trial produce new building materials. But new materials may
be extensively used only after testing and examination. All large
key projects, especially big and medium-sized dams which concern
the lives and safety of the people, must give the greatest attention
possible to ensuring the quality and safety of the projects. Materials for such projects must strictly meet the quality and standards
specified by the designs. If no qualified materials are available, it
is better to suspend the work for the time being, and under no circumstances should carelessness be tolerated. The production and
installation of equipment is even more important than are the building materials to the quality of the project, so we should certainly
pay even closer attention to this in designing and building the projects and must never be careless.

To ensure the quality of the capital construction projects, we
must raise the political consciousness and technical level of the
staff and workers and strengthen technical control work. To reasonably ensure the quality of structural work, building materials
and the installation of equipment, as mentioned above, is closely
related to the political consciousness and technical level of the
workers and staff. The higher their political consciousness and
technical level, the better they understand the importance of project quality and the easier it is to solve the problems in this respect. We must attach great importance to the training of the capital construction departments' workers and staff, both politically
and technically, so as to increase greatly their sense of responsibility toward the cause of socialism, enrich their knowledge of science, and raise their technical skills. As for the shortage of workers doing certain highly skilled jobs, such as electrical welders,
hoisters, and installers of large equipment, all kinds of efficient
methods must be adopted and every interval in the construction
must be utilized to conduct special and intensive training.

Ensuring the quality of projects is also closely related to
strengthening construction management, especially technical control. We should teach all the workers and staff to follow strictly
the regulations, technical procedures, and rules of operations with

regard to designing, construction, and materials to ensure the quality of the project. Where there are no such rules and regulations,
they must be instituted quickly; where they have been cast aside,
we must see to it that they are restored as soon as possible and
carried out conscientiously.

VI. COMBINING CENTRALIZED LEADERSHIP
WITH MASS MOVEMENTS

Practice in the past one year and more has proved that the centralized and unified leadership of the Party and the Party's mass
line must be maintained in capital construction as in other work.

The Party's general line for socialist construction is the application and development of the Party's mass line in the course of socialist construction. For this reason, the policies and plans on
capital construction (such as first building a national industrial system and developing local industries in provinces and autonomous
regions in an appropriate way, the proper dispersion instead of over
concentration of enterprises, the simultaneous development of
large-, medium- and small-scale enterprises, and the arrangement
of projects in order of importance and urgency) must all be first
submitted to the Party committees at various levels and the departments concerned for careful deliberation before decisions can be
made and must all be tackled fully in accordance with the requirements of the mass line. In other words we must, on the one hand,
carry on repeated and serious discussions among the cadres of various levels in order to reach a common understanding and, on the
other hand, mobilize extensively the masses to participate in construction, bring into full play the activism of the masses, and tap
the potentials in all fields to the fullest extent. Moreover, in the
course of practice, leading bodies should continuously supplement
and amend the policies and plans in light of the experience and inventions of the masses so that under the guidance of correct policies progress can be made in capital construction with greater,
faster, better, and more economical results.

After a decision is reached on a capital construction project, the
Party committees of the construction unit should strengthen their
leadership and conscientiously carry out the mass line in choosing
the location for the project, making designs, arranging construction, and formulating necessary rules and regulations to ensure the
speed of construction and quality of the project. By so doing, we
will truly pool the wisdom of the great masses of technical person-

nel and workers and staff and greatly arouse their initiative and
enthusiasm.

The policy of combining the Party's leadership with the mass
line requires the designers, when working on designs, to go deep
into reality and immerse themselves among the masses to get ac-
quainted with the situation, listen to suggestions, and study new experiences and inventions. Discussions should be arranged among
the designers to encourage the engineers, technicians, and trainees
to air their views, and all the rational suggestions, after comparison and analysis, should be pooled together for the design plans.
Then, the tentative plan should be handed over to the technical personnel, workers, and staff in the relevant departments, enterprises,
and work sites and to the teachers and students of relevant schools
for discussion, examination, revision, and supplement. Also, in
the process of organizing the project all workers and staff should
be informed of the project tasks and quality requirements and be
encouraged to hold extensive discussions. Only after all this should
schedules and methods of the construction be decided. In every construction unit, the system of "the two participations, one reform
and three combinations"[a] should be enforced earnestly. Each and
every cadre should show himself as a common laborer and associate closely with the masses, paying attention to their thinking, taking charge of the production, and taking care of their living. Just
as pointed out in the "Resolution on Problems Concerning People's
Communes" adopted by the Sixth Plenary Session of the Eighth Central Committee, "We must take good care of the people and correct
the tendency of caring for property rather than for man. The
harder the masses work, the better the Party should look after
them; the better the Party looks after them, the greater will be
their enthusiasm."

As the masses are mobilized more and more extensively, it is
all the more necessary to strengthen leadership, perfect the administrative system and augment the system of job responsibility. The
leading bodies at all levels in capital construction departments
should conduct among the workers and staff propaganda and education on general and specific policies on capital construction so that
they will understand better the overall and long-range interests,

a) I.e., cadre participation in productive labor and worker participation in
management; reform of irrational and outmoded rules and regulations; close
cooperation among workers, cadres, and technicians. — Eds.

implement conscientiously the general and specific policies of the
Party and the state, strengthen labor discipline, and comply with
rules and regulations. We should supplement and revise the existing rules and regulations in the light of practical needs and the
changing situation, but this does not mean at all that one can negate
all rules and regulations. All the reasonable rules and regulations
in the capital construction departments concerning administration
and technical supervision must be observed continuously, and those
that have proven unreasonable through practice should be revised
after discussion among the masses and with the approval of the
leadership. Based on the experience accumulated by the masses
in practice, we should gradually improve and finally perfect the
various rules and regulations.

13

A LETTER TO COMRADES IN THE CENTRAL
FINANCE AND ECONOMICS SMALL GROUP
(April 1959)

Recently I have had several opinions in regard to the issue of markets and the issue of planning methods, but they are not mature yet. I present them for your reference when you consider these issues.

I will first talk about the issue of alleviating shortages in the market.

1. We should eat and use grain economically. After the summer and autumn harvests last year, the estimated output was too high, and we ate and used too much. Since this year the urban and rural sales volume is continuously increasing (this year we will sell 18 billion jin more grain than we did last year) and the volume of reserves is decreasing, there is a widespread shortage. Therefore I think, that no matter how much grain production this year increases, we must eat and use grain economically, and we must control the sales volume. It is quite important to grasp this point. In our country, the problem of adequate grain production has not yet been solved. If the grain problem is settled, the whole situation will be stable; if grain is tight, the market will be tense. Now grain is still the most important item for stabilizing the market. We must do work in this field well.

2. Organize supplies of pork, chicken, duck, eggs, and fish. A shortage of pork, chicken, or duck in city markets is very different from a shortage of industrial products. To improve life, eating is the first thing. It is very difficult to use other things to make up a shortage of one billion yuan of pork, chicken, and duck by putting other commodities in the market. We cannot alleviate these shortages in the market even if we make it up with one billion yuan of industrial products. Why? If we have one billion yuan of pork, chicken, eggs, and fish, and if we make some dishes through processing, altogether it will amount to 1.4 or 1.5 billion

yuan of commodities. Today, most public houses and restaurants are run by the state, so these things will soon become a very great resource for withdrawing currency from circulation for the state. This year, there is about 4 or 5 billion yuan difference between the supply of materials on the market and purchasing power. It would be very helpful for making up this difference if we could find a way to increase pork, chicken, duck, fish, and eggs by one billion yuan, namely, to add 10 million pigs, 200 million chickens and ducks, 200 million jin of eggs, and several dozen thousand tons of fish to the supplies on the market. That would alleviate market shortages to some extent. To organize the supplies of pork, chicken, duck and fish, we must start with production and work out effective methods. We simultaneously can use the three forms of state, collective, and individual to develop pig, chicken, and duck raising. We should walk on these three legs. At present, since state farms and people's communes do not have much experience in raising animals, probably it is best and most reliable to let peasant households raise them privately. Within communes, there should be very good arrangements of private plots. We should ensure that the families raising animals get feed, especially to allocate to them a certain amount of feed grain, strengthen management, and seriously improve conditions for raising cattle and poultry. I suggest that the Fifth Staff Office of the State Council[a] and the Ministry of Commerce separately convene professional meetings concerning the issues of pork, chicken, duck, and vegetables in the near future and seriously grasp this work. Though this will not solve the problems of this year, it will help to improve the market supply of next year.

3. We should specially arrange the production of consumer goods. When we plan industrial production, we should specially allocate some raw and processed material and arrange for the production of daily use products. We should ask those factories that used to produce small goods but have already been transformed to 'come back to the team" and resume production. Especially because handicraft cooperatives became local state-owned factories or cooperative factories, their production tasks came under unified arrangement and they cannot have individual production and management, a great amount of production of small goods has been stopped. Now we should organize them to return to their own fields of production. They can still be state-owned factories

_____

a) In charge of finance, trade, and food. Headed by Li Xiannian. — Eds.

or cooperative factories in name, but under the leadership of the local industrial department they can have independent accounts and sole responsibility for profits or losses in order to provide incentives to those handicraftsmen and to increase the quantity and variety of handicraft industrial goods. As to the original handicraftsmen in people's communes in the countryside, we should go through the communes to help them solve difficulties of raw materials and markets so as to increase the production of different kinds of handicraft industrial goods in the countryside.

4. Cut down purchasing power and carefully whittle down the ranks of the workers, too many of whom were recruited last year. If enterprises increase employment, purchasing power will be increased accordingly. If we increase labor power in the countryside, we do not have to worry that purchasing power will increase accordingly, because the supply of some agricultural and subsidiary products will increase at the same time. There are two situations in urban industry. One is to increase labor normally and also increase the production of commodities so we can balance them against increased purchasing power. The other is to increase laborers abnormally by an excessive amount, which causes labor productivity to decrease and commodity production to not increase, while only increasing purchasing power. This only increases the pressure on the material supplies on the market and is disadvantageous for both production and the market. In 1956 we recruited too many workers, and this caused shortages in the market, so we have had a lesson in regard to this matter. We must seriously cut the numbers of more than 10 million workers that we over-recruited last year and assign them to the countryside in order to reduce the existing purchasing power. From now on, we must strictly control the number of workers. The plan for increasing urban labor power must be controlled by the Party committees of the Center, the provinces and the cities.

5. In regard to the transportation shortage, we should give first consideration to arranging the transportation requirements for supplying the goods needed by the market. Especially, we should arrange well the laborers needed for short distance transportation. When industry and commerce both need transportation, we should arrange the means of transport, such as horse carts, pushcarts and wooden sailing boats, to meet the needs of commerce first, and we should increase the flow of commodities between urban and rural areas. Industry should not compete with agriculture and

commerce for short distance transportation resources.

Next, I will talk about the issue of the method of drawing up the plan for 1960.

1. We should fix next year's industrial production targets on the basis of the capacity of the complete sets of equipment that enterprises have already installed by the end of this year (including power, transportation, etc.). We will take this as the starting point for drawing up next year's plan and deciding the production targets of next year that we must complete. In addition to this, we will calculate targets for industrial production that we hope to fulfill on the basis not only of the production capacity of existing equipment but also the productive capacity that we can count on adding as a result of capital construction next year. Thus, we can make the production plan of next year reliable as well as positive by setting two production targets and keeping a difference in between.[a] The production target that is based on the capacity of complete sets of equipment is calculated not only on the capacity of major equipment but also on the capacity of the equipment of enterprises as a whole and each link in the professional fields. For example, as to the productive capacity of the iron and steel industry, we should not only calculate the productive capacity of blast furnaces, open hearths, and converters, but also we should calculate the production capacity of mining, coking, refractory materials, and steel rolling. We should not only calculate the production capacity within the department, but also calculate the production capacity of the departments concerned, such as the calculation of the production capacity of coal, power, transportation, and other departments. In general, we should calculate comprehensively.

2. The difference between production and demand is very great in several weak industrial links, such as copper, aluminum, petroleum, wood, and rubber. This can be solved in the near future. Ours is a big country. In industrial construction, we cannot rely on imports to make up the difference between production and demand for these several kinds of necessary materials. Owing to the very large amount, we cannot solve it completely. Therefore, when we compile the plan each

---

a) Chen is describing the so-called "double-track system" (sheng gui zhi) of planning introduced in 1959. For more details see Wang Guiwu, "A major reform in the method of compiling annual plans" in Jihua jingji (Economic Planning), 1958, no. 9, pp. 13-15. — Eds.

year, we should pay attention to the production of these several kinds of materials, strengthen these weak links, reduce the difference between supply and demand, and gradually solve the problem.

14

THE PROBLEM OF MAKING PRACTICABLE
THE STEEL TARGET
(May 1959)*

There are now two situations that are prominent in the industrial field: the first is the plan for the distribution of 2.5 million tons of steel in the second quarter, which was approved at the Shanghai Meeting in the spring of this year. It cannot be achieved since production has not gone up, and there are only 2.05 million tons of steel available for distribution. Thus the fulfillment of the original plan for industrial production and capital construction in the second quarter will have to be postponed for a month or even longer. The second is that once the plan is changed, it will cause instability in the production sequence of enterprise units. Somebody said that the situation in production in the most recent period is like "the back waves cover the front waves in the Changjiang [Yangtse River] — work work, stop stop, work work, stop." In many departments, factories, and units of capital construction, there is a common desire for stability. There is a common demand for an amount of steel that is actually distributable to one's unit, and a quick decision so that production can be arranged.

Based on the above situation, the Central Secretariat,[a] at the meetings of April 29 and 30, instructed the Central Finance and Economics Small Group to study three issues: (1) The target for iron and steel production this year is divided into two: one is a reliable target and another is a target to strive for. (2) Steel distribution for this year should be carried out according to the reliable figure which we can certainly produce this year. (3) If the amount of steel distributed decreases, it will be necessary to cut down some production items. Now we have decided in principle: we will cut down capital construction, guarantee the needs of production, and

---

*This is a speech by Comrade Chen Yun at a meeting of the Politburo.

a) That is, the Secretariat of the Central Committee, at that time headed by Deng Xiaoping and second only to the Politburo in importance. — Eds.

guarantee the needs of market and maintenance; in the capital construction field, we will guarantee absolutely necessary items of construction in the oil and chemical industry and so on. The general idea is to stabilize our position and then go forward so as to avoid being continuously passive.

After the Secretariat meeting, the Finance and Economics Small Group listened to six reports by the Ministry of Metallurgy (one report on the general situation in iron and steel and one report each on ore, coke, refractory materials, iron and steel smelting, and the assortment of steel products), and had one focused discussion. Now I will divide my talk about the report of the Ministry of Metallurgy and the discussion by the Finance and Economics Small Group into two parts: the first is the question of the reliable target and a target to strive for in steel; and the second is several issues on which we now need to focus attention

I. THE ISSUE OF A RELIABLE TARGET AND A TARGET TO STRIVE FOR IN STEEL PRODUCTS

For the steel product production target, the Ministry of Metallurgy put forward three figures: 9 million tons, 9.5 million tons, and 10 million tons. Corresponding to this, the steel production figures are 13 million tons, 14 million tons, and 15 million tons. The Ministry of Metallurgy also put forward a figure of 16 million tons of steel, but gave no detailed explanation.

In discussion, the figures put forward by the Heavy Industry Planning Bureau of the State Planning Commission are: the reliable target for steel products is 8.5 million tons to 9 million tons, and the target to strive for is 9.5 million tons. Corresponding to this, the reliable target for steel is 12.5 million tons to 13 million tons, and the target to strive for is 14 million tons. The reliable target put forward by the Metallurgy Bureau of the State Economic Commission is 13 million tons, and the target to strive for is 15 million tons. These figures are all smaller than that planned at the Shanghai Meeting.[a] The targets planned at the Shanghai Meeting were 11.5 million tons of steel products and 16.5 million tons of steel.

In the Finance and Economics Small Group, several comrades who often attended the report meeting referred to above — Fuchun,

---

a) Refers to the Seventh Plenum of the Eighth Central Committee, which convened in Shanghai on April 2-5, 1958, and the preceding Enlarged Meeting of the Politburo on March 25-April 1. — Eds.

Yibo, Zhao Erlu,[a] and I — all agreed that the reliable target for
steel products could be fixed at 9 million tons, then the production
target for steel would be 13 million tons.[b] As for the figure to
strive for, we will consider it again after we have listened to the
reports from the Ministries of Coal, Machinery, Railroads, and
so on, and after we get a clear idea of the production and transportation capability of these departments. We will not discuss
this for the time being.

Why are steel products fixed at 9 million tons, and why do we
take this as a starting point? There are the following several
reasons:

First, looking at each link inside the iron and steel industry,
this target is relatively reliable and truthful. But it is not an easy
job; we will have to make very great efforts to fulfill it. In order
to produce 9 million tons of steel products, we will have to produce 13 million tons of steel and 20 million tons of iron (it includes
13 million tons of steel for steel-smelting, 5.5 million tons for
casting and increased inventories, plus 1.5 million tons for preparing poor-quality iron). Now we will explain five aspects: ore,
coke, refractory materials, smelting, transportation, etc.

About ore. We need 3.5 tons of ore to produce 1 ton of iron,
thus 70 million tons of ore to produce 20 millions of iron. The
existing 14 large-scale enterprises that have machinery and equipment and railway transportation are able to mine 53 million tons
of ore (34.6 million tons were mined last year). Among 19 existing
medium-scale mining enterprises, there are 6 that have semi-
mechanized equipment and railway transportation. The other 13
utilize manual extraction and lack railroads. If this year we try
to equip them with some machines, use pneumatic tools to drill
and explosives to blast, "punch a hole and blast," and lay light
track railway, we can mine a total of 8 million tons of ore in the
whole year (6.8 million tons were mined last year). The existing 214 small-scale mining spots with indigenous production
can mine a total of 10 million tons (6.06 million tons were
mined last year). Adding up the large, medium, and small-
scale enterprises above, we can produce 71 million tons of

a) I.e. Li Fuchun, chairman of the State Planning Commission; Bo Yibo, chairman of the State Economic Commision; Zhao Erlu, minister of the First Ministry
of Machine Building. — Eds.

b) The actual steel target adopted in August 1959 at the Eighth Plenum of the
Eighth Central Committee was 12 million tons. — Eds.

ore, and we will be able to ship out 70 million tons.

In order to guarantee the mining of 70 million tons of ore, we need to add more air compressors, power shovels, hoisters, ball mills and such equipment, and explosive materials. Of this equipment and materials, some have been ordered, but they have not been completely decided on.

According to calculations, we need 2.1 million tons of rich ore (containing more than 58 percent iron) to be used by open hearth furnaces for the whole year. We can only produce 1.7 million tons, so there is a shortage of 400 thousand tons. In order to make up this difference, we are planning to ship out an additional 100 to 150 thousand tons of rich ore from Hainan Island; we will produce 200 thousand tons by the pelletizing method.

Considering the circumstances illustrated above, mining 70 million tons of ore in a whole year is not an easy matter, since we will have to do capital construction work on large and medium-scale enterprises and add much equipment. But looking at the situation of 17.8 million tons of ore shipped out in the first quarter, it is possible to fulfill the task of 70 million tons as long as we continuously pay close attention to the work in this field.

About coke. We need on average 1.5 tons of coke to smelt 1 ton of iron; we need on average 1.5 tons of washed coal to produce 1 ton of coke; we need on average 2 tons of coking coal to produce 1 ton of washed coal. To produce 20 million tons of pig iron, therefore, we need 30 million tons of coke, the equivalent of 45 million tons of washed coal or 90 to 100 million tons of coking coal.

Washed coal is the key to improving the quality of iron and steel. The quality of some iron and steel is not good, because it contains too much sulphur, while the origin of 70 to 80 percent of the sulphur is owing to the sulphur in coal not being washed off. Therefore we must give energetic support to washing coal well, otherwise we will waste resources of manpower, material and finance, and we will not even get good iron and steel. To solve the problem of the quality of coking coal, the first step is to solve the problem of coal washing.

The condition of coal washing capability is: large-scale coal washing factories that are mechanized will be able to produce 19.5 million tons this year, and newly built coal washing factories (they are mostly simple coal washing factories, and the problem of equipment is being solved as a special case) will be able to produce 5.5 million tons. The two will total 25 million tons. In addi-

tion, we will still produce 20 million tons using indigenous methods. The coal washed by indigenous methods, according to an
estimate, will need 600 thousand labor days. From now, it will
take 200 days to fulfill and will also require pulverizing equipment
and other necessary tools. We must also point out that the output
of 25 million tons of washed coal by Western methods mentioned
above is not constant in each quarter. Four million, one hundred
and fifty thousand tons have been fulfilled in the first quarter, and
there will be only about 4.64 million tons which can be fulfilled in
the second quarter. Also only 5.47 million tons can be fulfilled in
the third quarter, and the remaining 17.14 million tons (making up
40 percent of the total) will be fulfilled in a concentrated way in the
fourth quarter. Thus it will not meet the needs of iron smelting in
each quarter. If we cannot produce some more washed coal by the
Western method in the second and third quarters, then the coal
washed by indigenous methods will have to increase in these two
quarters.

The condition of coking capability is: the original existing large-
scale production by Western methods can amount to 10 million tons,
newly built mechanized coke ovens and simple coke ovens can produce
10 tons, and the plan for indigenous coking calls for producing 10 million tons. These three amount to 30 million tons. Among newly built
coke ovens there are 36 mechanized ones, of which 19 can be built in
this year. These will produce 2.43 million tons. There are 1,700
Red Flag No. 2 simple coke ovens. They can produce 5.3 million
tons. There are 800 Red Flag No. 3 simple coke ovens that can
produce 1.7 million tons after they are completed. At present the
Red Flag No 2 coke oven basically has manual production; its
technical problems still need further solution.

It should be noted that the scale of construction (including mechanized coke ovens and simple coke ovens) in the coking field is
not small. Only two-thirds of the needs can be satisfied, even if we
we are able to finish building all of them on time, plus making the
most of the original existing coking capability. The remaining
one-third, i.e. 10 million tons, still needs to be undertaken by indigenous production. The washed coal, of course, can also be
coked into good coke, but we still need to master the local coking
technique. We must pay enough attention to this matter.

About refractory materials. According to the Ministry of Metallurgy's calculation, for the whole year we need 4.2 million tons of
different kinds of refractory materials (including clay brick, silica

brick, magnesia brick, high alumina brick, etc.) and 6 million tons
of raw materials (clay, silica, magnesia, high alumina, etc.).
Of these materials, only 20 percent will be mined mechanically;
the remaining eighty percent will be basically operated manually.
Therefore, in the field of mining and carrying we need to use a
great deal of manpower.

About the equipment for iron-smelting, steel-smelting, and steel-
rolling. To produce so much pig iron, steel, and steel products,
we do not need to add too many things. It can be settled by basically relying on existing equipment (partially needing to be formed
into complete sets). The Planning Commission and the Ministry of
Metallurgy already have explained this condition, in more detail,
so I will not repeat it again.

About transportation. Besides transporting 90 to 100 million
tons of coking coal, the freight volume of ore, refractory materials,
and other goods and materials must also be very large in order to
produce 20 million tons of pig iron. The Ministry of Metallurgy
requests laying 500 kilometers of railroad branch lines and special
lines, laying 500 kilometers of light railway, adding 150 locomotives, adding 1,500 railroad cars, and also adding small locomotives and mine cars.

Owing to the needs of iron and steel production, the present
short distance transportation is in unusually great demand. In
quite a few provinces, vehicles are being used for transporting raw
materials and materials for iron and steel. It is difficult to maintain this situation. It will not work for a steelworks that has an
annual production of several thousand tons to rely only on vehicle
transportation.

The above-mentioned multifaceted situation shows that it is possible, within this year, to produce 9 million tons of steel products
and, accordingly, to produce 13 million tons of steel, although we
need to make a great effort.

Second, the situation of production in the first four months of this
year also indicates that it is possible to fulfill the production target of 9 million tons of steel products, 13 million tons of steel, and
20 million tons of iron. The important question is to guarantee the
quality of products.

In the past four months, we produced 2.27 million tons of steel
products, 3.36 million tons of steel, and 6.03 million tons of iron
(part of which was indigenous iron and unqualified second-rate
iron). During the next eight months, we still will have to produce

6.73 million tons of steel products, 9.64 million tons of steel, and 14 million tons of iron. With effort it is possible to fulfill this task but we need to pay special attention to improving the quality of iron. Now among iron produced by all the places, not a little amount of it is unqualified. It is completely correct that the Ministry of Metallurgy proposed that we emphatically stress the quality problem in the field of iron and steel production.

Here we will talk a bit about the problem of small blast furnaces. The construction of blast furnaces must honor the principle of combining large, medium, and small scales with large ones as the dominant factor. At present, small blast furnaces are necessary; to produce 20 million tons of iron, 9 million tons depend on small blast furnaces. Small blast furnaces should improve their technology, and some should develop toward large and medium scales. All this is an inevitable trend. In those areas where there is a shortage of coal and iron resources and where transportation conditions are difficult, some small blast furnaces will have to stop production. In those places with difficult conditions, small blast furnaces should not be rebuilt. For those small blast furnaces that are presently working, we must take powerful measures to improve their technology, strengthen management, and conscientiously improve the quality of pig iron.

Third, as to production of steel products, we can roll 9 million tons of steel products as long as we smelt 13 million tons of good steel this year. But there is still a problem of the variety of steel products. Newly added rolling mills this year are all medium or small size. The proportion of small-scale steel products to be rolled has increased, namely, from around 24 percent in the past few years to around 29 percent, and from 1.49 million tons to 2.6 million tons in terms of absolute amount. On the other hand, large rolling mills and important rolling mills have not been produced yet, so eight kinds of important steel products (heavy rails, large-sized steel products, medium-thick steel plate, thin steel plate, seamless steel tube, seamed steel tube, silicon steel, and high-quality steel) cannot be increased very much. In addition we will import much less than last year, so there probably will be only 4.86 million tons available for distribution in the whole year. A large increase in small-sized steel products and a small increase in large-sized and important steel products will certainly influence the manufacture of important equipment and the construction of important engineering projects.

It is a good thing to produce more steel. The main problem at
present is to work hard for increasing the output of eight kinds of
important steel products in order to meet the needs of production
and construction. For this reason, we should produce some more
large rolling mills and important rolling mills as soon as possible.

As regards each link within the iron and steel industry and the
situation of iron and steel production in the first four months of
this year, as well as the variety of steel products, there are good
grounds for fixing the output of steel products at 9 million tons.
It is probably relatively appropriate. Of course we should not be
satisfied with this target and stop going forward. The purpose of
standing firm is to go forward. If we stand firm at this starting
point, we will be able to go forward steadily, and only then will it
be possible to exceed this target. We need further study before
we can put forward how much it can be exceeded and how high the
target to strive for should be.

The present study of the production target for iron and steel is
limited to the links inside the iron and steel industry. We have not
yet done a comprehensive study on the relations between the iron
and steel industry and other industries, and furthermore, a complete study on the relation between whole industry and the other
departments of national economy. It cannot be completely correct
to decide the production target for steel and steel products by only
considering iron and steel as they stand. Since iron and steel are
just one link in the whole industry and the national economy, we
can only see more clearly whether the target for iron and steel
has been decided correctly after a comprehensive study. The
present opinions given by the Finance and Economics Small Group can
be only preliminary, and only for the consideration of the Politburo. We do not hope to make a final decision. Even if the Politburo agrees to preliminarily set the steel products target at 9
million tons and the steel production target at 13 million tons, we
still request the Politburo to give the Finance and Economics Small
Group some time to consider the opinion of setting steel production
at 15 million tons as proposed by comrades in the Ministry of
Metallurgy, and to comprehensively study the relation between iron
and steel production and the whole industry and the national economy.

In order to return to a reliable position, and to go forward after
a firm stand, we must have realistic planned arrangements for
production and construction. Meanwhile, we should let vast num-

bers of cadres and people understand that advance after standing firm is a more solid advance, so they will not feel discouraged about this.

The Finance and Economics Small Group still needs to consider how to arrange plans and to explain to each enterprise unit. The target of steel product production has been cut down, and the amount of distribution has been reduced. Production and basic units may now ask: what should we do if the original tasks cannot be completed? We feel that whatever is accomplished with the materials actually required plus subjective efforts will be the right amount.

II. SEVERAL ISSUES ON WHICH WE SHOULD FOCUS ATTENTION AT THE PRESENT TIME

First, we should stress improving quality. For iron and steel we stress improving quality, and for equipment manufacture, the production of manufactured goods for display use, capital construction, and the others, we should also stress improving quality. Many things for export had relatively good quality in the past, but our quality has now declined and is in ill repute abroad. Though the amount is great, if the quality is very bad and things produced cannot really function, they will not only fail to meet the needs of production, construction and the market, but also cause extremely great waste. Any product that had good quality that declined later on should return to its previous level as soon as possible; for any product whose quality has not been good, we should take active measures, setting time limits to improve it. The State Planning Commission and the Finance and Economics Group are planning to devote several days to discussion of the issue of improving product quality and are planning to work out some practical measures.[a]

Second, we should guarantee the key points and also consider the overall. Those key production and construction points such as iron and steel, coal, electric power, machinery, and transportation must be guaranteed. But we should also give realistic consideration to oil, the chemical industry, important building materials, and light industrial products that are in great market demand; otherwise not only will the departments of the national economy be unable to move forward together, it also will be difficult to reliably guarantee the development of the key points them-

---

a) On May 28, 1959, the Secretariat took up the issue of product quality at a meeting. — Eds.

selves. In general, we must handle affairs according to the principle of having plans and proportions.

Third, we should consider next year as well as the long term. Present production and construction are important. We must not neglect them. But we cannot think only of the present and neglect the future. For example, large- and medium-scale rolling mills and rolling mills for tube and plate materials are absolutely necessary to provide steel product variety, so they should be guaranteed. Another example is the four large blast furnaces. They are being built this year by the four steelworks of Wuhan, Baotou, Taiyuan, and Shijingshan and are absolutely necessary for increasing the production of pig iron, so finishing their building in advance should be guaranteed. If the present steel products distributed to the Ministry of Metallurgy are relatively few, and if the steel products to be used on important rolling mills and sets of the four large blast furnaces are in conflict with the steel products needed in other fields, for long-term interests we would rather cut down the latter and ensure the former when the two cannot both be considered. In addition, we should have a long-term program for the construction of a new main coking coal base and a new coal base in Jiangnan, the construction of the Lanxin railroad main line,[a] the exploitation of the northwestern oil field, and other indispensible raw materials for industry such as the production of raw materials for alloy steel, carbon electrode, and so on. These should be arranged right now and each item of work should be actively carried out.

Above is the first report to the Center after I listened to the report on the iron and steel situation by the Ministry of Metallurgy. I am not familiar with industrial conditions, and I do not know very much. Also, I have not listened to the reports from other industrial departments. I therefore still do not have a very great certainty as to whether the opinions I have given are appropriate. I intend to present reports to the Chairman, the Politburo, and the Secretariat after I have listened to the reports from each industrial ministry and the other departments.

---

a) The main line from Lanzhou in Gansu Province to Xinjiang Province, terminating in Urumchi. Work on this line began in 1954 and it was opened to traffic in 1962. — Eds.

15

A LETTER TO COMRADE MAO ZEDONG
CONCERNING PROBLEMS IN THE STEEL TARGET
(May 1959)

The opinions of comrades who joined in the study of the iron and steel target are: fix this year's reliable production target for steel products at 9 million tons; take 9 million tons of steel products as the quantity to distribute to the ministries, provinces and cities; take a target in excess of 9 million tons as a target to strive for in the future. The comrades from the Ministry of Metallurgy at the meeting believed that a target of 9 million tons of steel products (that is, to fix the amount of steel at 13 million tons)[a] is too low and it will discourage people at lower levels. There are different suggestions as to what quantity of steel products and steel can be produced reliably this year. There are also different opinions not only in Beijing but also in every province and city. However, looking at the whole situation, in order to stabilize the production sequence and to keep the plan from changing too much, I think that it is relatively reliable to have a target of 9 million tons of steel products for distribution. If in one month the production exceeds the month's target, we can distribute the excess in the following month, and it will not affect production overfulfillment. It is doubtful that it would be correct to say that it definitely would be discouraging if we fixed a lower production figure. As Comrade Liu Shaoqi said at the Politburo: if the figure is too high and we cannot realize it, it will be even more discouraging.

More than 40 percent of the iron smelted by small blast furnaces contains sulphur exceeding the standard of two per thousand set by the Ministry of Metallurgy. Some say that this share is at least 50 percent. If this condition does not change, there will be 4 or 5 million tons of pig iron that exceed the standard for sulfur content.

---

a) The actual steel target adopted in August 1959 at the Eighth Plenum of the Eighth Central Committee was 12 million tons. — Eds.

This cannot be used for casting; nor it can be smelted into useful steel products after steel smelting. This is a waste of labor and materials. Now we should find a way to overcome the high-sulphur condition. If the key is coal washing, we should decide that we must wash the coal, and we should clearly establish the standard of sulpher content. There should not be iron smelting without coal washing (indigenous washing can be used). I am worried that if the quality of iron does not improve, we cannot caste iron, and the steel smelting will not amount to 13 million tons either. That is, we will not get 9 million tons of useful steel products. Thus coal washing and removing sulphur are the key to whether or not we can fulfill the steel product target that is being planned now.

I hope that several comrades of the Finance and Economics Small Group, including Comrade Heshou,[a] will report to you soon. Please call us when you are free.

Since some comrades have different opinions representing the views of quite a large group of comrades, the Finance and Economics Small Group is planning to study their opinions once more. Following your instruction, we are being resourceful so as to be decisive.

---

a) Wang Heshou, Minister of Metallurgy. — Eds.

16

SPEED UP DEVELOPMENT OF THE
NITROGENOUS CHEMICAL FERTILIZER INDUSTRY
(May 1961)*

The Center has decided that speeding up the development of the nitrogenous fertilizer industry is one of the important tasks for industry to support agriculture.

In order to fulfill this important task, two issues now need to be decided. The first issue is whether we should build large-scale or small-scale nitrogenous fertilizer factories. The second issue is the disposition of nitrogenous fertilizer factories. Should the annual plan list a dozen centers that we have already started and go forward together, or should we concentrate our strength to let them go one group at a time and construct a productive capacity that increases by 200 to 250 thousand tons of synthetic ammonia annually?

From April 4 to 10 of this year, at the Hangzhou Forum held by Comrade Chen Yun and joined by some comrades of the Central Chemical Fertilizer Small Group, we did detailed research on these two issues and important related work and reached a unanimous opinion. We believe that within the three years between 1962 and 1964, the scale of nitrogenous fertilizer factories should be large, the arrangement of construction should be to concentrate strength, and that this will enable us to increase production capacity by 200 to 250 thousand tons of synthetic ammonia annually.

Why should we make this choice but not the other?

About the question of the size of nitrogenous fertilizer factories. Under the technical guidance of the Ministry of Chemical Indus-

---

*This is a report to the Party Center [a term usually referring in fact to the Politburo, but here may refer to a Central Work Conference convened in May-June 1961 in Beijing — Eds.] drafted by Comrade Chen Yun for the Central Chemical Fertilizer Small Group. This report was approved by the Party Center and it was issued as a central document [i.e., as a document issued in the name of the Central Committee — Eds.].

try, from 1959 to 1960 we started building a group of small-scale
nitrogenous fertilizer factories that annually produce 800 to 2,000
tons of synthetic ammonia. By the end of 1960, we finished building
and put into production more than 20 factories that annually produce 800 tons. Among them, 5 work normally. We finished building and put into production 7 factories that produce 2,000 tons
every year, and among them 3 work normally. At that time we had
planned to build many small-scale nitrogenous fertilizer factories
on a widespread basis. This was because we considered that
small-scale nitrogenous fertilizer factories needed relatively less
important materials, the manufacture of their equipment is relatively easy, and province-owned machinery factories can take the
responsibility for its manufacture; they suit the dispersed conditions of the countryside, it is easier to meet the general demand
for nitrogenous fertilizer in each place, and it is helpful to arouse
the initiative of the localities at each level and even certain of
people's communes to develop chemical fertilizer; the time of construction is short and development is fast. But the test of experience
of one year showed that this kind of plan lacked a sufficient basis.

Looking at the situation that we know about most recently, the
current production of the eight small-scale nitrogenous fertilizer
factories that work normally is unstable, because the quality of
their equipment is not good, it is very hard to master technical
operations, and there are a considerable number of accidents.
Actual production does not fulfill the designed capacity, and the
consumption of raw materials and power is also very great. Generally, the construction and production of small-scale nitrogenous
fertilizer factories have not met technical requirements. We still
have to make a great effort, and we need a certain amount of time
to meet the requirements completely.

The opposite of small-scale nitrogenous fertilizer factories are
the large-scale nitrogenous fertilizer factories that annually produce 25 or 50 thousand tons of synthetic ammonia. They are mature in terms both of construction and production and of technology.
There are six of these large-scale factories, located in Dalian,
Nanjing, Jilin, Lanzhou, Taiyuan, and Chengdu. All of these large
factories have been in production for a relatively long time,
and their production has been quite normal. With only a few
exceptions, the machinery and complete sets of equipment required in these large-scale factories have been successfully
trial-manufactured within China and have been put into regular

production. By the end of 1961, we will be able to produce three sets annually of the equipment required to produce 25 thousand tons of synthetic ammonia.

Meanwhile, by having large-scale nitrogenous fertilizer factories, we can save labor and can utilize technical resources in a concentrated manner; the quality of products is good, and the cost is low. In these respects, the large-scale factories are superior to small-scale factories.

As to the comparison between large-scale and medium-scale factories, the technology of the latter is not as mature as the former either. A medium-scale factory that annually produces 10 thousand tons of synthetic ammonia was built and put into production by the end of 1959. But until now its production is still unstable, and the level of output has still not reached its designed capacity. Particularly since we have not solved the technical problem of ammonia processing very well, ammonia losses are relatively large, and the product decomposes easily and is hard to preserve. Therefore, we cannot popularize very many medium-sized factories at the present time.

Of course small-scale nitrogenous fertilizer factories have their advantages. However, we should continuously experiment and improve them, since they have not met their design requirements. We should not build large numbers of them on a widespread basis before they meet their standards.

One way to build large-scale nitrogenous fertilizer factories which annually produce 50 thousand tons is to divide the construction into two periods, and build one plant of 25 thousand tons in each period. The other way is to build once. The construction period of a factory with 25 thousand tons annual production and a factory with 50 thousand tons annual production is two to two and a half years. If we build a factory with 50 thousand tons annual yield once, compared to constructing a factory with a 25 thousand ton capacity in the first period, it will use only one-third more material and equipment; thus compared to simultaneously building two factories each with a 25 thousand ton annual capacity, we will use one-third less. In order to economize on material and equipment, and to use technical resources in a concentrated way from now on, we should finish building the factory with an annual yield of 50 thousand tons of synthetic ammonia once, namely, we should not build it in two separate periods or build it as two separate factories.

Within the next three years the plan for developing the nitrogenous fertilizer industry should be to construct large-scale nitrogenous fertilizer factories with an annual yield of 50 thousand tons
of ammonia by years and in groups.

During the research on the size of nitrogenous fertilizer factories, we also investigated and studied the varieties of nitrogenous fertilizer. Owing to limitations on raw materials and capacity
for producing sulphuric acid, and because the sulphuric acid radical easily destroys the soil structure in certain areas, it is not
appropriate that we produce too much ammonium sulfate, either
at the present time or in the future. Ammonium bi-carbonate and
urea are now in the stage of small-scale trial production, so they
cannot be popularized much either. We think, therefore, that we
should mainly produce ammonium nitrate within the next two or
three years.

About the question of the disposition of construction of nitrogenous fertilizer factories.

Throughout the country we started to build more than ten large-
scale nitrogenous fertilizer factories one after another from 1958 on.
Since there are many scattered centers and we do not have a sufficient supply of material and equipment, so far we have not finished building one. Most of these items are not listed in this
year's plan, and we cannot continue their construction.

We should quicken the development of the nitrogenous fertilizer
industry as much as possible in order to develop agricultural production and increase grain output. Our opinion is unanimous in
regard to this issue. The question of the disposition of construction of nitrogenous fertilizer factories is to make the size large
enough that there will be enthusiasm as well as reliability. From
the beginning to the completion of construction, it takes about two
to two and a half years to construct a factory with an annual capacity of 50 thousand tons of synthetic ammonia. According to the
lesson that we cannot finish any if there are too many, we think
that it is proper, within the three years from 1962 to 1964, to build
four to five factories each year with an annual capacity of 50
thousand tons of synthetic ammonia. Specifically, in 1962, we will
build four in addition to the construction items completed in the
first half of the year that were in the state plan; in 1963, while we
complete the four started in 1962, we will begin five new factories;
similarly, in 1964 we will finish these five and at the same time
begin five new factories. Thus, beginning in 1963, the annual size

of the construction program, including the factories that we are
continuing to construct and the factories we are starting, will total
eight to ten factories. This means that we will be constructing
synthetic ammonia factories with a scale of 400 to 500 thousand
tons at the same time. The productive capacity of the synthetic
ammonia factories that we will complete and that will enter production every year will be 200 to 250 thousand tons. If they produce normally, there will be more than 400 to 500 thousand tons of
ammonium nitrate produced every year (one ton of synthetic ammonia can produce more than 2 tons of ammonium nitrate), which
equals 800 thousand to 1 million tons of ammonium sulfate (1 ton of synthetic ammonia can produce nearly 4 tons of ammonium sulfate).

Under the present conditions in our country, it is already very
large scale to increase productive capacity by 200 to 250 thousand
tons of synthetic ammonia. From 1950 to 1960 we added productive
capacity of 510 thousand tons of synthetic ammonia. It increased
140 thousand tons from 1950 to 1957, averaging 18 thousand tons
each year; it increased 365 thousand tons from 1958 to 1960, averaging 122 thousand tons each year. Yet in the next few years, we
will increase capacity by 200 to 250 tons every year, equaling four
or five times the average annual increase of the past 11 years. It
cannot even be mentioned in the same breath if we compare this
increase with the pre-Liberation period (the highest synthetic ammonia production capacity before Liberation was 50 thousand tons).

Can we further increase the construction scale of synthetic ammonia in the next three years? Under present conditions, we cannot. It is completely necessary to develop the nitrogenous fertilizer industry as fast as possible and to have a relatively higher
speed of development of agricultural output. It is already a much
bigger step than other industries have taken to increase production capacity by 200 to 250 thousand tons of synthetic ammonia.
We should not and can not use the method of cutting down the construction of other departments in order to accelerate the construction of the nitrogenous fertilizer industry; instead, we must properly arrange the nitrogenous fertilizer industry and the other departments on the base of a comprehensive balance of the whole national economy and a comprehensive arrangement. In regard to
the distribution of investment, material arrangements, and equipment manufacturing, we should consider the needs of nitrogenous
fertilizer industrial construction as well as the construction needs
of other departments. Only this can make us stand firm and go

forward on a solid base, and make the nitrogenous fertilizer industry develop in a healthy direction. It should be pointed out that we still have to make a very great effort to construct the nitrogenous fertilizer industry according to the scale mentioned above. We need a few years' experience to decide whether we can finish the construction on time.

Given this construction scale, how should we locate centers? We feel that we should locate them first in the areas where economic crops are concentrated and in the high-yield grain areas, and then locate them in other areas by stages and in groups. This kind of distribution allows us to postpone construction of nitrogenous fertilizer factories in scattered areas of economic crop production and ordinary grain production areas. Even in areas of concentrated economic crop production and high-yield grain areas, construction must be carried out by steps. This is contrary to the request to quickly develop the nitrogenous fertilizer industry on a widespread basis in the whole country. However, this is what we can do under the present conditions of materials, equipment, and technical resources. Experience shows that if we adopt the opposite way — construct on a widespread basis and go forward together — it will definitely cause the limited materials, equipment, and technical resources to be used separately, the construction period to be prolonged, the productive capacity not to be formed in time, and even cause great waste. The method of concentrated construction and construction in stages avoids the shortcomings mentioned above and greatly increases the speed of construction.

The above is our opinion concerning the principles of quickening the development of the nitrogenous fertilizer industry after our research and comparison.

In order to carry out the above principles and strive for the fulfillment of the construction plan of large-scale nitrogenous fertilizer factories, we suggest adopting the following measures:

First, import important materials. To build a factory that annually produces 50 thousand tons of synthetic ammonia, including a self-provided power station, a self-provided coke furnace, ammonium nitrate processing equipment and so on, requires about 10 thousand tons of different kinds of metal materials. Present domestic production of these materials is insufficient or they cannot be produced at all, so they must be imported and should be listed in the national annual import plan and the required foreign exchange should be guaranteed. According to the calculation of the

Ministry of Chemical Industry, we need about U.S. $3.2 million of foreign exchange for the important materials needed by a factory that annually produces 50 thousand tons of synthetic ammonia, and we need a total of 16 million for five factories. It is much more advantageous to import these important materials to build nitrogenous fertilizer factories than to import grains. With $3.2 million, we can only buy 45 thousand tons of grain, and it will be consumed very soon. But if we use this to buy the important materials for building a factory that annually produces 50 thousand tons of synthetic ammonia, the chemical fertilizer produced annually will increase grain production by 500 or 600 thousand tons of grains. In order to organize the import of these important materials, we suggest letting the Ministry of Chemical Industry, the First Ministry of Machine Building, and the Ministry of Foreign Trade establish a special small import group, and draw up a detailed list of import goods. They should also prepare other works, try to send people abroad to order goods by the end of May or early June, and purchase sufficient complete sets in groups and according to variety and standard. In addition to meeting this year's needs, we should gradually accumulate reserves equal to the quantity of a year's imports of important materials. The Ministry of Chemical Industry will establish a specialized warehouse to manage these imported materials and guarantee that specialized materials are applied to specified uses, in order to be able to manufacture the machinery and equipment and complete construction engineering for nitrogenous fertilizer factories according to plans.

Second, fix points for the manufacture of machinery and equipment. In order to guarantee the normal production and supply of complete sets of machinery and equipment of nitrogenous fertilizer factories, the factories that in the past have produced the specialized machinery and equipment for nitrogenous fertilizer factories should continue to undertake their original manufacturing tasks. At the same time, we should ask the First Ministry of Machine Building to designate an additional group of factories to manufacture the ordinary machinery and equipment (such as oxygen generators, refrigerators, air-blowers, valves, and so on) and electrical equipment needed by nitrogenous fertilizer factories. Designation of this group of factories does not mean that they can only manufacture the equipment needed by nitrogenous fertilizer factories, and that they cannot manufacture equipment for other industrial departments. These factories' tasks of manufacturing specialized equipment for other industrial departments should be carried out according to the originally decided plans. We just need to fix the tasks of manufacturing equipment for nitrogenous fertilizer factories on these factories to prevent a situation in which we can't guarantee the supply or the timely delivery of the ordinary machinery and equipment needed by existing nitrogenous fertilizer factories. After the points for the manufacture of machinery and equipment have been fixed, the Ministry of Chemical Industry and the First Ministry of Machinery Building should take charge of the supply of special materials, so manufacturing factories can fulfill their production tasks in time, ensure supply, and continuously improve the quality. Additionally, the tasks for manufacturing nitrogenous fertilizer machinery and equipment undertaken by the factories belonging to the Third Ministry of Machine Building should still be undertaken by the Third Ministry of Machine Building. This will not change for several years.

Third, supply complete sets of machinery and equipment for nitrogenous fertilizer production. There are many varieties and large quantities of machinery and equipment required by nitrogenous fertilizer factories, and the cooperative relations among these are very complex. In order to guarantee the smooth construction of nitrogenous fertilizer factories, we must organize the manufacture and supply of complete sets of machinery and equipment according to the detailed list of machinery and equipment in the design documents for a large-scale synthetic ammonia factory. Meanwhile, we must enlarge the range of supply of complete sets of nitrogenous fertilizer machinery and equipment, that is to say that besides ensuring the supply of complete sets of the main production equipment and the supply of complete sets of equipment for all the supplementary workshops for nitrogenous fertilizer factories, we should also ensure the supply of complete sets of the equipment needed for related coal washing, coking, power station, transportation, public utilities, and related projects. We suggest that the State Planning Commission list the complete sets of machinery and equipment specified in the design documents for the large-scale nitrogenous fertilizer factories in the plan, and ask the General Bureau of Complete Sets of the First Ministry of Machine Building to be responsible for their supply. In regard to the necessary accessories for nitrogenous fertilizer equipment, all of the electrical products subject to the unified distribution by the state or by the ministries and all of the five metals and electrical equipment (the so-called category three commodities) that can be purchased on the market should be supplied by the General Materials Bureau and the Ministry of Commerce, which should separately establish special organs to be responsible. The construction units building the large-scale nitrogenous fertilizer factories are not required to attend the national goods-ordering meeting for electrical products once complete set supply has been implemented for the machinery and equipment for nitrogenous fertilizer factories and these supply relations are fixed.

Fourth, guarantee the supply of domestic materials. In total we need more than 30 thousand tons of all kinds of metal materials for a factory with an annual production of 50 thousand tons of synthetic ammonia. Among these materials, we import nearly 10 thousand tons, and domestically produce and supply more than 20 thousand tons. The First Ministry of Machine Building and the Ministry of Chemical Industry should calculate the quantities of these domestically produced materials on the basis of the needs of the nitrogenous fertilizer factories being built each year, submit these distribution targets to the State Planning Commission for examination and approval, enter them in the annual plan, and guarantee supply. In order to manufacture the machinery and equipment as soon as possible the materials for the manufacture of machinery and equipment should be prepared half a year in advance and specialized materials should be applied to specific uses and allocated directly the the factories. The supplied materials, especially smelted pig iron, must be up to standard to guarantee the quality of equipment.

Fifth, eliminate weak links in the manufacture of complete sets of machinery and equipment. The whole country needs a very large number of oxygen generators, refrigerators, compressors, high-pressure valves, medium-pressure valves and large generators, but production is low and supply falls short of demand. This is the weak link in our present machine building industry. In order not to affect construction in other departments for the sake of ensuring the needs of nitrogenous fertilizer factories, we should take effective measures, including enlarging existing enterprises and strengthening the trial-manufacture of new products, to increase the capacity for manufacturing this equipment within two or three years. The First Ministry of Machine Building should propose a specific plan for this work and carry it out after it is examined and approved by the State Planning Commission.

Sixth, strictly follow the capital construction sequence. When we build large-scale nitrogenous fertilizer factories in the future, besides fulfilling the task of well-designed plans, we must follow the sequence of materials first, then machinery and equipment and finally building construction. That is, first organize well the supply of important imported and domestically produced materials. On the basis of completely fulfilling material supplies, organize the manufacture and supply of complete sets of machinery and equipment. Finally, arrange the pace of factory construction and organize building construction. Based on past experience, this will not prolong the time of construction, but will increase speed and ensure the quality of construction.

17

MANAGE FOREIGN TRADE WORK WELL
(May 1961)*

We always wanted to procure more agricultural products in the past. But because we procured too much and left too little to the peasants, finally the peasants did not want to work and we didn't collect anything. As a result, the supply for export and for cities was significantly decreased. After going back and forth for several years, experience in the procurement of agricultural products shows that a little slack is better than tension. That means that we would rather leave more to the peasants and procure less. For example, if a peasant raises one chicken that produces five or six jin of eggs, we will purchase just one or two jin; if he has two pigs, we will purchase just one. Thus, the peasants will be happy and will like to work. "Fertile water does not flow into outsider's fields." It will be easier to handle things if more is produced. Now the peasants are still very poor. If we leave more to the peasants, actually they will not just consume it but they will still want to sell some of it. There will be more goods if there is more flexibility. We can also consider adopting this method in regard to edible vegetable oils. The problem now is that we are too strict, as more and more kinds of things come under unified control, and less and less is procured. If we are more flexible, there naturally will be more things procured after production is developed.

I hope that you comrades will pay special attention to the production, procurement, and export of agricultural commodities. It is not easy for our industrial products to compete with capitalist countries in the international market, breaking into new markets is not easy, and the amount we can export is limited. Nevertheless, agricultural products are different. Our compatriots in Hong Kong

---

*This is a speech made by Comrade Chen Yun at the foreign trade specialists meeting.

and Macao and overseas in Southeast Asia all like to eat and use
our agricultural and subsidiary products, our local and special
products. The market is reliable, and the production period of
these products is short and the effect is fast, so we should strive
for more exports.

DO FOREIGN TRADE WORK WELL
AND STABILIZE THE DOMESTIC MARKET

Every place must try to find ways to make the market supply a
little better. We should, however, not ignore foreign trade. Goods
that can be exported should be exported as much as possible, and
we should first manage foreign trade well. Of course, we retain
something for the domestic market and ensure the most necessary
supplies in the cities. We should not be too cruel when we procure
agricultural products. We should pay attention to improving the
livelihood of the peasants and arousing their production initiative.

In recent years the urban population has increased by more than
30 million, the wage bill has increased from 13.7 billion yuan in
1956 to 26.3 billion yuan at present. On the other hand, because
of two years of continuous disasters, the production of agriculture
and light industry has decreased significantly; therefore there is
a great difference between social purchasing power and the quantity
of goods and materials that can be supplied. In order to solve this
problem, we have already adopted some measures, such as selling
high-price candies, cakes, etc., but these are temporary measures.
But the cardinal measure is to increase production, especially
agricultural production, to reduce urban population, and to cut down
purchasing power. There needs to be a period for solving this
problem; basically it will take two or three years.

The sequence for solving the supply problems of the domestic
market is food first and clothing second. In food, grain is first,
subsidiary food products second. We can import raw materials
to produce daily use industrial goods and put them on the market
after the contradiction between purchasing power and the quantity
of goods and materials that can be supplied is more relaxed. By
then, except for grain, oil, cloth and a few other things, we will be able
to supply other commodities without control; coupons will not be
necessary. I think this is possible.

To stabilize the market, the key is to import grain. In order to
import grain, we should make up our minds to make things available
for export, foreign first, domestic second [i.e., meet foreign trade

demands first, then domestic market demands]. To bring in grain
is an important matter that relates to the whole situation. If we
bring in grain, we can take less grain from the peasants; it will
stabilize the production morale of the peasants and increase their
production initiative. If we spend two or three years developing
agriculture, the problem of the domestic market will be also solved.
If the grain in peasants' hands is sufficient, they can raise more
chickens, ducks, and pigs and produce more economic crops and
various kinds of agricultural subsidiary products, and increase exports. In general, at the present time only if we grasp grain work
well can we stabilize the overall situation, relax the relationship
with the peasants, and improve the diversified economy. It is most
dangerous not to have grain. It is of course embarrassing if we
lack other commodities in the market — it is already embarrassing
now. Actually, department stores are commodity exhibition halls,
and except for stationery, cosmetics, and small commodities that
people can buy without control, coupons are needed to buy many
things. Comparatively, however, grain is much more important.

ESTABLISH COMMODITY EXPORT BASES

All export products should have their production bases. The
production of certain kinds of agricultural products is fixed with
several counties, and the production of certain kinds of industrial
products is fixed with several factories. These several counties
and these several factories are the production bases for these
specific export commodities.

Exporting whatever we produce is fine if talking about the significance of whether we have the natural resources. For example, we
can export tungsten ore if we produce tungsten ore. We cannot export a product that we cannot produce. This is from the
angle of products that are products in relatively large quantities
and that hold a certain position in the international market, but we
can't say this with regard to ordinary commodities. There is vitality in the international market; there is not just one country but
there are many countries. In the competition between each other,
commodities of good quality and low price will find a market. In
order to win the competition, those who trade can only follow the
needs of customers, not subjective decisions made by the producers. In order to export more, we must organize production
and manage well the bases for export commodities according to
the requirements of the international market.

In the past famous brand commodities, both those for export or those for domestic sale, all had their own bases. Quan Jude's roast duck, Dong Laishun's instant-boiled mutton, Zhang Xiaoquan's scissors, the sandalwood fans of Suzhou, the silk umbrellas of Hangzhou, and others all had comparatively fixed bases of material supply. Things produced in the bases have stable production, high production, good quality, and low cost. Destroying all these systems and practicing average distribution is inconsistent with economic principles. This method cannot last long. If we do not restore them soon, export will be neither economical nor stable. For example, there is a special kind of chicken that is worth $U.S.3.00, with which we can buy 100 jin of grain. That is economical. Many people like to eat this kind of chicken, so there is a good market. That is stability. To ensure exports we must work on commodity bases.

We should spend one and a half years to establish bases for export commodities. For each kind of export commodity that totals more than $U.S. 200 or 300 thousand, we should discuss for each how much to produce, how much to export, how much to retain for domestic sale, how to supply raw and processed materials, and so on. Moreover we should convene meetings of specialists to decide each item. Meanwhile, we should study and practice making direct contact between production and sale, and arranging foreign trade departments' contact with people's communes or factories.

We must guarantee the quality of commodities we export. In trading with foreign countries, we must be accountable for the products we export, guarantee changes and returns, and establish credit. We should establish brands with this kind of high quality. In the past, businessmen sold goods even if they lost money in order to establish a new brand and credit. Now some of our commodities are below standard and their quality is deficient, and our credit on the international market is very poor. Therefore we must establish a system of strict quality inspection of exports, and export of commodities that do not meet standards should uniformly be prohibited. The advantages of doing this are not just in the next three or four years but in the forseeable future as well. Only in this way will our exports and foreign trade be strong and develop.

To do economic work, we must have a sense of strategy and must consider big accounts. At the same time, we should also consider small accounts. We cannot only do big business and have huge imports and exports. That which should be big will be big; and that which should be small will be small. In general, no matter whether goods are for export or domestic sale, we should all work like businessmen. Now our state-owned stores look like a public house run by the King of Hell, so who dares come in? We must get rid of this kind of bad practice of the "official merchant."

18

AN IMPORTANT WORK THAT
RELATES TO THE OVERALL SITUATION
(May 1961)*

I will now talk about the issues of cutting back on workers and staff and sending urban residents to the countryside.

Why should we cut back on workers and staff and mobilize people in cities to go to the countryside?

Today is May 31, in another month this "grain year" will end.[a] If we estimate the situation in the countryside, I think that this year will be somewhat better than last year. Within this year, the Party Central Committee and Chairman Mao grasped the "Twelve Articles"[b] and later the "Sixty Articles,"[c] and the situation in the countryside gradually improved. At this meeting, we have further solved some policy problems, so I think that next year will be even better than this year. There will be a production increase, although the rate of production increase will not be very great, but it <u>will</u> increase because the peasants' initiative has been aroused.

The situation in the countryside has been improved, and the economic condition of the whole country is also improving. However, we see now that for grain controlled by the state, next year will be more tense than this year because reserves have decreased. If

---

*This is a speech by Comrade Chen Yun at a Central Work Conference.

a) The grain year refers to the procurement year. In the 1950s and early 1960s it began July 1 and extended through the following June 30. — Eds.

b) This refers to the "Letter Concerning the Urgent Directive of the Central Committee of the CCP Concerning the Problems of Present Policy Toward the People's Communes," issued by the Central Committee on November 3, 1960. The full text is available in Japanese in: Ajia Kenkyūchō, Jinmin kōsha sōran (Survey of People's Communes), Tokyo, 1965, p. 573. This Central Committee document provided concrete guidance for the People's Communes. — Eds.

c) This refers to the "Draft Regulations Concerning Rural Communes," originally drafted in March 1961. See Feiwei nongcun renmin gongshe tiaoli caoan (Draft Regulations on Bandit So-called People's Communes), Taipei, 1965. A revised Sixty Articles was adopted in September 1962. — Eds.

the state-purchased grain handed over to higher authorities by the provinces and prefectures this year is 11.6 billion jin, it will be reduced to 8.4 billion jin next year. Why? Because the various locales this year could turn over 11.6 billion jin to higher levels only by taking part of it from reserves, but next year there will be no reserves from which to draw.

We want to resolve four problems concerning grain shortage that we are now facing.

1. Continue adjusting the Party's basic policies in the country-side, that is, carry out the "Twelve Articles" and the "Sixty Arti-cles," plus the four articles put forth at this meeting (investigation and study, the mass line, return what was unlawfully taken away or pay compensation for it, and rehabilitation and punishment). This is very important. If we do not solve the problems of policy, the peasants will not display their initiative, and no matter how many other measures there are, agricultural production will not go up.

2. Industry should provide great support to agriculture. This is also very important. But the production of chemical fertilizer, tractors, irrigation and drainage machines, etc., will not increase very much immediately. So we will not see the effect of this mea-sure in a short time.

3. Import grain. It is very important to import grain. But in terms of the present situation, it is difficult to exceed 10 billion jin because we do not have that much foreign exchange or that much transport capacity.

4. Mobilize urban residents to go to the countryside to reduce the volume of grain sold in cities.

Of the above four articles, the first is the basic one. The second and the third are limited in time and quantity, and the fourth is in-dispensable and must be adopted.

The essence of the present problem is this: we will have to squeeze the peasants' rations if urban residents do not go to the countryside. Though the whole country is currently discussing and carrying out the "Twelve Articles" and the "Sixty Articles," the "Twelve Articles" and the "Sixty Articles" will not serve their function unless the burden of grain producrement is reduced, because ultimately the peasants still want to see how much we will procure. If the amount procured is still large, then peasants will not have enough to eat and their initiative will remain low. Therefore, there are two roads in front that we need to choose: one is to continue

to squeeze the peasant's rations; the other is to send urban residents to the countryside. We must choose one of the two roads, and
there is no other road we can take. I think that we can only take
the road of reducing the urban population.

Why must urban residents go to the countryside? We will understand this if we look at history. Relatively serious grain shortages
have occurred four times since the founding of the People's Republic. Three of these four times shortages were caused by excessive growth of the urban population, that is, the growth of the population exceeded what commodity grain could support at that time.
The other time was because of mistakes in our work. I will next
discuss the concrete situation during these four occasions of shortage.

The first time was in 1953. We decided to carry out unified procurement and unified sale of grains in October of that year. Before that, we lived on the grain tax, and we could stabilize the
market by levying a grain tax of 30 to 40 billion jin. In 1953 however, the state grain tax and procurement from peasants' surplus
grain totaled 83 billion jin but could not still ensure the market
supply. Why? Because the urban population in the first half year
of 1952 was no more than 61 million. Beginning in the second half
of that year, we prepared to carry out the First Five-Year Plan,
the governmental organs were enlarged, the workers and staff
in capital construction and enterprises all increased. Therefore
the urban population of 1953 increased to 78 million, a sudden increase of 17 million people. Thus we could no longer rely on the
grain tax and the peasants selling surplus grain to maintain market
supply.

The second time was in 1954. In that year we suffered great
floods and the grain production decreased. In the grain work of
that winter there was a mistake (my mistake first) — we over
procured, compared with the previous year we procured 7 billion jin more, and total procurement amounted to 90.2 billion
jin. One was a disaster, the other was a mistake in our work.
As a result, in the first half of 1955 "every family talked
about grain and every household discussed unified procurement."

The third time was in 1957. That time the shortage of grain
supply was not obvious. Only by careful analysis of statistics and
figures can we see that grain reserves decreased. Grain reserves

increased in 1954 and 1955. Owing to excess growth of the urban population in 1956, grain reserves decreased from the original 42.7 billion jin to 36.4 jin by the end of June of 1957. The decrease of 6.3 billion jin was because the amount of grain procured was no longer suited to the size of the urban population. That problem did not surface at that time because we had relatively more reserve grain then.

The fourth time started in 1959 and is still with us. We procured much but we sold even more in these two years. During this period, the urban population greatly increased from 99 million in 1957 to 130 million now [1961]. Thus grain reserves have decreased every year, and by the end of June reserves will probably decrease to 14.8 billion jin, of which there will be 10.1 billion jin of carry-over.[a]

This shows that the scale of industrial construction and cities depends on the amount of surplus products the countryside can provide to the cities. The key among these is grain. We already have had that lesson several times.

Of course, we should recognize that it is very difficult to mobilize urban residents to go to the countryside. People have already come in, and also urban life is much better than rural life, so it is very difficult to convince them to go back again. There could be a big fight if we do not handle this well. We should recognize this difficulty.

Then will it work if we do not mobilize city people to go to the countryside? No. Because that would create even more serious problems.

First, it would hurt the initiative of those production brigades, communes, counties, special districts, and provinces that have high-yield production of grain. If urban residents do not go to the countryside, there will be many more people asking for food from the countryside. Can we ask it from disaster areas? They do not have it. We can only ask it from those brigades, communes, counties,

a) Carry-over (literally "old grain") refers to grain procured from the harvests prior to 1961. Thus of the stocks expected to be in hand at the end of the grain year 5.05 million tons would be carry-over and 3.75 million tons from procurement of the 1961 crop completed prior to June 30. That procurement would probably be of overwintering crops, primarily wheat, planted in north China in the fall of 1960 and harvested in the late spring and early summer of 1961. — Eds.

special districts, and provinces that have high-yield production. It is
actually very egalitarian to ask them for more. Not allowing them to
eat more because they produce more but leaving them only 300 jin of
unhusked grain[a] is possible for a year but it will not work in the
long run. In the areas of commercial grain production such as
Heilongjiang, Hangjiahu,[b] and others, the grain consumption standard has been very low for a long time, and the initiative for increasing production has disappeared, so high-yield production areas
have become low-yield production areas. There are not many
high-yield production counties. There are 23 in Zhejiang Province,
and they are responsible for 74 percent of the grain procured in
the whole province. There are 6 in Suzhou Special District of
Jiangsu Province. We mainly rely on that special district to procure 1.2 billion jin of paddy rice to remit to central control and to
supply Nanjing City. It will be very disadvantageous for the agricultural development of our country if we hurt the initiative of these
high-yield areas.

Second, livestock will die continuously in large numbers. If little
feed grain is left (80 jin for large cattle, and 60 jin for a pig), the
livestock will not win the war of struggling for grain with human
beings. People will eat up feed grain and livestock will continue to
die in large numbers, and this will cause severe damage to agriculture. The reason is that we still rely on domestic animal power
instead of machinery for agricultural production.

Third, the production of economic crops will decrease continuously. If we procure more grain from the countryside and sell
less, peasants will not get enough food. They will cut back on economic crops in order to live, without regard to your cotton plan
and whether you give them cloth coupons or not. If we do not want
to cut back on economic crops, we must provide grain. For example, it would not be difficult to restore the area sown to peanuts
in Shandong; we need only provide 500 million jin of grain and stip-
ulate a proper price. Otherwise, even though you tell them that
cultivating economic crops is a "political task," they will just grow
a little on the edge of the land and still grow grain in the middle.
Thus, not only will it be difficult to maintain the urban market, but
it will also be disadvantageous to the overall development of agriculture. What do you give to peasants after you take away their

---

a) Literally "original grain." — Eds.
b) The area of northern Zhejiang around the cities of Hangzhou, Jiaxing and
Huzhou. — Eds.

grain? It will not work if you always give them high-quality candies. They still need to wear clothes. Therefore, the continuous decline in economic crops will be very disadvantageous for both the people's livelihood and the development of the whole national economy.

Fourth, grain imports will have to increase. If urban residents do not go to the countryside, we will have to import 10 billion jin of grain. This is a very heavy burden. We exported grain several years ago, and we spent the foreign exchange earnings mainly on importing complete sets of machinery and equipment and important raw and processed industrial materials. Now, if we spend the most part of our foreign exchange to purchase grain, it will definitely cut down the import of complete sets of machinery and equipment and important raw and processed industrial materials, and it will greatly affect national industrial construction.

In general, there will be many kinds of difficulties mentioned above if we do not mobilize city people to go to the countryside. The base of the national economy is agriculture, so industry and other aspects will improve only if agriculture is improved. Therefore industry and cities cannot squeeze agriculture, but instead, they should yield to agriculture and the countryside. Now we are facing a such condition: it is difficult to have too many people in the cities and also difficult to mobilize them to go to the countryside. Considering the whole situation and comparing the two difficulties, the difficulty of too many urban residents is more serious. Therefore we can only take the road of mobilizing urban residents to go to the countryside. Only if we do so we can stabilize the whole situation and ensure an improvement in agriculture.

We must be very determined in order to mobilize large groups of urban residents to go to the countryside. There are probably two issues that lead us to make such a decision.

One is the estimation of the pace of agricultural recovery. If we think that agriculture will recover very soon, people will ask why it is necessary to mobilize urban residents to go to the countryside since agriculture will recover very soon, and why make such an unnecessary move. In regard to the issue of the recovery of agricultural production, Premier Zhou has already prepared an analysis that shows that it will not be very soon. Even if agricultural production recovers to the pre-1957 level, we still will be unable to maintain grain supplies. Production will have to recover to at least the 1958 level. In order to reach that level, it will take

three or four years even if the production increases by 20 to 30
billion jin of grain every year starting now. Can we adequately increase the means of promoting agricultural production such as
chemical fertilizers, irrigation machines, etc.? Premier Zhou
addressed this issue, and I also considered it; it is impossible.
Therefore, the issue in front of us is whether to let many people
eat food in the cities while waiting for the development of agriculture, or to send them down right now. I do not think that we can
wait — people should go down right now.

The second is the fear that industrial production will be affected.
Will industrial production be greatly affected by the mobilization
of urban residents to send them to the countryside? I think there
will be some effect, but not much. Industrial production will not
rise if we don't cut down the number of people; if we cut down the
number of people, production will probably improve. For example,
in regard to the production of coal, iron and steel, we should say
that we have made a very great effort, but up to now it has not increased. The big problem is insufficient supply of raw and processed materials. Cotton production fell, so many textile factories
have stopped working. That shows that whether or not industrial
production can go up is not subject to how many people there are.
Can we end the situation of stopping work and waiting for materials
by the end of December 31 of this year and have a great improvement starting from January 1 of next year? I do not think that will
work either. We cannot expect the difficult situation of industrial
production to be improved suddenly.

I will first use coal production as an example. The plan drawn
up last year stipulated that daily raw coal production this year would
be 650 thousand tons in the first quarter, 700 thousand tons in
the second quarter, and 850 thousand tons in the third quarter. I
once estimated that production would probably reach 600 thousand
tons in February and probably reach 650 thousand tons after March
15. However, now it is already the end of May and daily production
is only little more than 513 thousand tons. Why can't coal production go up? I went to talk with several comrades in the Ministry
of Coal and also with some comrades from other places, and they
told me that coal production could not go up mainly because of these
problems: one is an imbalance in the proportions between exploitation and the quantity of reserves; the second is that much machinery
and equipment is in disrepair and being used despite "illness"; the
third is insufficient supplies of grain and subsidiary foods for

workers; the fourth is the necessary adjustment of some links in production relations. All of these practical problems need to be solved; otherwise production still will not go up even if we do well on rectification in the next two months. Nevertheless, these problems cannot be solved quickly.

In regard to the quantity of reserves of the coal industry, there are problems in the front as well as the back, on the left as well as the right, and in the upper level as well as the lower level. The problem in the front and the back is that the digging volume should exceed the mining volume under normal conditions, but now it is just the opposite — there are no reserves. The problem on the left and the right is: workers should turn into the second tunnel as soon as they finish the first, and if there is an accident in that tunnel they should be able to turn into another; but now the situation is that there are no new tunnels prepared on the right while they are mining on the left, or there are only a very few in reserve. The problem in upper level and in lower level is: there should be preparation in the lower level while workers are mining in the upper level in order to mine continuously level by level. It can be called up and down when the old tunnel is expanding downward and workers open another tunnel in place of the old finished one. Now the problem is that we only consider the present condition and mine on one level without considering and preparing for the future. Here the front-back problem can be solved in two or three months, the left-right problem can be solved in five or six months, but the upper-lower problem will require two or three years to be solved. As to how many front-back, upper-lower, and left-right problems there are in the coal industry, I do not have detailed information. However, coal production definitely will not go up very much in the next few months, and it might go down if something goes wrong; also, we have not mentioned here the unrepaired equipment and other problems affecting production.

Next let us look at ore mining. During these years of promoting iron and steel production, we have mainly paid attention to smelting, but we have not paid attention very well to iron ore mining, or to the manufacture of smelting equipment. Because of the shortage of steel products little mining equipment is manufactured, and the mechanization of iron ore mining has not kept up, and mining methods are backward. In the system of the Ministry of Metallurgy, about half the mines are small mines using indigenous methods and half the mines are large mines using Western methods. It is

very difficult to solve the problem of mechanizing iron ore mining.
In the past, we promoted small native mines using manual mining,
and we produced some ore from the surface. Now we have finished
mining ore on the surface and need to mine underground, so we
need capital construction to install the equipment for water pump-
ing, ventilation, elevating, and so on. In the past iron ore transportation relied mainly on manpower, and the tool was just a push
cart. Now we can't let so many people continue to work on transportation, so we need to mechanize manual work. Another problem
is that a poor deposit should become a rich deposit. Now, no matter whether ore contains 30 percent iron or contains 40 percent
iron, it is all considered useful, so a lot of coal is being wasted.
In order to increase the content of iron in furnace material, we
have to pulverize ore and to do magnetic selection, then finally
smelt it into rich ore. It will require three years to complete such
a process of from working on the surface to underground, from
manual work to mechanized work, from poor ore to rich ore,
namely to convert small mines using indigenous methods to small
mines using Western methods.

It is also a big problem to build railroads for ore transportation.
So-called mining is nothing but moving stones. We cannot work
just by using our hands to push carts; we must build railroads.
The Niushoushan Iron Mine is a small mine 20 li from Nanjing.
There are 1,300 workers, among whom 1,000 move stones. The
Longyan Mine in Hebei was opened during the Japanese occupation.
It has an annual production of 2.9 million tons of ore and has 300
thousand meters of underground mine rails. It takes a very long
time to build a mechanized mine.

Moreover, it also takes a while to solve the problem of coking.
Currently there are many factories coking without thorough coal
washing or coking by using indigenous methods, so much coal is
used and the quality is poor. If we want to wash the coal and
Westernize indigenous coking, we have to add a great deal of equipment.

If we do not greatly increase coal production and do not increase
iron and steel production, light industry, heavy industry, and capital
construction will all be unable to increase. The total number of
workers and staff in the whole country increased by more than 25
million in the past few years. Among the units in which workers
increased, first is the department of capital construction, which
increased by more than 4.2 million workers; second is the machinery

industry, which increased by 3.2 million workers. If the iron and steel industry does not enlarge, capital construction will not increase by much, other departments too can barely develop very much owing to a lack of raw and processed materials, and there will not be much for productive enterprises and capital construction units to do. We are not able to rely on imports of raw and processed materials either, because we spent foreign exchange on buying grain and there is not much left. Because of these various aspects I think the readjustment of industry is not a one year undertaking. Actually the situation in which there are people but there is no work has already appeared. In textiles 5 million spindles have stopped, and workers have nothing to do after they eat. The food industry increased by 550 thousand people in the last three years, which could be considered a small number, but again many people have nothing to do. Therefore, it will not affect industrial production and capital construction if we mobilize large groups of workers to work for agriculture in the countryside. In the future, after agriculture has taken a turn for the better and peasants are able to supply more grain, this can be discussed again.

We recruited more than 25 million workers and staff in the last three years, causing the urban population to increase to 130 million. This is not proper if we consider the present situation. At that time, we had no experience and overestimated grain production, and we thought that it would be better if everything was smaller and more indigenous — even though we would use a great many people, it was good as long as we could produce things. Thus we recruited a great many people. Can we promote industry by using handicraft or semi-handicraft — semi-mechanized methods? At certain times and under certain circumstances we can as long as we have a sufficient supply of grain, but we should consider its economic effect. The present circumstance is not like this. We do not have enough grain, the industrial scale is too large, we use too many people, and there are more people than jobs. Under these conditions it is unsuitable.

Somebody has said that if workers are sent to the countryside they still have to eat, and they eat there if they do not eat here. Actually, eating in the countryside is very different from eating in the cities. How big is the difference? I think it is very big. In the first year workers are in the countryside, we can supply 150 jin less per person; that will be 1.5 billion jin if 10 million people go to the countryside, and 3 billion jin if 20 million people go. This is the difference in the first year. The more obvious difference is in the second year. Workers who are originally from the countryside will go back home, and the workers whose homes are originally in the cities will go to the countryside to set up their homes. They will join collective production and distribution, and because of the harvest gained from private plots they will not need grain supplied by the state. Thus, we can supply 4.5 billion jin of grain less if 10 million people go to the countryside, and 9 billion jin less if 20 million people go.

  Will workers have nothing to do if they go to the countryside? I don't think so. There are many things to do in the countryside, and they can do this little bit or do that little bit. They can always produce something. They also can produce products for export. Many agricultural capital construction projects, such as leveling land, building canals, as well as fine plowing, farming, etc., will increase the production of grain and other agricultural and subsidiary products.

  The situations mentioned above show that we should decide to mobilize urban residents to go to the countryside. Making this decision earlier is better than making it later. I think that generally we should convince all those who came from the countryside in the last three years to go back to the countryside, to go back to where they came from. Of course it might be difficult for all of them to go back, but the majority should go back. As to those small retailers and capitalists who are originally from the cities, we do not have to mobilize them to go to the countryside. Only if we do well this important task of cutting back on workers and staff and mobilizing urban residents to go to the countryside, which concerns the whole situation, will we definitely gain remarkable results.

19

AN INVESTIGATION OF RURAL
QINGPU [COUNTY]
(August 1961)*

I spent fifteen days from late June to early July in Xiaozheng
People's Commune of Shaghai's Qingpu County[a] carrying out rural
investigations. I am quite familiar with the situation there since
that is the place where I participated in the peasant movement in
1927, and I have been in frequent contact with this area since Liberation. Before I went there, Comrade Xue Muqiao led a working
group to investigate the area for a week. Two comrades in his
group had participated with me in the peasant movement in 1927.
The peasants knew us and dared speak the truth. I listened to two
reports by the Party committee and convened ten discussions on
special subjects, viz. (1) pig-raising by the collective, (2) pig-
raising by individuals, (3) cropping arrangements, (4) private plots,
(5) returning or paying compensation for (what had been unduly
taken in) the movement of eqalitarianism and indiscriminate transfer of resources,[b] (6) rural commerce, (7) commune industries and
handicrafts, (8) quotas stated in grain contracts, state purchase
quotas and enthusiasm of peasants, (9) the problem of cadres and
their supervision by the masses, (10) guarding against pilfering and
protecting production. Some of the discussions were arranged
mainly to undertake investigations among the peasants, and some
were for exchanging ideas with the Party committee of the commune. Several times I went personally to the houses of the peasants to see how they raise pigs and work their private plots and
to study the situation of their housing and food. The peasants have

---

*This is a letter and three investigation reports written by Comrade Chen
Yun to Comrade Deng Xiaoping on the situation in the rural areas.

a) Qingpu, originally a county in Jiangsu that in the 1950s was annexed to
Shanghai Municipality. — Eds.

b) A manifestation of leftism during the Great Leap Forward. — Eds.

both commendations for and criticisms of our Party. Their criticisms and complaints may be summarized as the following four:
first, they do not have enough to eat; second, the cadres at the
grass-roots level set high quotas arbitrarily in disregard of re-
alities, and they have failed to participate regularly in work and
have led privileged lives; third, the cadres have given wrong orders
in production and refused to make self-criticisms; and fourth,
because collective production has not been organized well, the peasants lack enthusiasm — while by contrast, they show great enthusiasm for private plots and sideline production. Nevertheless, the
peasants think that since Liberation they have benefited greatly,
mainly in five respects: (1) With the redistribution of land, "it is
easy to get through the New Year" (i.e., they do not have to worry
about not being able to pay their debts at the end of the year);
(2) marshland has been filled in (the commune has a total cultivated
area of 24,000 mu, 7,000 of which are considered marshland);
(3) more land has come under electric irrigation (which accounts
for 80 percent of the cultivated land); (4) more chemical fertilizer
is available (averaging 30 jin per mu in the last two years); and
(5) though they are still sometimes bossed around by the cadres,
things are now much better than they were under the rule of the
Guomindang.

   Later on, I went to Hangzhou and Suzhou to visit a few counties
(Jiaxing and Jiashan) in Jiaxing Prefecture and a few (Wuxian,
Wujiang and Kunshan) in Suzhou Prefecture where the conditions
are similar to those in Qingpu County. I discussed the growing of
double cropped rice as well as wheat with the Party secretaries of
the county committees and Party secretaries of a number of production brigades and asked in passing about pig-raising and private
plots. I also visited comrades of the county committees of Xiaoshan and Wuxi. These counties differ from Qingpu County in land,
population, and climate. I did some research on questions concerning cropping arrangements by investigaging cropping and
making comparisons. Finally, I exchanged ideas with the Shanghai Municipal Party Committee and the Zhejiang and Jiangsu
Provincial Party Committees on questions of pig-raising, cropping arrangements, and private plots. The investigation reports
on these three questions are enclosed herewith for your reference.

SOWS SHOULD BE RAISED BY INDIVIDUAL PEASANTS
Investigation Report (I) of Xiaozheng
People's Commune, Qingpu County

The policy concerning pig-raising has already been defined, i.e., pigs are to be raised both by the collective and by individuals, with priority on the latter. But it is yet to be explicitly stipulated who should raise sows, the collective or the individuals. A rapid resolution is needed. From what we have seen and heard, most of the communes have transferred the job of raising pigs to the individual commune members, but most sows are still being raised collectively by the communes, production brigades, or production teams. Many communes are still hesitating over whether sows should be raised by individual commune members and are taking a wait-and-see attitude. After we personally observed ten of the fifteen pig farms of Xiaozheng People's Commune and convened two discussions on pig-raising, we found that sows are growing very well under the care of the individuals and that these bear more piglets with high survival rate. On the contrary, there are more nonpregnancies and miscarriages among the sows raised by the collective, and the death rate of piglets is high. We got the same impression from the discussions with cadres of a number of communes in Jiaxing and Suzhou prefectures. Facts have proven that in order to restore and develop pig-raising rapidly, more piglets are needed and, in order to get more piglets, sows must be raised by individual commune members. This is the key to whether pig-raising can be rapidly resumed and developed in the future.

I. SOWS UNDER THE CARE OF INDIVIDUALS GROW WELL AND BEAR MORE PIGLETS

Peasants in Xiaozheng have a tradition of raising sows, and three out of ten households used to raise sows. Before the commune was established, the 2,400 households raised a total of 700 to 800 sows that gave birth to more than 10,000 piglets a year. Some piglets were kept for raising pork, and the rest were sold to the neighboring areas in exchange for feed. After the sows were transferred to the collective, the total number of sows in the commune increased to 1,500 in 1960, but they only bore 6,704 piglets. On average, one sow gave birth to only four-and-a-half piglets a year. What's more, 5,993 of the piglets died, the death rate reaching 89 percent. Moreover, 710 sows had miscarriages with a loss of

4,196 piglets. When sows were raised by individuals before the
commune was set up, each sow bore an average of 14 or 15 piglets
a year, and the death rate of piglets was only 6 percent. According
to the administrative personnel of the pig farms, sows raised by
individuals grew because each sow was under the care of several
people. Sows raised by the collective can hardly grow well, as
several sows are taken care of by only one person. (One stockman
looks after an average of ten sows. If those who grow, harvest,
and transport feed and the administrative personnel are included,
the average number comes to 4 sows under each person.) Peasants with experience in sow-raising said that when they were raising sows, they could make a lot of money only if the sows were
well raised; otherwise they would suffer losses. So, they would
look after sows as if they were lying-in women and look after piglets as if they were babies. They listed the following advantages
of individual raising of sows in comparison with collective sow
raising:

1. Better feeding. Feed is arranged according to differing needs
of the sows and piglets in different periods, with more concentrated
fodder at some times and more greenfeed at other times, more
dry feed at some times and more liquid other times. The peasants
can observe the sows and piglets as they eat to see what kind of
feed they like. This also enables the peasants to determine
the sick pigs, which eat little. When pigs are raised by the collective, the feed is always bland, like "food in a mess," without dis-
tinction between dry and liquid feed, and nobody cares how much
the pigs eat.

2. A better job is done in bedding down the pigs. When pigs are
raised by individuals, green grass is used to bed down the pigs.
The pigsties are clean and comfortable. The sows and piglets are
kept clean, and they seldom fall ill. When pigs are raised by the
collective, only a little rice straw is used to bed down the pigs
because there is nobody collecting green grass. Sows and piglets
are always muddy all over in a wet pigsty and easily fall ill.

3. Special attention is given to the pregnant sows, and they are
protected from being frightened. Some peasants do everything possible to make the sows less disturbed by thunder and firecrackers.
They let the sows out when they are cleaning out the pigsties lest
the sows get disturbed.

4. Attention is given to delivery. When the sows are about to
give birth, the peasants sleep by the pigsty and see to it that

no piglets suffocate under the body of the sow.

5. Piglets are under special care. Special care is given to the last-delivered, smallest, and weakest piglet. It is put on the third nipple, the one with most milk. After a few days, the piglets get used to being nursed on the same nipples, and they grow up without some being too big and some being too small.

6. Measures are taken to prevent heatstroke in summer and to preserve heat in winter. In summer, waterweed is put in the pigsty, and sows feel cool on it. Dry grass is used in winter, and it is easy to preserve heat for the well-covered small pigsty. When pigs are raised on the collective, pigsties are big and cold in winter. The piglets, jammed in the rice straw or under the belly of the sow to hide from the cold, are easily crowded to death.

As it is more difficult to raise sows than porkers, some comrades are afraid that peasants may not be able to do a good job in raising sows. But as far as we know, all the households that want to raise sows are those with rich experience in the job. When they raise sows, they try to prevent nonpregnancies and miscarriages and to help the sows bear more piglets, with a high survival rate. Owing to proper feeding, a sow under individual care will bear and bring up at least two times as many piglets a year as compared with a collectively raised sow.

II. INDIVIDUAL BREEDING HAS SEVERAL ADVANTAGES OVER COLLECTIVE BREEDING FOR BOTH SOWS AND PORKERS

1. Relatively ample feed is available for pigs raised by individuals. It is impossible now to rely solely on concentrated feed to raise pigs. A great proportion of greenfeed has to be used. Privately bred pigs have a much better supply of greenfeed than collectively bred ones. When households raise pigs, waterweed and fresh grass can be collected by auxiliary laborers or in off hours. Tender and fresh weeds are for pigs to eat, and the old ones are for the pigsty. On the very evening and the following morning when it was announced in Xiaozheng People's Commune that most sows, piglets, and porkers were to be raised by individual commune members, many households that wanted to do the job vied with each other in collecting waterweed and fresh grass which would be dried and stored as pig feed in winter. It is thus obvious that with the same amount of concentrated feed supplied by the state, privately raised pigs will have better feed and more feed than the collectively raised ones.

2. Privately raised pigs grow faster than collectively raised ones. Owing to good feed and good sleep, privately bred pigs grow faster. A porker grows an average of half a jin per day, and a piglet weighing over 20 jin will grow to a pig of around 100 jin in four or five months. With the same amount of concentrated feed, a collective pig will gain an average of only 5 or 6 jin per month.

3. More manure will be collected when pigs are raised by individuals. Because a great amount of green grass is used to bed down the privately raised pigs, more manure of better quality is collected. When pigs are raised by the collective, only a little rice straw is used in the pigsty, so that less manure is collected and its quality is not as good. Some 200 dan of manure per privately raised sow per year can be collected, while in the case of collectively raised sows, only 100 to 120 dan per sow per year are collected, with a fertilizer equivalent of 60 to 80 dan.

4. Auxiliary laborers and off hours can be used when pigs are raised by individuals. A peasant raising a porker does not have to absent himself from work if he has an auxiliary hand at home, and one sow will cost him only 10 to 20 working days a year. Able-bodied workers are needed when pigs are raised by the collective. One worker in Xiaozheng Commune can look after only four sows or ten porkers. Some 300 workers are engaged in the raising of 2,400 pigs (including piglets) of the commune and the brigades, one worker looking after only eight pigs.

5. Less rice straw is used when pigs are raised by individuals. At least 2 jin of rice straw per pig per day is used up for cooking feed and bedding down the collectively raised pigs, which totals 7 dan per year, a little bit more than the rice straw collected on one mu of paddy field (600-700 jin). When individual breeders cook their food, they can use the hot fire left in the stove for preparing pig feed, thus saving on fuel (through doubling up).

For the above reasons, privately bred pigs can bring profits while collectively raised ones cause losses. According to the peasants, a sow can give birth to 12 to 16 piglets a year which could be sold at 180 to 200 yuan. A porker of over 100 jin could be sold at 30 to 40 yuan. If they raised two porkers a year, they would make 60 to 80 yuan. Losses are a common phenomenon in the case of collective pig raising. Last year, Xiaozheng Commune suffered a loss of over 38,000 yuan owing to collective pig raising, each household bearing an average 16 yuan loss. The loss would have been greater if investment in capital construction were counted.

We also asked about the drawbacks when pigs are put under the care of individuals. The cadres pointed out the following two: (1) they are afraid that peasants might butcher pigs on the sly and sell them on the black market, and (2) they also worry that peasants might refuse to sell pigs when the state urgently needs pork for the market. Nevertheless, these two drawbacks can be avoided by the implementation of correct policies and by proper management. At the same time, the state and the collective could also raise some pigs to meet urgent demands of the market.

III. THE PIG-BREEDING INDUSTRY CANNOT BE RESTORED AND DEVELOPED UNLESS SOWS ARE RAISED BY INDIVIDUALS

When porkers are being raised by individual commune members and sows by the communes, production brigades, or production teams, can we say that we are now carrying out the policy that pigs are to be raised by both the collective and the individuals but with priority on the latter? In our view, the policy has not been carried out thoroughly, and the percentage of collectively raised pigs is still too high. We have the following two reasons:

First, at first glance priority has been given to private breeding, since there are fewer sows raised by the collective than porkers raised by individuals. Actually, that is not how things stand. Under normal conditions, each collectively raised sow nurses four or five piglets. Usually, sows and suckling piglets will account for one third to one half of the total number of pigs. Therefore, with sows being raised by the collective, piglets and boars being included, more than one third or even half of the pigs are still raised by the collective. Out of the total of 3,720 pigs of Xiaozheng Commune at the end of last June, only 1,437 were porkers — less than 40 percent. The remaining 60 percent are sows, boars, and piglets. Since most sows and a small number of porkers are raised by the collective, as of the end of June two thirds of the pigs in Xiaozheng Commune were raised by the collective and only one third by individuals. As of the end of June, only one fourth of the 850,000 pigs in the ten suburban counties of Shanghai were being raised by individuals.

Second, it is more difficult to raise sows than porkers. It has already been mentioned that when sows are raised by the collective there are frequent occurrences of nonpregnancies and miscarriages, and the death rate of piglets is high. Without more piglets, a rapid development of pig-raising is impossible. The total number of pigs in Xiaozheng Commune reached 15,000 to 16,000 in 1957. The year 1960, after the sows were transferred to the collective, witnessed a decrease of nearly two thirds, i.e., only 5,600 pigs were raised. According to the statistics of last June, the 909 collectively raised sows of the whole commune were nursing only 1,234 piglets, less than two piglets per sow. It is impossible to have a rapid improvement in the present conditions of raising sows by the collective. Therefore, if sows continue to be raised under the collective, the coming winter will probably see a fairly high death rate of piglets Only by a quick transfer of sows to individual commune members can the birth rate among sows and the survival rate of piglets be greatly increased and a large number of piglets be supplied to ensure a rapid restoration and development of pig-raising next year.

After encouraging individual commune members to raise sows privately, it is necessary to solve the problems in the market transactions for piglets. We can consider restoring the previous piglet markets under the leadership of state commerce or the supply and marketing coops. Peasants who have sold piglets should be rewarded with a certain amount of feed and meat coupons so as to induce a rapid increase in the supply of piglets.

IV. PRIVATE SOW BREEDING SHOULD
    PROCEED FROM ACTUAL CONDITIONS

The practice of raising most sows by individual commune members does not contradict the policy of raising pigs by both the collective and individuals. In areas with certain traditions of raising pigs, there is absolutely no problem in letting individual commune members raise most of the sows. However, peasants in about ten communes in the vegetable-growing areas near Shanghai do not know how to raise sows owing to lack of experience in this regard. Therefore, it is impossible at present to put most sows under the care of these individuals. In these areas, it might be necessary for the government organs or communes to continue to experiment in running pig farms to raise more sows and porkers. But plans should be drawn up in light of the feed supply possibilities, and efforts should be exerted to improve management and administration.

At the same time, efforts should be made to explore all the possibilities of private breeding and to help peasants raise more pigs.
Generally speaking, in order to improve the pig breed, communes
or production brigades should raise fine breed boars and some
fine breed sows. By doing so, priority is still given private breeding though combined efforts are being made by both the collective
and the individuals.

As the suburban areas of Shanghai have to supply pork to 7 million urban inhabitants, it is imperative that various methods be
adopted to rapidly develop pig-raising. Pigs can be raised by
government organizations, communes, and production brigades or
by individual commune members. What exactly is the best way to
raise more and better pigs? Relevant experience has not yet been
accumulated. At present, a great potential for pig-raising exists
among the peasants. Private plots have now been reallocated in
the rural areas; the grain rations have been arranged down to
household level and the chaff from grain processing is now retained by the peasants. All this has provided the great masses of
peasants with conditions for raising pigs and has greatly boosted
their enthusiasm. Up till the end of last June, there were only
210,000 privately bred pigs among the over 800,000 households in
the suburbs of Shanghai, one pig per four households. The total
number would be four times as big if each household raised one
pig. To tap the great potential among the commune members,
most collectively raised sows and piglets must be transferred to
the commune members to meet their demands. This problem has
not been thoroughly solved in many areas. The solution to it might
be of great significance to the rapid development of pig breeding
in the future.

DOUBLE CROPPING OF RICE IS NOT AS GOOD
AS PLANTING A SINGLE CROP OF RICE PLUS
A CROP OF BROAD BEANS
Investigation Report (II) of Xiaozheng
People's Commune

Xiaozheng People's Commune is located in an area with low-lying
land. The average per capita cultivated land of the agricultural
population is 2.4 mu. In the last few years, the agricultural production there has remained quite stable. Grain output in 1960 went
beyond that of 1957 and even reached approximately the bumper
harvest level achieved in 1956. There are two controversial questions concerning the cropping arrangement: (1) Should two crops

of rice be planted? (2) Should more wheat or more broad beans be planted? The peasants do not like the idea of double cropping rice and planting more wheat, which in their view will result in a "nominal increase and actual decrease, the loss outweighing the gain." After repeated discussions with the cadres of the commune and brigades, we think the peasants are right.

I. WHY DOUBLE CROPPING OF RICE IS NOT AS GOOD AS PLANTING A SINGLE CROP OF RICE

In double cropping rice in the Xiaozheng area, per mu yield of the early crop is about 500 jin and of the late crop is about 300 jin, totaling some 800 jin. The land used for double cropping of rice is all upland fields. Single cropping of late rice grown in upland fields yields about 580 jin per mu. In comparison, per mu output of double cropping of rice is 220 jin higher than that of single cropping. Superficially, then, more grain can be produced by double cropping of rice. However, when we look at things in an all-around way, we see that double cropping of rice incurs great losses in many respects and that it in fact does not pay well.

1. Output of the fields with extra seedlings for the late crop will be affected. It is the custom here that seedlings for the late crop of double cropped rice be planted in the fields of the single late rice crop — that is to say, more seedlings are transplanted to the fields for single cropping rice and in early August half of these are pulled up and transplanted again into the fields for the late crop of the double cropped rice. As a result, fields with such seedlings will yield about 150 jin less per mu. (If the output of a single crop of late rice is 580 jin per mu, then that of the field that includes seedlings for the late crop of double cropped rice is only 430 jin per mu.)

If seedlings which are fully developed in the seedling beds are used, fewer seedlings can be grown per seedling bed, and one mu of seedlings is sufficient for transplating onto only four mu of paddy field. Even so, the seedlings are quite thin and weak. The late crop of rice grown out of such seedlings can yield only about 250 jin per mu, 50 jin less than the late crop with seedlings retransplanted from the single-cropping field. Only the late crop of the double cropping can be planted in seedling-bed fields; the early crop cannot. Because of the lateness, per mu output is only some 250 jin, 330 jin less than the per mu yield of 580 jin of the single cropped late rice. The 330 jin, shared by the other three mu of

land, come to 110 jin less in per mu output. The two add up to
160 jin, a little bit more than the per mu loss (150 jin) of the field
with seedlings for the late crop of the double cropped rice.

2. More seeds are used. Twice as many seedlings are used for
the early crop of double cropped rice. What's more, cold weather
causes low survival rates. Thus, 40 jin of seeds are needed per mu
for the early crop. Plus 15 jin for the late crop, the seeds used
total up to 55 jin per mu. In comparison, one mu of single cropping
of late rice needs only 15 jin of seeds, 40 jin less than double
cropping rice.

3. No summer crops (beans, wheat) but only safflower can be
planted if double cropping of rice is done. But in the case of single cropping of rice, one crop of broad beans or wheat can be
planted. The per mu output of these is 80 to 100 jin, or 60 to 80
jin after deducting seeds.

The above-mentioned figures add up to 250 to 270 jin, which are
more than the 220 jin by which double cropping of rice tops single
cropping. Therefore, double cropping of rice does not pay as well
as a single crop of rice plus one crop of beans or wheat. Furthermore, double cropping of rice suffers the following indirect losses.

4. More manure is applied. Owing to the short growing period
of early crop of double cropped rice, more manure has to be applied. The late crop needs about the same amount of manure per
mu as does single cropped late rice. The above-mentioned output
of double cropped rice can be obtained only when at least an extra
15 dan of night soil or barnyard manure and an extra 15 jin of chemical
fertilizer are applied per mu. At present, the fertilizer applied to the
single cropped rice is not adequate. Should the extra amount of fertilizer used on double cropped rice be applied to single cropped rice, the
per mu output of the latter will increase by at least 40 jin.

5. More manpower is required. This is an area with small
population and large acreage. If double cropped rice is planted,
there will be a serious shortage of hands during the period of rush-
harvesting of the early crop and rush-planting of the late crop.
As a result, the fields of single cropped rice will be weeded one
time less. What's more, this is also the best period to collect
waterweeds and grass for feed and green manure. The manpower
spared from growing one mu of double cropped rice can be put into
weeding, collecting and applying green manure to the fields. By
doing so, the per mu yield of a single crop of late rice would be
further increased by at least 20 jin.

6. Less straw is harvested. Because the stem of the double cropped rice is short, there is less straw from one <u>mu</u> of the double ble cropped rice than from one <u>mu</u> of single cropped rice.

Taken as a whole, though the per <u>mu</u> yield of double cropped rice surpasses that of single cropping by 220 <u>jin</u>, the various losses caused by the double cropping add up to 310-330 <u>jin</u>. Comparing the two, the loss obviously outweighs the gain.

II. WHY GROWING MORE WHEAT IS NOT AS GOOD AS GROWING MORE BROAD BEANS

As this is an area with low-lying land and a high water table, it is not suitable for growing wheat. The reason why the peasants want to grow less wheat and more broad beans is that the income from growing wheat is less than that from growing broad beans.

1. One <u>mu</u> of upland field here can yield only about 80 <u>jin</u> of wheat. (It is only 62 <u>jin</u> this year.) The net output is 60 <u>jin</u> or so after deducting 20 <u>jin</u> for seeds. Per <u>mu</u> output of wheat in low-lying land is merely 30-40 <u>jin</u>, and little is left after deducting seeds. One <u>mu</u> of upland field can yield some 100 <u>jin</u> of dry broad-beans. Eighty <u>jin</u> of wheat are worth about 9 yuan, while 100 <u>jin</u> of broad beans are worth 11 yuan.

2. More fertilizer is needed to grow wheat. Fifteen <u>dan</u> of barn-yard manure have to be applied to one <u>mu</u> of wheat, while 5 <u>dan</u> are enough for one <u>mu</u> of broad beans. Wheat consumes more of the fertility of the soil than do broad beans because the root bac-teria of legumes are nitrogen-fixing. With the same amount of fertilizer, per <u>mu</u> output of rice grown in the broad bean field is 50 <u>jin</u> higher than that grown in the wheat field. Another 20 <u>jin</u> are possible if the 10 <u>dan</u> of barnyard manure saved from the broad bean field are applied to the rice field. The two figures add up to an increase of 70 <u>jin</u> of rice per <u>mu</u>.

3. If broad beans are planted, people can eat some green broad beans, which works out better than eating only dry broad beans. The beanstalks left over from the green broad beans can be used as green manure, and the beanstalks from one <u>mu</u> of broad beans can be applied as base fertilizer to two <u>mu</u> of paddy fields with more or less the same fertilizer efficiency as one <u>mu</u> of safflower. As the green broad bean harvest is 20 days earlier than the dry broad bean or wheat harvests, its timing is relatively advantageous for planting paddy rice. Income from green broad beans is much higher than that from dry broad beans. One <u>mu</u> of green broad beans

with beanstalks, which is about 500 jin, is worth 25-30 yuan. Green broad beans can serve as vegetables, and consumption of more green broad beans means consumption of less grain. It is stipulated in Shanghai that one jin of grain can be deducted from the quota of grain sold to the state for every 6 jin of green broad beans sold. Therefore, the per mu output of 500 jin of green broad beans is equivalent to over 80 jin of grain.

4. It is profitable to export broad beans to pay for the import of wheat or barley. The export price of one ton of broad beans is £30, the import price of one ton of wheat is £22-23, and that of barley is £16. So, 1.32-1.36 tons of wheat or 1.88 tons of barley can be imported by exporting one ton of broad beans.

In recent years, the fertility of soil has tended to decline owing to the large acreage devoted to wheat and double cropping of rice and the small acreage planted in broad beans and safflower. Though the per mu output of grain has somewhat increased as a result of more chemical fertilizer, the fertility of the soil is not as good as it used to be. Long-term interests demand that such an irrational cropping system be changed resolutely and rapidly.

III. THE ARRANGEMENT OF CROPS MUST
BE IN LINE WITH LOCAL CONDITIONS

Farming customs that have evolved over a long period of time should not be changed rashly. In the past, there was no double cropped rice and little wheat planted in the Xiaozheng area. Before Liberation, a peasant household would grow in winter, out of 10 mu of land, about 7 mu of safflower, 2 mu of broad beans, 0.5 mu of wheat, and 0.5 mu of rape. The acreage devoted to double cropping of rice last year increased to 14 percent of the total, that of wheat to 24 percent, and fewer broad beans and safflower were planted. Owing to this cropping arrangement, which ran counter to the specific conditions of the area, agricultural production suffered, peasant income declined, and the masses were very unhappy. Though the acreage of double cropping of rice this year has been cut down to 7.5 percent of the total, the peasants still think it is too much.

The frost-free period in the suburbs of Shanghai as well as Jiaxing and Suzhou prefectures is not long enough. Thus, generally speaking, it is not suitable for growing more double cropped rice. Areas like this, where there is a small population with a large amount of cultivated land, have shortages of manpower and fertil-

izer. So, the losses from double cropping of rice outweigh the
gains. The average per capita cultivated land among the agricultural population in Jiaxing area is 2.8 mu. Acreage for double
cropping of rice last year amounted to 60 percent of the total paddy
field acreage. Shortages of manpower caused delays in farming.
Thus, the two crops altogether yielded only 450 jin per mu, 48 jin
less than the per mu output of the single cropped rice. Therefore,
it is not realistic subjectively to practice "changing single-cropping
to double-cropping" as the main measure to increase grain output
without studying the objective conditions.

In certain areas, it might be profitable to double crop some rice.
For instance, Xiaoshan County of Zhejiang Province double cropped
rice in 60 percent of its fields, and it is said that it will probably
have a bumper harvest. The reasons are as follows:

1. The frost-free period in this area is quite long so that it is
possible for early sowing and early harvesting of the early crop,
and the transplanting of the late crop can be finished by the end of
July (it is finished 7-10 days later in other areas). Frost comes
late in this area. Therefore, output of both early and late crops can
reach over 500 jin.

2. In this area, the per capita cultivated land is less than one
mu, so there is enough manpower. There is also plenty of fertilizer because it is located near Hangzhou and a lot of manure can
be obtained in the city.

3. This is a half rice, half cotton and hemp area so the time to
plant rice and to plant cotton and hemp can be staggered. To double
crop some rice will not cause delays during the busy period of rush
harvesting the early crop and rush planting the late crop, and the
single cropped late rice will not be affected too much.

It is not suitable to double crop rice too much even in this kind
of area. The peasants were very unhappy about too much double
cropping of rice last year.

Thus it can be seen that whether to double crop rice and how
much it should be done depend mainly on the length of the frost-
free period, the ratio between population and land, and so forth.
Under the current circumstances, in the southern part of the Changjiang [Yangtze River] delta, more double cropping of rice can be
done where the per capita cultivated land is less than one mu; a
small amount can be done if the per capita land is about 1.5 mu,
and it would be better not to double crop rice at all if the per capita
land reaches about 2.5 mu. In the northern part of the delta (such

as Wuxi), it might not be suitable to double crop rice even if
per capita land is less than one mu.

How much wheat should be grown depends mainly on the physical
features of the land and the quality of the soil. Generally speaking,
it is not suitable to grow a lot of wheat on low-lying land. Take
Qingpu County for example. With the eastern sector generally
higher than the west, more wheat has grown in the east over the
years, with a higher per mu output than in the west. The Shanghai,
Baoshan, and Jiading counties of Shanghai and Jiangyin County of
Suzhou Prefecture are high-yielding areas of wheat, and wheat has
been grown in large acreage over the years. But this kind of area
should also grow some broad beans and green manure crops to improve the fertility of the soil.

IV. IT IS NECESSARY TO CHANGE THE TIMING
FOR ARRANGING GRAIN RATIONS

It is a desire shared by all the peasants in the Xiaozheng area
not to double crop rice, to grow less wheat, and to grow more
broad beans and safflower. It is for the provision of grain that quite
a lot of wheat last winter and some double cropped rice this spring
were planted. The grain provided last year only lasted till the end
of June this year, and grain for the third quarter of this year must
come from the wheat and the early crop of rice. If there is no double cropping of rice and less wheat is planted, the third quarter
grain must come mainly from the autumn harvest of the previous
year. That is to say, the grain ration must be arranged such that
it is enough to last till September of the following year. Thus, the
"grain year" has to be changed from July-June to October-Septem-
ber. In the long period since Liberation, the grain-ration of the
peasants in this area has been from October to the end of September.

There are some areas in the suburbs of Shanghai and in Jiaxing
and Suzhou prefectures where conditions are similar to those in the
Xiaozheng area. In the discussions with the cadres of the counties,
communes, and brigades in Jiaxing, Jiashan, Wujiang and Wuxian
counties, most comrades, after weighing the advantages and disad-
vantages, asked not to double crop or to double crop less rice and
to grow less wheat but more broad beans. But they held that in order
to change the cropping arrangement, the problem of providing grain
for the third quarter of the year must be solved. They calculate
that by growing some wheat and some red rice and indica rice

(where harvest time is 45 days earlier than that of single cropped late rice) in the low-lying land which is liable to waterlogging, and by substituting some broad beans for grain, the third-quarter grain ration for all but a month and a half is covered. If the state reduces the unified procurement quotas by 60 jin per person in the first year, then the timing of the grain ration arrangement could be changed. The total amount of state-purchased grain will not be reduced, because the 60 jin could be made up in the following year.

The population in the areas similar to Xiaozheng Commune is 550,000, of which 250,000 is in Jiaxing Prefecture, 100,000 in Suzhou Prefecture and 200,000 in the suburbs of Shanghai. If the unified procurement quota per person is reduced by 60 jin, the total reduction is only 33 million jin. By simply reducing state purchase quotas by this small amount in the first year, real output of grain and the net income of the peasants in this area will probably increase. Moreover, such an arrangement could help gradually improve the fertility of the soil. The restoration and improvement of soil fertility in two or three years will constitute a sound base for increasing grain output in the future.

SET ASIDE ENOUGH LAND AS PRIVATE PLOTS IN ACCORDANCE WITH THE REGULATIONS OF THE PARTY CENTRAL COMMITTEE
Investigation Report (III) of Xiaozheng
People's Commune

When these were advanced agricultural producers' cooperatives, over 700 mu of land were private plots, which made up only 3 percent of the total cultivated land. Out of these 700 mu, about 500 mu were on large pieces of land and the rest were small plots by the side of houses, roads, ponds, etc. When the people's commune was set up, all the private plots were turned over to the collective. After the Zhengzhou Conference in 1959,[a] some 300 mu of fields were set aside as private plots of the peasants. However, these spring distributed fields were turned over to the collective again in the autumn, and the grains produced in these fields were also turned over to the collective (though the peasants were paid at the market price). Later on, even the small plots of land by the side of houses, roads, ponds, etc., which had been retained by the peasants were turned, one after another, into vegetable gardens for the [collective] canteens.

---

a) An enlarged meeting of the Politburo that convened from late February to March 10, 1959 (usually called the "Second Zhengzhou Conference"). — Eds.

This spring, after the promulgation of the "Sixty Points" concerning the work in the rural areas,[a] 726 mu of land were redis-
tributed to the peasants as private plots, less than 8 li per person.
Only 120 mu of the private plots, less than one fourth of that in the
period of the advanced agricultural producers' cooperatives, are
on large pieces of land, which are 0.5 percent of the total cultivated land. According to the cadres of the communes and brigades,
it is obvious that the present private plots can hardly meet the
various needs of the peasants. The peasants, instead of having
smaller private plots than during the period of advanced agricultural cooperatives, should have somewhat larger ones.

In the discussions, the cadres of communes and brigades pointed
out the following advantages of letting the peasants cultivate more
private plots:

1. More grain will be available. Owing to the shortage of grain,
most peasants eat gruel four times a day. Such a situation
should not last long. The grain portion in the suburbs of Shanghai
is already bigger than that in other areas, so an increase is impossible in the near future. Therefore, to give the peasants more
private plots to grow grain, melons, and vegetables is the main
method at present to add additional grain to their portions.

2. It will help pig breeding and manure collecting. Fertilizer
plays a very important role in increasing grain production. More
fertilizer comes mainly from raising more pigs and growing more
green manure crops. Nowadays, one cannot rely on bean cakes and
bran supplied by other areas to raise pigs. Bran from processing
one's own portion of grain is not enough. So it is necessary to
grow some grain for feed on private plots.

3. Peasants will be able to grow vegetables for their own consumption. The vegetables consumed by Xiaozheng used to be supplied by other areas. Now, only a small proportion is available.
The peasants have to grow vegetables on private plots for their
own consumption.

4. Peasants will earn some pocket money. At present, the peasants have to borrow money from the production teams in case of
need, and they "have a harder time than a young daughter-in-law
in front of the matriarch." With private plots at their disposal,
they can grow something for sale. They can also raise chickens

---

a) See Note c) p. 144 above. — Eds.

and ducks and sell eggs for money. It will save the cadres a lot of
trouble when peasants have some money on hand.

5. Bamboo gardens could be resumed and enlarged. Because
there were not enough private plots, some peasants chopped down
bamboo to clear the land to grow grain and vegetables. Consequently, there are now far fewer bamboo gardens than before Liberation. This is by no means advisable. As timber is now in short
supply, bamboo has more uses. Especially, there should be no
shortage of bamboo for weeding rakes and the handles of harrows
which need to be replenished every year. It is not easy to buy
bamboo from other areas. Therefore, peasants should have some
private plots to restore and enlarge bamboo gardens, and they
should also grow more bamboo around their houses.

The cadres of the communes and brigades, on the one hand,
deemed it necessary to give the peasants more private plots, but
on the other hand, they still had all kinds of worries in this regard.
They mainly worried that the state grain requisition quotas might
not be fulfilled owing to the reduction of land under collective cultivation. They also worried that the commune members might only
care about their private plots and not participate actively in collective production. After discussion, they came to realize that
these were unnecessary worries. The reasons are that peasants
can do a very good job on private plots and obtain a higher per unit
output than the production teams. With some increase in private
plots, the peasants could obtain some supplement to their grain
ration and somewhat improve their livelihood. Furthermore, the
enthusiasm of the peasants for collective production is likely to be
boosted as a result of implementing a series of measures, such as
making production contracts for fixed outputs, rewarding those who
have overfulfilled the production target, and generally distributing
more to those who have contributed more. With the enhancement
of the peasants' enthusiasm, instead of hindering collective production, the distribution of some private plots for the peasants to
work on will help promote collective production and, with the development of production, the state purchase quotas will be fulfilled
more easily.

The cadres of Xiaozheng Commune suggested in the discussion that the size of private plots be increased to 6 percent of
the total cultivated land (the Shanghai Municipal Party Committee has made the decision recently to increase it to 7 percent).
Of these private plots, only 3.5 percent are on large pieces of

land. Another 700 <u>mu</u> of land are to be distributed to reach
this target. As there are 374 <u>mu</u> of land growing feed for the
collective pig farms and vegetables for canteens which can be
distributed to the commune members, actually only another
326 <u>mu</u> of land will be enough. This is not a very large
amount.

20

TALK AT THE FORUM ON COAL WORK
(October 1961)

Basically, the work of the Ministry of Coal is good. Coal production has increased a great deal in the last three years. The coal production of the mines directly under the Ministry increased from 90 million tons in 1957 to 200 million tons in 1960. The increase of coal production played an important part in economic development. The great increase of coal production in the last three years is due to: old mines brought their potential into full play, this made up more than half of increased production; there were relatively more new mines put into production, this made up one-third of increased production; some "satellite mines" also were opened, and they made up one-tenth of increased production. In these three years, the level of mechanization improved to a certain extent, technical innovation had a certain effect, and workers were very full of vigor. All of these played an important role in increasing coal production. However, quite a large amount of coal was mined by improper methods and this had several consequences. We should notice that average daily coal production decreased from 630 thousand tons in the second half of last year to 520 thousand tons in the first half of this year, and it has now decreased to 440 thousand tons. The basic cause of the decrease in coal production is that the production target is too high and the scale of capital construction is too large. As a result mining is uncontrolled, equipment is unrepaired, part of the equipment is just barely working, and the supply of materials and equipment is insufficient. Meanwhile, the living standard of workers has declined and this affects their health and production initiative and causes an increase in the mobility of production workers. Chaotic management, poor ideological work, bad styles of cadres and other factors also directly cause coal production to decrease.

There are positive experiences as well as negative experiences in coal work. To sum up well these experiences is good for improving our future work.

I will next talk on several issues.

I. THE ISSUE OF THE PLAN TARGET AND MATERIAL SUPPLY

We should decide the plan target according to the conditions of each aspect. The size of the capacity should determine the target; it cannot be set according to our subjective will. The socialist economy is planned, which means to be in proportion. It must be proportional not only in the present year, but also for the next five years or even twenty or thirty years from now.

In order to be in proportion, the first thing is accounting. We should calculate separately and clearly how much major machinery and equipment, general equipment, subsidiary materials and the three kinds of goods and materials are necessary for production and capital construction.

The second is to determine plans based on the results of accounting. The target should be consistent with the supply of materials; the amount of work we can handle is determined by the quantity of materials we have, and we must not promise what we cannot deliver.

The third is that the plan targets can be readjusted based on actual conditions. If materials are not sufficient after the target is planned, departments and enterprises can request the comprehensive organs to lower the target.

The planning target and material supply absolutely cannot create a "vicious circle" within the links of the coal industry departments or within the coal industry and other departments. If there is a gap and the target is raised again, the gap will be bigger and bigger; if we cut it down, the gap will be smaller and smaller. It will stop reducing when it reduces to a certain extent, and it will develop forward according to the condition of proportion.

In the past few years, the target was too high and there was too little material, production depended on past reserves, and there were not complete sets for capital construction. The present problem is that the scale is still too large and we have not made up our minds to cut down.

Even if the target is lowered but more things are produced it will not matter. If there really are more things in the second half of the year, we can revise the original target.

II. THE ISSUE OF CAPITAL CONSTRUCTION

Construction scale. Without counting in increasing potential and innovation of original mines, we need to build new mines that annually produce 20 million tons in order to raise coal production 20 million tons. Thus the construction scale needs to be 80 million tons. During the years of the First-Five Year Plan, coal mining capacity in mines under the Ministry of Coal increased at an annual rate of ten million tons and in the first three years of the Second-Five Year Plan the capacity increased by an average annual rate of 26.9 million tons. At one time mine construction relied on foreign machinery and equipment; later we manufactured it by ourselves, but not in complete sets. Now we should completely rely on domestically produced machinery and equipment and strive to produce complete sets. We should clearly calculate the quantity of complete sets of machinery and equipment we can produce every year.

Construction standard. We must have appropriate investment, materials, and machinery and equipment when we decide the construction scale. Of course, it is not good if the standard is too high and it causes waste. The result will be even worse, however, if the standard is too low: we will not have normal production after construction. If we engage in so-called simplified investment and afterward carry out repair and form complete sets not only will production not go up, but also we will use more material and spend more money.

Time of construction. The time of construction should not be planned too tight. We cannot hope to be too fast, since we are now producing equipment by ourselves and each profession and field must form complete sets. It is comparatively realistic to estimate that it will take four or three and a half years to complete building a large-sized mine. In the last three years large amounts of machinery and equipment were in incomplete sets, and much more work will be required to change this situation. There is a problem of complete sets of machinery and equipment, and there is also a problem of complete sets of materials.

Proportion of large, medium and small-scale mines. In regard to the construction of large, medium and small-scale mines and how much each takes, we should not only consider the needs of the state, but more importantly, it should be based on actual conditions. Mines with rich reserves should be built somewhat larger if it is

possible. However, we should also see the technical condition as
mainly the capacity for manufacturing mechanical equipment
domestically. We should build mines somewhat smaller if we are
not able to build large ones. In addition, we should also consider
the production environment of workers under mines. We should
do our best to increase the level of mechanization and safety and
to use fewer people.

Industrial distribution. Now the north is actually responsible
for the coal supply of the whole country so investment should
be somewhat more. The southern areas are new, therefore production cannot start without investment. Now we all say that it is
not economical to transport northern coal to the south. There are
really places with coal resources in the south, and we should provide some investment to build new bases. Of course, it is best
to build the south and the north together, but we do not have that
much investment. In the end, should we build the south first or the
north first? We can get the area balanced one or two years earlier
if we forget the north and build southern bases, but the speed of
overall industrial development will decrease since the coal production will not go up in these years. Thus we must still invest more
in the north and transport northern coal to the south for a certain
period of time. We will build the bases in the south when we have
greater capacity.

Generally speaking, industrial construction in the northeast
should not be expanded further and they should be self-sufficient
in coal. The northwest needs 23 million tons of coal every year,
but it only produces 12 million tons. The newly built industrial
base in Lanzhou will meet a great difficulty without coal so we
should solve that problem.

III. THE ISSUE OF THE SYSTEM OF WAGES AND
INCENTIVES AND THE LIVELIHOOD OF THE WORKERS

The Jingxi Mine practices an hourly wage system and provides
bonuses based on fixed quotas. This is actually a piece rate wage.
Some places practice a piece rate wage system in form, but the
wage becomes average after many things are counted in, so actually it becomes payment by the hour. It seems that basically the
piece rate wage system is practiced for excavating workers since
it is advantageous for developing their initiative. We should eliminate the problems that existed before 1957 and the equalitarianism
that has existed in recent years.

There are two forms of incentive grain. One is "to reduce people but not grain," the other is to distribute 40 percent of the incentive grain. We should select one of the two. The mining bureaus can decide by themselves whether or not to adopt the incentive method of "reducing people but not grain." In addition, after an enterprise fulfills the planned task, "one more jin of grain for one more ton of coal" is also a good method. It is very worthwhile to have 20 million jin of grain for 20 million tons of coal, but I am just afraid that it cannot be done.

Now we can only solve three problems related to the livelihood of the workers: (1) Each month one jin of vegetable oil for each person. For those who do not have enough oil, substitute meat, eggs and fish. (2) In regard to the grain rations, vegetables and firewood that are necessary for family members of workers, one way is to mobilize family members of workers to join production and work, the other way is to let production teams (the teams with surplus grain and the self-sufficient teams) take care of them in order to ensure the grain ration of family members of workers is not lower than the grain ration of those difficult families with many members but few laborers, but they should pay by themselves. As to those whose families are in the teams lacking grain, the state will provide unified supply. (3) Properly adjust the varieties of grain.

The present cause of worker mobility is: dangerous working conditions, a low living standard, and illnesses of workers and staff. The increase in mobility is mainly due to problems of livelihood. To stabilize mining teams, we should pay attention to: (1) Raising the degree of mechanization of mine construction and the conditions of health and safety. (2) Raising the level of wages and giving more consideration to living conditions in order to make mining attractive and peasants willing to come. (3) A certain proportion of family members should live at the mines and for those who do not live at mines should be given home leave vacation. (4) Recruit children of miners to work at mines.

IV. THE ISSUE OF TECHNICAL PERSONNEL

Now technical personnel basically consist of three groups of people: one is the old technical personnel; another is those who just recently graduated from colleges and secondary technical schools; the third is those promoted from workers. Now old technical personnel are the important component and we cannot work without them. These people studied engineering and they are different from those who studied law and politics and planned to be officials. They hope that industry will save the country and they want our country to be good.

To bring to bear the initiative of technical personnel, especially old technical personnel: (1) We should let technical personnel have position as well as authority. We should handle well the relations of the leadership of the Party committee, the launching of mass movements, the authority of professional departments, and so on. We should reestablish the production command system, which should not have been disrupted but was disrupted. (2) We should carry out correct intellectual policies. Among these one important question is that we should have a proper view of present and past family class status and the personal class status of technical personnel. The organization departments should give a clear provision of the correct view on family class status, personal class status, historical questions and social relations of technical personnel who came from the old society. (3) We should have an enthusiastic attitude to help old intellectuals to change and improve and clean off bourgeois ideology gradually.

V. THE ISSUE OF THE ENTERPRISE
   MANAGEMENT SYSTEM

In order to carry out the system of factory manager responsibility under the leadership of the Party committee, on one hand, we should perfect the system of production, administration and command, assign and distribute more capable cadres to take charge of leading administrative positions at each level, strengthen technical offices, and establish a strict system of responsibility. Now the administrative leaders of many enterprises are too weak, and the system of factory manager responsibility under the leadership of the Party committee cannot be carried out if we do not have more capable cadres. The Party committee should concentrate on dealing with important issues and manage the Party well. On the other hand, we should remove all shortcomings in the work of the Party committee leadership, such as undertaking administrative affairs, little establishment but much abolishment of regulations and rules, emphasizing politics in command without carrying out material incentives, emphasizing settling so-called political accounts without working out economic accounts, not respecting scientific and technical personnel, and so on.

An enterprise can have a mass movement when it is necessary. However, the mass movement must be advantageous for strengthening the management of the enterprise and cannot weaken enterprise management. Mass movements should be under the unfied leadership of the Party and there should be serious investigation and study before they are gradually spread. Also, we must fully develop democracy and we cannot issue arbitrary orders.

We cannot promote production without a system of regulations. We should systematically restore the systems of regulations that should not have been abolished but that were abolished. We should get rid of shortcomings and retain the good features of the past system of regulations.

21

HOW WE CAN ACHIEVE A SOMEWHAT MORE COMPREHENSIVE UNDERSTANDING
(February 1962)*

At this enlarged Central Work Conference,[a] Shaanxi comrades who participated in the conference convened large meetings and small meetings, and they all went very well. What was good was that higher levels and lower levels communicated with each other. On the one hand, comrades from district and county Party committees presented their opinions to the provincial committee, and on the other hand, comrades in charge of the provincial Party committee made self-criticisms twice. Criticism and self-criticism are an essential condition for communication between higher and lower levels. We can unite only if we have communication, and we can centralize only if we have democracy.

In recent years, our internal Party life has not been normal. "He just tells one-third when he meets people, thus he cannot give his whole heart to people" is a very dangerous situation. One cannot avoid saying wrong things, and it is impossible not to say anything wrong. Within the Party, we are not afraid of anybody saying something wrong, but we are afraid of no one talking. There are some "clever people" whose greetings are simply "Aha, today's weather ..." when they see people. They do not mention short-comings and mistakes even if they see them. If it goes like this, our revolutionary course will not succeed but will definitely fail.

This enlarged conference has won a very great victory. Do not underestimate it. As long as we dare to develop criticism and self-criticism, and insist on truth and correct mistakes, our Communist Party will be invincible anywhere in the world.

---

*This is a part of a speech by Comrade Chen Yun at the large group meeting of Shaanxi Province at the enlarged Central Work Conference.

a) A conference attended by seven thousand cadres that convened at Beidaihe from mid-January to early February 1962. — Eds.

It is not enough to rely only on a few leading cadres to discover problems, shortcomings, and mistakes in our work. We must develop democracy and mobilize the vast numbers of the masses and cadres to give opinions on our work. We can arouse people's initiative and really do well in our work only if we honestly correct shortcomings and mistakes in our work according to people's opinions.

The leading cadres especially should listen to negative opinions. Anyone dares to voice the same opinions. Usually, owing to the closed-mindedness of leaders, it is not easy to hear different opinions, and people dare not speak. Therefore, we must be open-minded and listen more to different opinions. We should also see that things are very complex, so we must listen to each different opinion and collect them together through careful and detailed analysis, in order to arrive at a comparatively comprehensive and correct understanding. There are many different ways to engage in investigation and study. To go to exchange opinions with people who have different views is one important way. We Communists should strengthen self-cultivation and should cultivate the good practice of patiently listening to different opinions.

What methods shall we use in order to make us understand more correctly? I will suggest the following several methods; you comrades can try them and see if they work.

Comprehensiveness. In seeing problems, it is always easy to be partial. For example, there is a teacup on the table. The person across the table can see its picture but not its handle, and the person on this side can see its handle but not its picture. The two only see one of the two sides of the cup and they are one-sided, so neither of them is comprehensive. If these two persons "exchange" their views, they are comprehensive. We often say seek truth from facts. Facts means to understand the factual situation clearly; to seek truth means to put forth correct policies based on the results acquired in such studies.

In fighting a war, if we judge the situation of the enemy incorrectly, we will lose the war. It is the same as a doctor seeing a patient. He cannot cure the patient, or can even kill him, if he misjudges the patient's condition. What method shall we use to understand the situation clearly? One method is to exchange opinions with other people more. This will make the original one-sided view gradually become comprehensive; the original vague objects will gradually become clear; the original different opinions on issues will gradually become unified. What should we do if there is no opposite opinion? I think that we can make assumptions and consider the problem from the opposite aspect and each side and study the possibilities of each different condition. This will make our understanding more comprehensive. We make mistakes just because we do not handle affairs according to objective facts. However, it is not true that people who make mistakes do not have facts at all, they just take one-sidedness as comprehensive. When the leading organs make policies, they spend 90 percent of their time in investigation and study work. It is enough to spend less than 10 percent of the time for final discussions and decisions.

Comparison. We should compare different kinds of plans when we study problems, make policies, and decide plans. We should not only compare with the present, but also compare with the past and compare with things abroad. Such many-sided comparisons can make things clear and make judgements more accurate. It is only good, not bad, for us to compare more.

Repetition. We should not decide right after we compare. We need to consider repeatedly. Decisions on some issues seem to be correct at one time, but after a while we might find out that they are not correct or that they are not completely correct. Therefore, we should not make decisions rashly, and we should leave time for consideration. We had better reconsider things after a while, and then decide. When Chairman Mao and I work together, he also does not decide some issues right away. When you discuss matters with him he says oh, but that does not mean that he agrees with your opinion.

The provincial Party committee made self-criticism twice at your meeting. Were their self-criticisms good enough? I have not worked in Shaanxi and do not know the situation very well, so you should judge whether they were good enough. However, I think that we should take a welcoming attitude toward the self-criticism of the provincial Party committee, because it is better to make a self-criticism than not to make one. All of you can give opinions to the provincial Party committee, and you can give any kind of opinion. However, you should allow the provincial Party committee to have some time for consideration, and some problems can be discussed in the future. The reason is that there were many questions raised that were unexpected. Also we have not had enough time, so we have not had a chance to make a thorough study. In addition, only half of the leaders of the provincial Party committee are here so we cannot discuss and decide many issues.

Someone said that we can raise any opinion because we are now in Beijing but it probably will not work back home. I do not really think this is so. Why? Because this is the general trend. Starting from this meeting, from now on the door of criticism will be totally open and it should be opened more and more. Comrade Shaoqi[a] said in his report that we should seriously carry out democratic centralism and make criticisms and self-criticisms. This is not a new question. Developing democracy and making frequent criticisms and self-criticisms are all old traditions in our Party. We just lost this tradition in recent years and now we will reestablish it. Comrades! If the Communist Party does not engage in self-criticism and all of us just say good day, I do not think people will join the revolution; nor will they respect Communist Party members of that kind. Certainly I cannot guarantee that all the leaders are open-minded and will accept criticism, but after all, a few people cannot block the way. Some comrades say that I still need to think. We should allow the others to think. Since our democratic life within the Party has not been normal in recent years, it is not strange that some people doubt whether we can really develop democracy.

Who is responsible for the shortcomings, mistakes, and faults of the work in recent years? The Center and the provincial Party committees each have their own responsibility, but the Center is primarily responsible. The provincial Party committee also has its own responsibility, and lower down, the district Party committees have their own responsibilities, and the county Party committees have their own responsibilities. We all should draw on the experiences and lessons and do work in the future well.

---

a) Liu Shaoqi, Chairman of the People's Republic after Mao stepped down in 1959. — Eds.

22

THE CURRENT FINANCIAL AND ECONOMIC SITUATION AND SOME METHODS FOR OVERCOMING DIFFICULTIES
(February 1962)*

Today I shall talk about present financial and economic conditions and certain measures to overcome difficulties.

At the present time there exist difficulties in the fields of finance and economics. Of course, we have advantageous conditions
that will allow us to overcome the difficulties and improve the
situation, but we should recognize that the situation is difficult.

We are unanimous in the opinion that difficulties exist. Views
among high-level cadres are not unanimous with regard to the degree of difficulty and the speed for overcoming difficulty. I think
this kind of disagreement is normal and inevitable. Do not cover
up this kind of disagreement. In the great change of recent years,
people naturally have different views on the situation. Time and
the proof of facts are needed to get unanimity of understanding. I
believe that our understanding will come together through the
process of practice. It is a good thing rather than a bad thing to
raise different opinions and to discuss them. It is advantageous
to move our understanding toward unanimity. It is very important
that the views of high-level cadres differ. We can keep the opinions that are different after discussion, and we can consider them
again. To maintain different opinions is allowed.

I will talk about five aspects of present financial and economic
difficulties.

1. Agricultural production decreased greatly in recent years.
Compared with the output of 1957, grain output in 1961 decreased
approximately by more than 80 billion jin.a Cotton, other eco-

---

*This is a speech by Comrade Chen Yun at a meeting of Party members of
the Ministries and Commissions of the State Council.

a) Official data released in 1981 showed the decline was 95.09 billion jin.
Since Chen was speaking in early 1962 his assessment of the change in the harvest compared to 1957 was based on an estimate of 1961 output. — Eds.

nomic crops, and livestock products also decreased a great deal.
There is not enough grain to eat. We imported more than 10 billion jin of grain last year, and we still need to import 8 billion jin
of grain this year. We lack oil in our stomachs and we lack clothes
to wear. This result is caused directly by the decline in agricultural production.

Is the difficulty in agriculture large or small? There are different estimates. Recently, I heard some comrades say that in
some villages the peasants eat very well, there are a great many
chickens and ducks, and so on. That kind of village exists, but is
a tiny minority. It is not like that in most areas of the whole country; peasants do not have enough grain to eat.

Is the speed of agricultural recovery fast or slow? There are
also different estimates. In the first half of last year, I expected
that we could increase grain output by 20 billion jin annually for the next
several years. In order to understand clearly the prospects for
increased production we asked the Agriculture and Forestry Office
of the State Council and several other units to organize a small
group to study the basic conditions of agricultural production, such
as land, farm animals, fertilizers, farm tools, seed, water conservancy, machinery, the possibility of industry supporting agriculture in the next few years, and so on. They will examine
the difference between present conditions and those of the past,
to see what conditions are better than in the past and what
are not as good as in the past. I cannot answer these questions today. However, we can make estimates: balancing the good
conditions against bad conditions, I fear we cannot say that present
conditions are better than those of the First Five-Year Plan period.

How much did grain output increase on average every year during
the period of the First Five-Year Plan? According to the material in "The Handbook of Agricultural Economics Materials"
[Nongye jingji ciliao shouce] published by the Planning Bureau in
1959, compared to the previous year, grain output increased 5 billion jin in 1953, 7.1 billion jin in 1954, 28.7 billion jin in 1955,
15.4 billion jin in 1956, and 5 billion jin in 1957. In five years
grain output cumulatively increased 61.2 billion jin; the average
annual increase was 12.2 billion jin. If there is "water" in the
grain output announced for 1957, then the average annual increase
in production is not even this much.

Compared with the period of the First-Five Year Plan, water
conservancy and machinery have improved, irrigated area has in-

creased, flood control capacity has been strengthened, irrigation and drainage equipment have increased, and also tractors and other agricultural machinery have increased. Meanwhile, the industrial base has been enlarged, and the possibility of supporting agriculture has increased compared to the past. This is one aspect. In the other aspect, the conditions of land, farm animals, fertilizer, farm tools, and seed are worse than before. Take land as an example. In the last four years the capital construction for water conservancy, industry, and transportation occupied about 200 million mu of cultivated land, and vegetable land enlarged by 50 million mu, while newly cultivated wasteland was only 150 million mu. Balancing the increase and decrease, the land for grain and other crops was reduced about 100 million mu. It is an important matter that the 1.6 billion mu of cultivated land in the whole country has been reduced by 100 million mu. Furthermore, the land we lost in these years was mostly high-yield good land, while the increase in cultivated land was mostly in outlying areas such as Heilongjiang, Xinjiang, and Nei Monggol, and therefore its yield is relatively low. There are fewer farm animals and pigs than before, a part of our seeds have degenerated, and crop rotations are out of sync in some places. Based on the general situation, the speed might be faster in the recovery period, but we should also see how conditions develop. Generally, good and bad conditions are balanced, and the present condition is not as good as that of the past. This is a reliable judgment. We need one year to see how fast agricultural recovery can be. We cannot make a judgment at the present time. Practice will show whether or not it can be a little faster after one year.

The starting point of our work should be: strive to be fast and prepare to be slow. We should do anything that is advantageous for increasing agricultural production, do as much as possible. However, we should also consider that it might still be slow even if we do all the work, so we should prepare to be slow. Chairman Mao has said: "It is completely necessary to prepare for the worst possibility, but this is not to give up the good possibility; instead, this is the very condition of striving for the good possibility and transforming it into reality."* We also should arrange agricultural plans according to this view in the future.

* "The Conclusion About Repulsing the Second Anti-Communist High-Tide," Selected Works of Mao Zedong, Vol. II, p. 784.

The steps we use in our financial and economic work will differ depending on agricultural output, primarily the speed of recovery of grain production. For instance, how much grain can be procured every year? Should we import grain? Should the speed of recovery of economic crops and pigs be faster? How much can we invest annually in the next few years and how large should the scale of capital construction be? Should we reduce the urban population and by how much? These issues need to be decided on the basis of agriculture, primarily the rate of increase of grain production. For capital construction, if we want to increase investment, in addition to increasing producer goods, we must appropriately increase grain and other consumer goods. The speed of recovery of agricultural production also directly affects the speed of recovery of industrial production. It is very necessary that leaders of central ministries and commissions all come to study somewhat the agricultural problem. The agricultural problem is a big issue for the whole country and it is related to the work of each Ministry and Commission. This problem should be studied not only by the ministries of agriculture, and forestry, and water conservancy, the industrial and transportation ministries, the ministries of Finance and Commerce, but also the ministries of culture, education, politics and law, and foreign affairs. We are people who undertake revolution and socialism. We must be concerned about such big issues that affect more than 600 million people in the whole country and that affect the whole socialist construction.

2. The scale of capital construction that has been started exceeds the national financial and materials capacity and cannot be balanced with the present level of production in industry and agriculture. There are different opinions in respect to this matter. Some people say that the construction scale of these years is appropriate and that the problems are just owing to disasters. Some other people also say that it is agriculture that obstructs us; otherwise it would be just right. According to their views, it seems that the industry is hurt by agriculture and industry itself does not have a problem. I do not think so. Instead, it is because the scale of capital construction is too large, and neither agriculture nor industry take this burden.

Such a big construction scale not only cannot be supported when agriculture suffers disasters, but it cannot be maintained even during normal harvest years. Suppose that grain production in 1961 did not decrease that much and it had been 370 billion jin as

in a normal harvest year?[a] Could we maintain such a big construction scale? I do not think we can.

We have experienced grain shortages four times since the founding of the People's Republic. Three times were owing to excessive growth of the urban population. The first time was in 1953,
namely the first year of construction of the First Five-Year Plan.
The increase in workers and staff was too great and, as a result,
we had to implement the state unified grain procurement. The
second time was in the spring of 1955. Because we overprocured
grain in 1954, shortages appeared, and this made "every family
talk about state unified procurement and sale." The Center and
Chairman Mao criticized that mistake in grain work. The third
time was in 1957. At that time, the grain shortage did not come
to the surface, but the volume of grain procurement that year could
not meet the needs and we had to take out 6 billion odd jin from
storage. This shows that at that time it was already difficult for
agriculture to maintain that large a scale of industrial construction.
The fourth time was from 1959 to 1961. Production decreased
but we requested much and procured even more.

The great development of industrial construction in the last few
years was based on the mistaken estimate that 700 billion jin of
grain and 70 million dan of cotton were produced in 1958. At that
time we thought that grain production had already made a breakthrough, so we could greatly encourage industry and recruit a large
number of workers and staff. According to past experience, even
if we return to an annual production of 370 billion jin of grain in
the next few years, it will still not suit the present scale of construction.

It is not only agriculture that cannot sustain the burden of the
scale of construction that has already been started; the scale also
exceeds the industrial base. The present condition in industry is
that workers are increasing too fast, while output value is not increasing much; industrial products cannot meet the needs from
every field in terms of volume, quality, variety, and standard.
Therefore, capital construction items have to be cut down group by
group, and semifinished goods have to be stockpiled in large
amounts.

How did the scale of construction become so spread out in recent

a) Actual 1961 production was 295 billion jin, according to official data released in 1981. — Eds.

years? Besides our mistaken thought that grain production had
achieved a breakthrough in 1958, it was also based on the premise
that steel production could quickly reach 50 or 60 million tons. We
all had no experience, and affairs became overextended, and workers were overrecruited. That meant the scale of construction was
not suited to the industrial base.

3. Too much paper money was issued, causing inflation. Though
the present inflation is radically different from the hyperinflation
before the Guomindang collapsed, it is still a kind of inflation. Is
it really true? Is it being taken too seriously? There might be
different views. In recent years we took out commercial reserves,
raised prices, used very large amounts of gold, silver, and foreign
exchange reserves, and we incurred a foreign trade deficit and in
addition issued 6 to 7 billion yuan in currency order to make up the
financial deficit. These are all expressions of inflation. The reason is very simple: on the one hand, much paper money was issued;
on the other hand, the production of agriculture and industry declined
and the state held few commodities, so the two cannot be balanced.

What will the tendency of inflation be? According to the present
condition, it cannot be stopped before we adopt strong measures.
We must firmly change the tendency of inflation. Otherwise, it
will not be advantageous to the recovery of production in industry
and agriculture, the stability of the market, and the development of
economic construction.

4. Since so much money from the cities moved into the countryside, some peasants have a great quantity of cash in their hands
and speculation is developing. In regard to this, there are also different opinions among our high-level cadres. The present condition
is that prices of both subsidiary products managed by peasants and
the three materials produced both by collectives and by individuals
have increased greatly. For the last year or so in the free markets
peasants sold goods and materials that are equal to 1 billion yuan
at normal prices, but that exchanged for about 3 billion yuan of
paper money. Now there are quite few peasants who hold a considerable quantity of currency and the tendency of urban money to
move into countryside still has not been stopped; it will still continue for a while. The cause is that the state did not distribute
enough goods to meet demand in cities. We let communes and
peasants develop agricultural subsidiary products, so it will not
work if we do not allow them to sell; nor will it work if we procure
too much. Because urban people still need to eat, prices will rise;

others will buy even if you do not buy. In the past, we supplied
more than 3 billion jin of pork to cities, but now it is less than 1
billion jin. Can it soon return back to more than 3 billion jin?
Impossible. The tendency of urban money moving into the countryside in large quantities can be stopped only when the state holds
a large quantity of goods and materials and the urban supply is
guaranteed.

Under the circumstance of few goods and materials and much
money, quite serious speculation appeared. We should distinguish
two kinds of people: one is peasants. They sell pork, eggs, and
other products they have produced themselves in the free market
where prices are high and earn some extra money. The other kind
is speculators. They make a lot of money by buying in and selling
out. As to the number of people, the former is the majority but
there are indeed quite a few speculators. Comrade Xiannian[a] has
just said that even if a bicycle was priced at 650 yuan, there are
still people who would rush to purchase it. We must take effective
measures to deal with speculators.

A great amount of money moves into the countryside, but the
state does not have enough industrial products to withdraw that
money from circulation. The collective producers sold a certain
amount of agricultural subsidiary products to the state, but they
cannot get industrial products back with equivalent value. According to what comrades of the Ministry of Commerce say, for each
100 yuan of agricultural products sold by peasants, we can only
provide them with 60-odd yuan of commodities, or only 70 to 80
yuan if we add haircutting, movies, and other servies. There is
still a difference of 20 to 30 yuan. It is very difficult to sustain
this only by political mobilization, without equivalent industrial
products to supply the countryside and without exchange of equal
value. To a certain extent, the free market is advantageous for
promoting production. However, if we do not find a way to change
back the money that peasants earned by selling high priced agricultural products, there will be more and more money in peasants'
hands, and there will be a danger that peasants will not like to continue to sell agricultural products.

5. The living standard of urban people has declined. There
isn't enough to eat, wear, and use. Prices rise, and the real wage
has decreased very much. There is no disagreement on this point.

_____
a) Li Xiannian, Minister of Finance. — Eds.

I have talked about above five difficulties among which the first and second are the basic ones. The other three are derived from the first two.

Are conditions advantageous for overcoming these difficulties? They certainly are. I will point out the following main points:

1. The general line of socialist construction in practice has already achieved a certain success. Under the leadership of the Party Center and Chairman Mao, we have already provided some specific policies in order to realize the general line. After the "Twelve Articles"[a] on the improvement of rural work and the "Sixty Articles"[b] on rural people's communes were carried out, the initiative of peasants was obviously improved and rural people's communes were further consolidated. The Center's order on re-adjusting industry and the "Seventy Articles"[c] on industrial enterprises also have started to produce results. After the recent convening of the enlarged Central Work Conference, the leading cadres above county-level of the whole Party greatly heightened their ideological consciousness, and work in all fields will make marked progress.

2. Doubtless the production of grain, poultry, and pigs is recovering. How fast is the recovery? We still need to observe some more. It still is difficult to determine whether the output of economic crops can recover quickly to a certain level of output. Because there is not enough grain to eat, peasants do not like to grow large amounts of economic crops.

3. The expansion of industrial and communications capacity in recent years in some cases will contribute to the economic recovery. That is, our strength for overcoming difficulties is greater than it was in the past.

4. People will cooperate with our Party during the period of overcoming difficulties and restoring the economy. Doubtlessly, people will cooperate with us as long as we clearly explain the existing difficulties and the methods for overcoming them. Of course, we cannot say that there will be no minor disturbances at all. Generally speaking, however, people will surmount the difficulties with our Party. This point is very important. We should be confident. People clearly understand the historic brave struggle that

---

a) See Note b), p. 144 above. — Eds.

b) See Note c), p. 144 above. — Eds.

c) This refers to the Seventy Articles on Industry, originally drafted by Bo Yibo and disseminated in September 1961. — Eds.

our Party carried out for dozens of years and the achievements of socialist construction that we gained in the more than ten years since the founding of the People's Republic. They probably have complaints with regard to some issues, but they still think that, compared to the old society, we are better. Comparing the mistakes we have made and the damage we created with our good points, including the revolutionary victory and the achievements of construction, certainly our good things are more numerous. With regard to this, people will make a fair judgement. Our present difficulties generally were produced by the mistakes made by good men with good hearts. The men are good and their hearts are good, but we just made mistakes. People will excuse us after we explain clearly, correct mistakes, and do our work well.

5. The Party's leading cadres have gained both positive and negative experiences. This point is also very important. The cadres' experiences are advantageous to overcoming difficulties and to economic recovery and are also good for future work.

The above five points are the favorable conditions that I have thought about. There might be others. What I have said is not comprehensive, so I ask all of you to study it.

In general, we have favorable conditions for overcoming difficulties, but the present difficulties are quite serious. We should point this out to the cadres at the levels of central ministries and the provinces, cities, and autonomous regions. It is inevitable, as well as permissible, to have different understandings. It will be good for overcoming the difficulties if we exchange opinions with each other and then unify our understanding. Should each Central Ministry and Commission in finance and economics raise these questions and let everybody express different opinions among the cadres at the level of ministry and department office? I think we should do so. Because there actually exist different opinions on these questions among the ministries and commissions and within them. It is good for exposing the shortcomings and improving our work if we exchange opinions with each other and listen to different opinions. The situation of "only telling one-third of one's opinions" and hesitating to speak out still exists. If speaking with a "bureaucratic tone" and no heart-to-heart talks continues, the revolution will fail. We revolutionaries should speak the truth. We should raise questions and express opinions once we have them and discuss them seriously.

Now I will talk about certain measures to overcome difficulties.

According to the situation mentioned above, what measures should we use to overcome difficulties in financial and economic work? I will give six opinions.

First, divide the ten-year plan into two stages. The first stage is a recovery stage and the second stage is a development stage.

Both agriculture and industry need a period of recovery. Recovery of agriculture requires about three to five years. In these three to five years industry also can only develop slowly; it can only readjust and recover. How many years are required for the recovery stage? In my personal opinion it requires about five years, starting from 1960. I ask you to consider whether it should be five years and finally let the Center decide.

Of course, during the recovery stage, there might be some development in certain fields. We all know that during the three-year recovery period after the founding of the People's Republic, annual production of steel not only recovered to more than 900 thousand tons, but also developed to 1.3 million tons. In general, however, the first stage of the ten-year plan should be mainly recovery. The task of this period is to overcome difficulties, restore agriculture and industry and strive for the radical improvement of the financial and economic situation. The recovery is for development. We will have development in the second stage only if we have recovery in the first stage.

If we divide the ten-year plan clearly into two stages and specify the first stage as one of recovery, it will have a very positive effect on the proper arrangement of the work of each of the finance and economics ministries. If that is not done and we generally ask people to carry out the ten-year plan, we will want to develop as well as cutting down, to enlarge the scale as well as having "better troops and simpler administration," and we will be trapped in these contradictions. Having divided the process into two stages, we can first cut down and then increase the target of capital construction and certain heavy industrial products, and the task will be clearer.

We should recognize that economic conditions during the recovery stage are very difficult. As Comrade Shaoqi[a] said, it is similar to extraordinary times. We should have ways to deal with extraordinary times. There are mainly two ways: one is to have more centralized

a) Liu Shaoqi, Chairman of the PRC since 1959 and Vice-chairman of the CCP. — Eds.

unification; the other is that every step should be firm and steady. Here centralized unification means to centralize and unify the forces after we give localities and enterprises necessary and flexible financial and material resources. The degree of this kind of centralization could exceed that at the beginning of the founding of the People's Republic because the situation now is more complex.

Second, reduce the urban population, "better troops and simpler administration."

This is a radical measure to overcome difficulties. We must do both according to a temporary plan and a long-term plan.

We should reduce the number of workers and staff who are from the countryside as well as some who are from cities. We should make proper arrangements after their numbers are reduced. For example, most textile workers are from cities. Now many textile factories cannot open, so we can only do more ideological work and clearly explain the facts to workers. It is very difficult to reduce the number of workers — it is easy to ask them to come, but it is difficult to ask them to go. But if we do not make reductions now, we will incur continuous financial deficits, the market will be in chaos, and we will be more passive. It is difficult to reduce now, but it will be more difficult to make reductions in the future. Comparing the two, I think it is still better to make reductions earlier.

For people who have families in the countryside, it is difficult to mobilize them to go home. However, it is still much easier than procuring grain from the countryside and supplying them in the cities. Last year, we reduced the urban population by more than 10 million. If these people had continued to stay in the cities they would have eaten more than 4 billion jin of grain. Now it is impossible to procure 4 billion jin additional grain from the peasantry. It is even difficult to procure an additional 1 billion, several thousand million jin. It makes things easier if we let workers who are from the countryside eat at home and eat regularly. All of us must make up our minds to reduce the number of workers; otherwise there will be no way out.

Third, we have to take all the measures to check inflation.

There are probably four measures that I can think of.

1. Strictly control cash and economize cash expenditures. Banks should control money well and must not use money that should not be used. We should resume the bank system of strictly controlling cash, and the degree of strictness should be higher than that in

the period of the First Five-Year Plan.

2. Increase as much as possible the production of daily goods that people need. We should transfer some raw and processed materials from heavy industry to light industry, import some raw materials, increase production of daily goods, and withdraw money from circulation. People have money, so we must make it possible for them to buy things. Only this can make them happy. If not, and if we just raise the prices of commodities, people will call us names.

3. Increase several kinds of high-priced commodities. There should be a few varieties of high-priced commodities that will withdraw much money. Be scattered and make everything high-priced and we will not make much money but instead we will get a bad reputation. If we do not carry this out, how will we be able to reliably withdraw a lot of cash? To increase the number of several kinds of high-priced commodities is primarily for drawing back the money people earn from selling high-priced commodities in the free market. Meanwhile, we can also use it to balance the difference between the volume of commodities supplied and purchasing power. Last year we produced high-priced commodities mainly in the cities, but this time it should be mainly in the countryside. We put high-priced commodities in those places where there is a lot of money. We should use this method first in experimental centers, wait and see the reactions, our steps steady, and popularize it after we are sure about it. To sell high-priced commodities is actually to devalue the currency, and people might have complaints. However, there will not be big problems as long as there is no price rise for means of subsistence. If we do not use this method, the excess money cannot be withdrawn; it will pound the market in many places, and this will be worse.

4. Firmly struggle against speculative activities. For this kind of struggle, there should be three strategies. The first is economic struggle. If you sell me eggs at the market price, then I also will sell you candies at the market price; if you sell high-priced eggs to me, then I will sell you high-priced candies; if you earn extra money, I will find a way to get it back. This means that there should not only be low-price against low-price, but also high-price against high-price; otherwise the method is not perfect. The second is business management. The established supply and marketing cooperatives in the countryside and consumer coopera-

tives in the cities will cooperate to manage the three kinds
of material and part of industrial production. Prices may rise
a little if these things are managed by supply and marketing
cooperatives and consumer cooperatives. But if we should not let
them manage these things, and it falls to the speculators to manage
them, people will lose more. It is better to let supply and marketing cooperatives and consumer cooperatives make profit than to
let speculators make profit. The third is administrative management. We should control the free market through market management, taxing, the price of transportation, etc. We should consider
this work repeatedly. We should have experimental centers and
gain some experience, and then spread it out.

In 1962 and 1963 we must strive to balance finance, credit,
fiscal revenue, and expenditure by every possible means, and check
inflation. We should not keep quiet this year and wait until next
year to check inflation.

Fourth, ensure the minimum susistence of urban residents.

At the present time, there are three measures that we can take
gradually.

The first is to supply 3 jin of soybeans to each person every
month step by step. We can supply less in the summer and in areas
where there are more vegetables. We need 3 billion jin of soybeans every year to apply this method to the urban population of
100 million people. The production of soybeans in our country was
about 19 billion jin before 1958 and has been 12 billion jin in these
last two years. Therefore, it is possible to supply 3 billion jin to
the cities. We should strive to fulfill this within two years. The
first step is to apply this in the large and medium-sized cities the
total population of which is 60-odd million. By using this method,
not only can we ensure urban people's health, but we can also raise
workers' actual wages somewhat. If people have soybeans to eat
or convert to bean curd they will not have to buy or they can buy
less high-priced nonstaple food in the free market. According to
calculations, each person every day needs at least 70 grams of
protein. One jin of grain contains about 45 grams of protein, 1 jin
of vegetable contains 5 grams, and 1 liang of soybeans contains
20 grams. Because we lack meat and egg products, we can use
soybeans to supplement nutrition. This is a relatively reliable
method.

The second is to supply dozens of million pairs of nylon socks

every year. We can say that this is also an important issue. For
families with many children it is a real headache to darn socks.
If we spend U.S.$4 million to import 1 thousand tons of nylon, we
can make 40 million pairs of nylon socks. If we make socks with
nylon bottoms, we can double the output. One pair of socks can
be sold for several yuan and buyers are happy, and the state can
also withdraw several hundred million yuan of currency every
year. This is beneficial for both public and private sides.

The third is to expand high-priced restaurants by using 40 to
50 million yuan worth of delicacies from the mountains and seas
and other high-quality subsidiary food products from all places
in the country, the selling price of which can be raised somewhat. The price of these things should also be high when guest
houses buy them. Thus, we can improve some people's livelihood,
and we can also withdraw much money.

In regard to ensuring the livelihood of urban residents these
are the only three comparatively feasible methods that I can think
of now. We cannot yet write other "checks." It is not very easy
to even carry out these methods.

Fifth, use all possible resources to raise agricultural production.

This is a fundamental plan. According to the present actual
situation, we should grasp the following three things:

The first is that besides increasing grain production, we should
reconsider measures to ensure an increase in economic crop production. Which measures should we take? How large a range
should we ensure? For how many years should these measures be
taken? All of these need to be studied. The present method of
reward for farming economic crops is like "202" mercurochrome.
That has some value, but it cannot solve the problem completely.
If the economic crops do not recover, the state will not have commodities to ensure the supply to cities and the countryside, the
worker-peasant alliance will not be consolidated, and there will
be no real exchange of equal value between the state and peasants.
The state spends 1 yuan to purchase cotton, and after it is spun into
cotton yarn and woven into cloth, the state can sell it for 4 yuan.
If it is processed into knit goods, even more money can be withdrawn. However, in order to encourage peasants to grow cotton,
we must ensure that peasants have enough grain to eat. Peasants now receive only 35 jin of award grain for each 100 jin

of ginned cotton that they sell to the state. The cotton growing peasants cannot get enough food with this method, so they have to convert cotton fields to grain fields. If this continues, not only will cotton production not increase quickly, it will probably decrease continuously. If we supply peasants with 2 jin of grain for each jin of ginned cotton sold, peasants will take the initiative and grow cotton. According to this method, we would have to use 5 billion jin of grain in order to purchase 25 million dan of cotton. The situation of other economic crops is similar. We have to supply adequate grain rations if we want to increase production. Now the state must import grain to supplement rations and we will need to import more grain if we want to ensure economic crops. Also, in the past we considered whether it was better to import grain or to import cotton. The study showed that our commodity supply is inadequate to import cotton and also it was not as worthwhile as importing grain. Importing 1 ton of cotton requires U.S.$700, while importing 1 ton of grain requires only $70. This means that the foreign exchange required to import 1 ton of cotton could be used to import 10 tons of grain, while we could use 10 tons of grain to encourage peasants to grow 5 tons more cotton.

The second is that we should study different methods of increasing production in different grain producing areas. In our country, the main areas of commercial grain production are Heilongjiang, Jilin, Nei Monggol, the central Shaanxi plain, the Changjiang Delta, the Jianghan plain, the Dongting Lake area, the Chengdu basin, the Zhujiang Delta, and so on. These areas have different characteristics. We should find effective methods for increasing production that are suited to the characteristics of these areas. We should supply more chemical fertilizer to the main commercial grain producing areas. According to our calculations, it is more worthwhile to import chemical fertilizer than to import grain. We should import more chemical fertilizer as long as our supplies of foreign exchange are adequate.

The third is to allocate some steel, iron, and wood to produce medium and small farm tools. Now the key point of industry supporting agriculture is not tractors but medium and small farm tools. We should actually calculate the possibility of supplying chemical fertilizers and agricultural machinery. We should fulfill what we can actually do and not make any infeasible plan.

Sixth, planning organs should shift their main attention from in-

dustry, transportation, etc. to increasing agricultural production
and checking inflation. This should be reflected in the national
plan.

I think increasing agricultural production, solving the problems
of food and clothing, ensuring market supply, and checking inflation are the primary issues. It is also important to produce annually 7.5 million tons of steel and 250 million tons of coal, but
this is a secondary issue. Certainly it is very good to produce so
much steel and coal, with the condition that the increase in
agricultural production is not obstructed and inflation is checked.
It will be just as well not to produce so much if it constitutes an
obstruction.

It will not do if we just rely on the Office of Agriculture and
Forestry and the Office of Finance and Trade of the State Council in
order to increase agricultural production and to check inflation. We
should mainly rely on the State Planning Commission, the State
Economic Commission, and the other comprehensive organs, and
we should put these things in a position of primary importance in
the national plan. Chairman Mao pointed out long ago that we must
take agriculture as the base in the development of the national
economy and must arrange the plan in the order of agriculture,
light industry, and heavy industry. Now we must study our planning
work and economic work, in order to know how we can really reflect this spirit.

The above six issues are the main methods for overcoming
present difficulties. What I have said is probably not complete,
so please discuss and supplement it.

What is the present financial and economic situation and what are
the methods to overcome difficulties? — these are important issues
that the whole Party and the people of the whole country are concerned with every minute. We should consider these issues carefully and work conscientiously for a few years. The disposition of
our work should be considered repeatedly, and we should understand it exactly. We should have experimental models and gradually spread them, and every step should be firm and steady. To
be somewhat more careful, to see somewhat more clearly, and to
solve problems somewhat better is preferred to being rash,
moving earlier, and moving without order. It is not only useless but also harmful if in a difficult period you just worry
or when you are critically ill you turn to any doctor you can
find for a cure. Of course, once we are sure about the really

effective methods, we must be concentrated and unified, and go all out. In the next few years we should strive to overcome difficulties faster and at the same time prepare for the possibility of not being fast. Doubtlessly, as long as we work hard, we will definitely be able to overcome difficulties and to strive for an early favorable turn in the financial and economic situation.

23

TALK AT A MEETING OF THE CENTRAL
FINANCE AND ECONOMICS SMALL GROUP
(March 1962)

Today I will talk about seven issues.

The first is the issue of long-term planning. We do not have to draft a ten-year plan now. We should first draft a five-year plan. Last time I said that the ten-year plan could be divided into two stages: the first is the recovery stage, and the second is the development stage. We can only talk about development after we have recovered completely. In the recovery stage we will gradually clarify the issues of the development stage. The situation now is too unclear to discuss development. That involves the problem of how we should move forward, which we must deliberate well. Should we say taking readjustment as the center and carrying out the "Eight Character Policy"[a] or should we say adjustment and recovery? This should be mainly decided by the Center. However, the leading organs must clearly understand that we should mainly recover at the present time.

Of course, some fields will develop during the recovery stage, and some fields will still be recovering during the development period. Take farm animals as an example. Grain is now in short supply so we should first consider the need of people to eat. We may not be able to recover to the previous peak level within five years.

Should the Central Work Conference that is prepared to open this July not discuss the plan targets of the Third Five-Year Plan? Because now we are still not sure about the situation it is very difficult to give relatively realistic targets or even to draw a line. I suggest that at the July meeting we mainly talk about the financial and economic situation, present problems, make issues

---

a) I.e., the general policy of readjustment, consolidation, filling out, and raising standards (tiaozheng, gonggu, chongshi, tigao). This phrase characterized the overall strategy for recovery from the Great Leap Forward in the early 1960s. It was first mentioned publicly in January 1961. — Eds.

clear and discuss policies, and study measures. We should
discuss seriously the estimation of the situation and the measures
to use, and we should unify our thinking.

How fast can agriculture really completely recover? We still
need to wait two years — this year and next year. Therefore, not
only can we not put forward the planning target this July, but also
it will still be difficult to put one forward even next year. Our
First Five-Year Plan started in 1953. We talked with the Soviet
Party and the government as well as with Stalin before putting
forward this plan. After the State Planning Commission was established at the end of 1952, we repeatedly studied the draft of
the First-Five Year Plan. The plan was put forward in the spring
of 1955. It was first passed in the spring by the National Party
Conference and in July by the National People's Congress, and announced afterward. It took us more than three years to put forward the First Five-Year Plan. As to the Third Five-Year Plan,
the situation is more complex. In order to understand the issues
clearly, I do not think that we should rush to work on targets. With
regard to the annual plan for next year, we can put forward an
outline at the July meeting this year. This will give people a general idea.

The second issue is that the annual plan this year needs quite a
large readjustment and rearrangement. This is very necessary.
We should not change any more in the following three quarters
once we decide. We should not, as in the past, "plan an annual
plan for a year," which really gives comrades of the State Planning
Commission a hard time. In the past, we had to calculate all over
again in order to change one or two figures. However, the figures
were not actually determined, so we had to concentrate on accounting and did not have time to study the situation and policies. We
cannot do this in the future. After the annual plan for this year is
readjusted, the State Economic Commission will take charge of
any change during its execution.

Now the plan readjustment actually slows down somewhat the
development of industrial production and capital construction to
facilitate really emphasizing agriculture and the market. The distribution of materials first should meet the needs of recovery in
agricultural production. Of course this should also be based on
actual possibility. For example, it is impossible to supply
the more than 5 million cubic meters of lumber needed by
the countryside. But we should primarily consider agriculture

as far as possible. The distribution of materials, secondly, should
meet the demands of the market, mainly the demand for the production of daily use industrial consumer goods. In accordance
with actual possibilities, we should provide if we can somewhat
more. We then can consider others after these two have been determined. To manage the annual plan, we should first make good
arrangements for agriculture and the market.

Supplies of staple as well as nonstaple foods for urban residents
are not sufficient, so the people's physical condition is deteriorating.
Can we allocate a somewhat greater quantity of steel products to manufacture motorized sailboats, add some fishing equipment, and ask the
aquatic product departments to go to sea and catch more fish? If
we can increase the supply of fish by 150 thousand tons annually,
each of the more than 60 million people living in large and medium
cities will have a jin of fish to eat. (Comrade Zhou Enlai: Chen
Yun's earlier proposal that we supply one liang daily of soybeans
to each person is very good. However, human nutrition requires
more than plant protein; animal protein is also needed. Perhaps
Buddhist monks and nuns who sit in meditation every day only
need plant protein. That will not suffice for people like us, and
certainly not for people who do more labor than we do. We should
have plant protein as well as some animal protein.) Each person
will have half a jin of fish and in addition we will open some high-
quality restaurants. If you have money, you can go to eat. Thus
the masses will not be able to complain too much when we give
preferential treatment to the cadres. It is reasonable that now
there are quite a few people who disagree with the method of preferential treatment of cadres. The target and measures for increasing fish production must be listed in the annual plan beginning this
year. This problem can be solved only if we make good arrangements.

In addition to each of the more than 60 million urban residents
of large and medium sized cities having half a jin of fish, can we
increase the supply of meat by half a jin a man by the end of next year?
According to what Comrade Yao Yilin[a] said, if each pig has 60 jin
of meat net, the 12 million pigs we plan to purchase this year will
in total weigh more than 700 million jin. Excluding exports and
other uses that must be ensured, there will be 6 jin of meat per

a) Deputy director of the State Council's Finance and Trade Staff Office (under
Li Xiannian) and probably director of the Party Central Committee's Finance
and Trade Work Department. — Eds.

person annually. We should ensure the purchase of pigs, and we should have appropriate distribution after purchases are made. For example, cut down exports. Thus, a family of five members will have 5 jin of meat and fish each month. At present, this is a major national issue. If 600 million people do not have good health and we do not find ways to solve their problems, people will have objections. People want to know whether the Communist Party is really concerned about them and can solve living problems. This is a political issue.

The problem of agriculture and the market is a great problem related to the livelihood of more than 500 million peasants and more than 100 million urban residents, and it is a problem of the people's livelihood. Solving this problem should constitute an important national policy. It is absolutely necessary that other fields "sacrifice" a little bit for agriculture and the market. In the plan for this year, especially in the distribution of materials, we should decide aspects of agriculture and the market first and then see how much material there is for industry. For industry, we should also primarily consider maintenance and forming complete sets in order to maintain simple reproduction. We will have capital construction after we meet the annual needs of production. We will engage in capital construction to the extent there are surplus resources. We should follow this procedure this year as well as in the future so we can improve the people's livelihood year by year.

Comrades, we spent dozens of years to achieve a successful revolution, and we must not let our revolutionary achievements slip from our hands. Now we are facing the problem of how to consolidate and develop our revolutionary achievements. The key point is to arrange well the livelihood of more than 600 million people and to really seek happiness for the people.

I think this year's annual plan requires quite a large readjustment. We should prepare to "fracture" the targets of heavy industry and capital construction. The key point is the four characters "to fracture." We should forthrightly cut down and should not refuse to "fracture." We cannot hesitate anymore now. (Comrade Zhou Enlai: we can write a parallel [vertical] couplet: the first line is grasp food, clothing, and goods for daily use; the second line is realize agriculture, light industry, and heavy industry — thus the couplet is comprehensively balanced when read horizontally as well.)

The third issue is comprehensive balance. There are many

arguments on this issue relating to the formulation of active balance and passive balance. There are different understandings of
what active balance is and what passive balance is. I think that
first we should make two things clear: one is, When should we
start to have comprehensive balance? The other is, Which "line"
should we start from to achieve comprehensive balance?

We will first talk about when we should start to have comprehensive balance. Some comrades think that we should not do it now
because conditions are not appropriate. They claim that we should
put forward a few long-range targets, then calculate every figure
and decide the construction plan. A leading comrade of the Ministry of Metallurgy originally planned for 30 or 25 million tons of
steel within 7 years. I asked him if we could have a complete
range of varieties of products then; he said that the range would
still not be complete. My view is that the comprehensive balance
must start now, and we should have comprehensive balance in the
annual plan for this year. We should not wait to engage comprehensive balance only after steel production reaches a certain number of million tons. It should be based on the present economic
level of comprehensive balance and undergo serious study and
calculation, and then we will see what level the long-range plan can
reach. We absolutely cannot do the opposite. What is called comprehensive balance is being in proportion, and to be in proportion
is to be balanced. Any one department cannot depart from other
departments. If a machine lacks some parts, it cannot run even
if it has all other parts. Being in proportion is an objective law;
nothing will work without proportion. According to domestic and
foreign experience, there accordingly should be nearly 50 thousand
tons of nonferrous metal in order to produce 1 million tons of steel.
Among the nonferrous metals, there is a certain proportion of copper, aluminum, lead, and zinc. It will not work without one metal,
or with an insufficient amount of metals. If we manage the economy without comprehensive balance, we cannot move a single step.

Now I will talk about which "line" we should use to work out a
comprehensive balance. There is only the long line or the short
line. In recent years comprehensive balance was based on the
long line. The biggest lesson was that we could not achieve balance. As a result, large quantities of materials and semifinished
goods remained in storage, which caused great waste. There have
been enough lessons in this respect. Only if we draw up comprehensive balance according to the short line will we be able to

achieve true comprehensive balance. The balance of the short line means to balance supply and demand with things that can be produced within the year, plus necessary reserves that can be used and imports on which we can actually rely. For example, we need a certain amount of nonferrous metal to produce a certain amount of steel. Therefore we need to calculate carefully how much of these nonferrous metals can be produced within that year, how much should be taken out of reserves, and how much should be imported from foreign countries. We then balance on this basis and fix the production targets. The comrade of the Ministry of Metallurgy wanted to convince me, saying that they were planning to produce 25 million tons of steel. If there is not enough nonferrous metals, we can import from foreign countries. I calculated a budget for them: calculated at 5 percent, an increase of 3 million tons of steel will require 150 thousand tons of nonferrous metals. Since the founding of the People's Republic of China the greatest quantity of imports of nonferrous metals in any single year was 130 thousand tons. Suppose we import the nonferrous metals that cannot be produced in sufficient quantities domestically in order to increase steel production by 3 million tons next year. Then we would have to import even more nonferrous metals in order to increase steel production by several million tons in the year after next. I think that it would be difficult to make those purchases even if we had that much foreign exchange. Therefore, we must draw up a comprehensive balance according to the short line. That way we can coordinate production and produce things in sets. We can only do a better job after things are formed in sets; otherwise they are just a pile of semifinished goods, and this is a waste.

What about the long line after we have drawn up a comprehensive balance and decided the planning targets according to the short line? One way is to continue production. Take the production capacity of the First Ministry Machine Building as an example. There are many long lines (within them there are many short lines), and machines manufactured this year cannot be used. However, we can arrange production for those that can be used next year or the year after and store them temporarily. Yet, we should also consider whether it is better to store them or to use raw materials for producing things that are in greater demand. That is to say, we can stop producing those things that are not needed or those that are needed but not badly needed, and therefore we can produce things of urgent need.

In general, planning targets must be reliable and must leave some margin. We should not worry that the targets are a little low as long as we have comprehensive balance. Though the target is somewhat low, it is much better than an unrealistically high target, and we can master the initiative and avoid being passive. For example, we should arrange the production target of coal according to actual capability. There will be no damage even if it is arranged somewhat lower than actual capacity. Things will still be in the People's Republic of China; we can produce more later. We should pay more attention to leaving some margin when we plan long-term targets. We should not just think of steel any more, we should draw up an overall arrangement on the basis of comprehensive balance.

Recently I checked the statistics on steel production in the last 90 years in the United States, Britain, Germany, Japan, the Soviet Union, and others. I found that these countries spent the longest time when their annual production of steel was below 10 million tons. The United States, Britain, Germany, Japan, and other countries became imperialist countries when their steel product was between 5 million and 10 million tons. The Soviet Union also became a strong industrial country on the basis of a similar production level. Generally, by the time steel production of these countries was between 5 million and 10 million tons, each kind of industry was largely complete, and this laid the foundation of industry. When Japan started the July 7 Incident [in 1937], its steel production did not even reach 7 million tons. We should start now according to historical experience. Within a certain time, we should strive to make the varieties of industrial products complete, their quality good, and the technology advanced in order to meet needs. We can go forward relatively faster after we have such a foundation.

Our stomachs are bigger these years. An annual investment of more than 10 billion yuan seems to be nothing. Starting from when Zhang Zhidong established industries until the founding of the People's Republic of China, the cumulative fixed assets of Chinese private industry were only around 2.2 billion yuan. Now, in only one year we spend 10 billion yuan on investment. If the arrangement is proper and we do well, one year will equal dozens of years of the past. Isn't this scale large? We need 2 million tons of steel products for an investment of 10 billion yuan. Now we annually produce 7 to 8 million tons of steel products, and we use 2 million tons on capital construction and will do many things. In addition, there are still 5 to 6 million tons of steel products for other uses.

The fourth issue is the system for managing materials. In general, the management of materials should be more centralized than it was during the period of the First Five-Year Plan. At present the materials are controlled separately by the state, each ministry, and each local government. From now on, there cannot be too many ministry-managed products. We let the Ministry of Metallurgy take care of steel products, but they "steal what is entrusted to their care," so the state should take centralized control. Now more than half the energy and time of the State Planning Commission is spent distributing and dispatching goods and materials. The process of production is also a process of distributing goods and materials. If you do not have the authority to control the goods and materials, you cannot concentratedly conduct production. We should have meetings with the comrades who are in charge of goods and materials and sum up experiences and lessons, including the experience and lesson of too much concentration and too much decentralization, then find out a set of methods of scientific management.

The fifth issue is to study the basic condition of agriculture. The State Planning Commission, the State Economic Commission, and the Office of Agriculture and Water Conservancy should solidly investigate and seriously study the various conditions of agricultural production and plan agricultural production targets on this basis.

The sixth issue is that the State Planning Commission should devote its main energy to agricultural production and to stabilizing the market. The State Planning Commission has a tradition of always starting with industry and capital construction. Fields such as agriculture, finance, trade, etc., are all offhand work. There is a historical reason for this. During the recovery period, the Finance and Economic Commission carried out unified management of finance and economics. After the State Planning Commission was established, agriculture and finance-trade have been separately controlled by the Office of Agriculture and Water Conservancy and the Office of Finance and Trade.[a]

---

a) The Finance and Economics Commission, headed by Chen Yun from 1949 to 1954, was one of four major commissions under the Government Administrative Council. It was the only commission that oversaw economic work. In the government reorganization of 1954 the State Council replaced the Government Administrative Council. The State Council had eight general offices concerned with domestic affairs, six of which were in the field of economics. Each oversaw the work of a number of related subordinate ministries. Chen's references above are to the 7th office, or Agriculture and Water Conservancy and the 5th office, Finance and Trade. — Eds.

I mainly concentrated attention on three fields when I was in the Finance and Economics Commission. The first was the socialist transformation of capitalist industry and commerce, handicraft industry, and small retailers. When Chairman Mao read the materials reflecting the objections of the capitalists, he wrote instructions on the documents, asking me to study them. Every time capitalists came to meetings in Beijing, we paid attention to studying the questions they raised. It was really a good thing if there was an opponent standing in front of us. It forced us to think through the questions. The second was the investment in capital construction. My method of doing this was to cut down. I cut down to the level that could be sustained by national capacity in finance and materials, especially agricultural production. The third was the labor force. Everyone wanted to increase recruitment every year, but I controlled it strictly. It was easy to let people in, but very difficult to let them out. Once they came in, we had to give them pay and supply food, clothing, and daily goods. Every time we increased the number of workers and staff, I had to calculate. If there were not enough goods and materials, I did not allow them in. If capital construction investment and labor power were controlled, the plan was also generally controlled and there would not be any problems. At that time, I did not manage agriculture. It was later that I was in charge of unified state procurement and sale of grain. Comrade Huang Jing[a] used to point out: bank credit funds are very large, and the working capital of the commercial system is very large. Why don't we take some money from these two to promote capital construction? He did not understand that if we took necessary credit funds and working capital to promote capital construction, material supplies would be in trouble. This would not work and was dangerous.

In the past we needed to count once a year how much purchasing power there was and how much commodity supply there was. We wanted commodity supply to exceed purchasing power. There should be several hundred yuan worth of commodities for each 100 yuan of purchasing power. If 100 yuan was against 100 yuan, there would be a shortage of market supply, because there would be some commodities that would not meet the demands of consumers. Only if the volume of commodity supply is greater than purchasing

a) Head of the First Ministry of Machine Building from its establishment in August 1952. After May 1956 simultaneously chairman of the State Technological Commission. Died in early 1958. — Eds.

power will consumers have a choice. An adverse balance between
the volume of commodity supply and purchasing power will definitely produce fiscal deficits or even inflation.

The seventh issue is to encourage people to express different
opinions. Actually there are different views on the present situation, policies, measures, and where we should locate the key points
of our work. Each ministry, commission, and unit should encourage two parties who have different views to express their opinions.
It is a good thing to have two groups of opinions in our Party and
in government offices. This can make us consider issues more
comprehensively, avoid one-sidedness, and make fewer mistakes.

ABOUT THE EDITORS

Nicholas R. Lardy is Associate Professor of Economics at Yale University. A member of the Yale Faculty since 1975 he received his B.A. from the University of Wisconsin-Madison in 1968 and his Ph.D. in economics in 1975 from the University of Michigan. He is the author of several publications on the economy of contemporary China that analyze economic planning, industrial production, and international trade. These include Economic Growth and Distribution in China (1978), Chinese Economic Planning (1978), and Agriculture in China's Economic Development (forthcoming).

Kenneth Lieberthal is Professor of Political Science at Swarthmore College, where he has been on the faculty since 1972. A graduate of Dartmouth College, he received his M.A., East Asian Institute Certificate, and Ph.D. in political science from Columbia University. His numerous publications on Chinese and Soviet affairs include A Research Guide to Central Party and Government Meetings in China, 1949-1975 (1975), Central Documents and Politburo Politics in China (1978), Sino-Soviet Conflict in the 1970's: Its Evolution and Implications for the Strategic Triangle (1978), The Strategic Triangle: Can the US Play the 'China Card'? (1979), and Revolution and Tradition in Tientsin, 1949-52 (1980).